August 1990.

To Margaret — from Sheila
- not much about our dad in here!
- interesting nevertheless.

HIGHLANDS AND ISLANDS

HIGHLANDS AND ISLANDS

A GENERATION OF PROGRESS

edited by
Alastair Hetherington

with the assistance of
John Kerr

ABERDEEN UNIVERSITY PRESS
Member of Maxwell Macmillan Pergamon Publishing Corporation

First published 1990
Aberdeen University Press

© Aberdeen University Press 1990

British Library Cataloguing in Publication Data

Highlands and Islands: a generation of progress
  1. Scotland. Highlands & Islands
  I. Hetherington, Alastair, *1919–*
  941.10858

  ISBN 0 08 037980 X

Typeset from author generated discs
and printed by AUP Glasgow/Aberdeen—A member of BPCC Ltd.

Foreword

In 1965 Sir Winston Churchill died, Alexei Leonov first walked in space and Wedgwood-Benn put up the price of a letter from 3*d.* to 4*d.* It seems like a long time ago!

Also in 1965 the Highlands and Islands Development Board was established by the then Secretary of State for Scotland, Willie Ross, since when a whole generation has grown up in the Highlands who have never known a world without HIDB.

The intervening years have seen a succession of ideas and projects come and sometimes go, as the challenge of stemming the long-term decline in the Highlands and Islands has been faced. It is a challenge of much more than local significance, since many countries also wrestle with the problems of remote rural areas in a world where it is the cities that attract the young. Many countries now see HIDB as a pioneering body, with experience relevant to, for example, the Falklands, Finland and Japan.

This book sets out to describe, from many personal points of view, the changes that have happened and been introduced to so many aspects of Highland life since the current generation was born. There have been many influences—oil, local government reform, European aid and the rise of 'green' concern are just some—but the people of HIDB have been much involved in all of it. You will assess their record for yourself, but I for my part take greatest satisfaction, not so much from the many successful and enduring developments, but from the new level of self-confidence now to be found in most Highlands and Islands communities. The self-confidence stems from the area's higher profile and a much increased range of amenities and opportunities for all who live in it.

In 1991 a successor organisation, Highlands and Islands Enterprise and ten local enterprise companies will take on new powers, and will find new ways of helping the area prosper during a generation ahead which faces even more surprises than we have yet seen. It is a fitting time therefore to celebrate twenty-five years of HIDB and to take stock.

This book is not an official history. Though HIDB has sponsored it we specifically did not seek editorial control. The many talents who have contributed to it, almost all with Highland connections, collectively demonstrate the real wealth of the Highlands and Islands.

SIR ROBERT COWAN
Chairman
HIDB

Contents

CONTENTS

Black and White Illustrations

List of Colour Plates

Acknowledgements

Among the many people who have helped us with advice or information—none of whom should be blamed for anything written in this book—we wish to thank:

Richard Ardern, George Campbell, Chris Dawson, Gordon Drummond, Arnold Duncan, Stuart Edmond, Miklos and Celia Etrz, Robert Fasken, Peter Ferguson, Dr Howie Firth, Kathleen and Uisdean Fraser, Inspector John Graham, Lord Grimond, David Henderson, Francis Keith, Tom and Lesley Kilbride, Roy McIver, Robert Maclennan MP, Elizabeth Murphy, Rev Alex Murray, Colin Paterson, Frank Spaven.

Also, of prime importance, the past and present chairmen of the HIDB—Sir Robert Grieve, Sir Andrew Gilchrist, Sir Kenneth Alexander, Rear-Admiral Dunbar-Nasmith and Sir Robert Cowan.

And we are grateful for frequent access to the library, University of Stirling.

Appendix

Tables compiled by Elizabeth Murphy, Economist, Policy, Planning and Transport Division, HIDB.

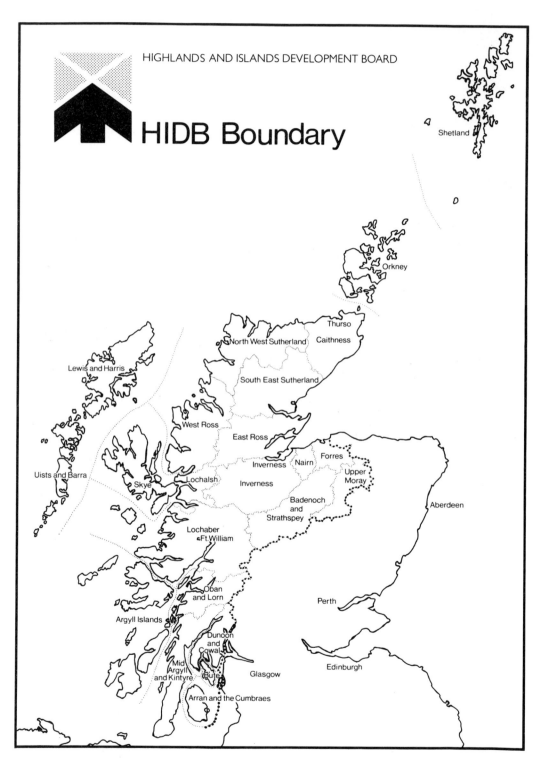

HIGHLANDS AND ISLANDS DEVELOPMENT BOARD

HIDB Boundary

Shetland

Orkney

Thurso

North West Sutherland

Caithness

Lewis and Harris

South East Sutherland

West Ross

East Ross

Forres

Inverness

Nairn

Uists and Barra

Upper Moray

Skye

Lochalsh

Inverness

Aberdeen

Badenoch and Strathspey

Lochaber

Ft.William

Oban and Lorn

Perth

Argyll Islands

Dunoon and Cowal

Mid Argyll and Kintyre

Bute

Glasgow

Arran and the Cumbraes

Edinburgh

'Until the Highland problem is looked upon as social rather than as economic, it is to be feared that we can expect little improvement.'

Frank Fraser Darling, Wild Country, CUP 1938

'For 200 years the Highlander has been the man on Scotland's conscience.'

Rt Hon William Ross, moving the Highland Development Bill, *Hansard*, 16 March 1965

'Glasgow is one joker in the Scottish pack; the Highlands are the other.'

Professor Sir Robert Grieve, BBC Television, April 1978

'I enjoyed my time at the Highland Board. It was the first time I'd felt I was doing a useful job, as opposed to Diplomatic work where all you see is the result of failures, whereas in this one could see the result of successes. I enjoyed it very much.'

Sir Andrew Gilchrist, interview, August 1989

Chapter 1

Northern Scotland—Real Lives

Alastair Hetherington

The time: the winter of 1979. The place: a discussion-dinner in London, not far from Downing Street. The question, put by one of the Prime Minister's policy advisers: 'Does it matter if Ardnamurchan, Applecross and West Sutherland become uninhabited? If people choose to live in such places, why shouldn't they pay something closer to the economic cost of the services they require? Why should taxpayers in Manchester, Derby, Nottingham and Southampton have to subsidise them? Will anything be lost if these areas revert to wilderness?'

It shook me at the time, even though it was no more than a provocative probe. My immediate reaction was that much would be lost. For a few hardy campers and mountaineers a total wilderness might be ideal. But looking even from a narrowly economic stance, city dwellers would be denied the Highland holidays and recreation that they enjoy. And if at a later date development of oil-related or nuclear or mineral industries was required, such growth must be much more difficult. No people, no shops, few roads, no pubs.

The reality, of course, has been quite different. Over the past twenty or thirty years there has been rebirth and growth in many parts of the Highlands and Islands. More people, more jobs, better schools, better roads, improved hotels, better B & Bs, new ferries, new fishing boats, fish farming, forest maintained, growth of cottage industries; overall, though with some failures and some exceptions, more money and better living. And, at the same time, a revival of the Gaelic language and continuing strength of the Churches, especially in the Western Isles. Shetland and Orkney, too, have flourished in these years.

All this has been supported by successive governments, in spite of Treasury objections to the costs. The idea of a Highland Board had been floated as early as 1928 and more strongly in 1938, but was deferred by the war. Post-war, the permanent secretary at the Scottish Office, Sir David Milne, came up with the proposal of an advisory Highland Panel. It was created in 1947, but was of little value in its early years. Milne, a master of window-dressing, did not want it to be too active. But in 1955 the forceful judge Lord Cameron became its chairman. From then onwards it generated more ginger than the Scottish Office had expected.

Bobby Fasken, seconded from the Scottish Office to be secretary to the Panel in the early 1960s (and later a board member of the HIDB) recalls Lord Cameron as 'the only chairman of a government committee whom I knew who announced to the press immediately after the meeting what the findings of the "advisory" committee were'. Since Fasken had to write the minutes of the Panel, that sometimes made him 'somewhat apprehensive'. Beyond doubt, Lord Cameron's gradual pressure for an authority with executive powers and finance helped to open the way for the Highlands and Islands Development Board in 1965.

Another force for improvement, launched in 1953, was the Highland Fund. Conceived by Lord Malcolm Douglas-Hamilton and financed at first by a whisky magnate, it gave—and still gives—loans chiefly to crofters and fishermen. It provided a modest but valuable rehearsal for the later work of the HIDB. But the big step forward—the primary attempt to tackle what many people saw as the 'insoluble' problem of the Highlands—came with the Highland and Islands Development Act of 1965 and the creation of the HIDB in November of that year.

The Scottish Office had been making discreet preparations even before the 1964 general election: not because its senior staff wanted an executive Highland Board— to them a 'rival' in the north was far from welcome—but because of the pressure from Lord Cameron and the Advisory Highland Panel, and from other quarters. The STUC (the Scottish Trades Union Congress) had come together with the Labour Party's Scottish Council in calling for a new deal. The promise of a Highland Board was in Labour's campaign manifesto. And the young Liberal Russell Johnston, about to become the MP for Inverness-shire, was a vigorous campaigner. Whatever the outcome of the autumn election, legislation was a possibility. And—whether because of Labour's tiny majority or in spite of it— the initiative at Westminster came barely five months after the election.

The Bill was put before Parliament in February, sponsored by the new Secretary of State, Willie Ross. He had two terms in that post—1964–70 and 1974–6, almost eight years in all and the longest holder of the appointment until equalled by George Younger in 1986. Ross latterly became Lord Ross of Marnock. Throughout his time in office, he was an enthusiastic supporter of the Board—and, unusually among Cabinet Ministers, was personally upset when things went wrong. (Younger, on surpassing Ross's long reign, was presented with a silver bed of nails by colleagues and staff.) Aspects of the Bill were much criticised by Conservatives during lively debates on the second reading in March and the third on 17 June, but in the end the Opposition did not vote against the legislation. The Shadow Secretary of State, Michael Noble, at one point referred to it as 'a Marxist enactment', though later he too became a clear supporter of the Board. Jo Grimond, for the Liberals, in welcoming the Bill, said that 'success depends upon the calibre of the people appointed to the Board'. George Younger, later a good friend of the HIDB, similarly said he hoped the Government 'will not skimp the provision of monies but will get the best possible people.'

One of many eloquent contributions to the second reading is worth quoting, from the member for Perth and East Perthshire, Ian MacArthur:

It is often quite easy, when considering the Highlands, to slip into a mood of romantic sentimentality. Like the reaction of the piper in Neil Munro's story, the heart leaps back over the years and yonder lies Glencoe. Romance and sentiment are very agreeable, but these emotions, which often cloud debate outside this House, distort judgment by obscuring reality with a tartan cloud ...

When we speak of the Highland problem today we mean the problem of depopulation, which should haunt the mind and conscience of every Hon. Member. Today there are fewer than 300,000 people in the Highlands. Great stretches of land lie nearly deserted except for the memory of generations scattered around the world and more often than not, a stone with too long a list of names of gallant men who died for their country. Against this background, any Measure which sets out to develop the Highlands is to be welcomed, provided that it is designed to meet the problem and is not simply an essay in theoretical socialism.

It was not 'theoretical socialism', as the Board's pragmatic approach and its rigorous first years soon proved. But it owes something to Labour's narrow margin in the 1964–6 Parliament, with a majority of only three at first and only one before the 1966 election. As James Shaw Grant argues in Chapter 3, it is only when governments have a slender majority that they will give time to such radical legislation for a peripheral area.

In parts of the Scottish Office, the Highlands and Islands were seen not just as peripheral but as impossible. On good authority it is said that the Permanent Secretary of the years 1965–73, Sir Douglas Haddow, had demonstrated this at a meeting some time before the new Board came. Leaning over a map, he laid his elbow on Fort William and stretched his whole forearm up the Great Glen, and made a great gesture westwards—a sweeping gesture north and west—and said 'so far as that area is concerned, it's out'. He saw it as a troublesome area that somehow had to be kept quiet by 'chucking buns across the fence' if necessary, and he was not alone in that view. But he was a just man, and once the Board had been established he gave it good support, while sceptical about its prospects. When officials from Inverness appeared at St Andrew's House (the Scottish Office) they were sometimes greeted as 'the Highland Mafia'. The Board had been given a brief unlike any before it in Scotland, and its approach had to be unorthodox.

The first chairman was Professor Sir Robert Grieve, a philosopher, academic and mountaineer of exceptional talent, and an excellent choice for the new post. A Glasgow man who had walked frequently in the Highlands—with a tent, or staying in bothies because he had next to no money—he began as a civil engineer but joined the Scottish Office in 1946 and became its chief planner from 1960 to 1964, then Professor of Town and Regional Planning at Glasgow University from 1964 to 1974. The university gave him leave to take up the HIDB post from the autumn of 1965, for five years.

Soon after the Bill became an Act in June of 1965, Bob Grieve was asked to see the Secretary of State for Scotland in his room at the House of Commons, following two or three telephone calls from the Scottish Office to explore whether he would accept the post. The Commons meeting was in early July and was the only substantial discussion that Grieve had with Willie Ross before the Board came into existence. Grieve made the point—with Sir Douglas Haddow present—that an entirely new approach was needed, one 'completely foreign' to the previous practice of the Scottish Office. It must be 'a new strategy', seen as being based in the Highlands, and it must be 'risk-taking and adventurous'. That was accepted. The Act gave the Board wide powers; but, as we shall see later, application of many of those powers—on investment or land use or major developments—was subject to specific approval from the Secretary of State. While not disputing the good constitutional reason for the 'reserved powers', Bob Grieve and others after him were to find that it frustrated some of their most important projects.

A minor but significant tussle with St Andrew's House came right at the start. It was agreed that there must be a press conference after announcement of the appointment. The officials said it must be held in Glasgow or Edinburgh. Grieve insisted that it must be in the Highlands, just as he had insisted that the HIDB headquarters must be there. The Scottish Office said it could not pay Grieve's fare to Inverness because he was not yet employed. He said that in that case he'd pay his own fare. The Board must be seen to be committed to the Highlands. A compromise was found, by which a press officer from Edinburgh drove Grieve to Inverness in his car, charging that to St Andrew's House. The press conference itself went well, with a warm welcome for the Board by all the newspapers, except for the always unpredictable *Inverness Courier*. Later, though, there were complaints from some of the local authorities about the 'colonial administration' that had been 'foisted' on them by the Government.

At this point it is worth listing the five chairmen who have served—each differing in character and background, but each effective.

1965–70 SIR ROBERT GRIEVE, as noted above. Born 1910. Educated North Kelvinside School, Glasgow, and Royal College of Science and Technology (now University of Strathclyde), Glasgow, as civil engineer. Local government posts, 1927–44; prepared Clyde Valley Regional Plan, 1944–46, Civil Service 1946–64; Professor of Town and Regional Planning, Glasgow University 1964–74, but on leave from University while chairman HIDB 1965–70. Chairman, Royal Fine Art Commission for Scotland 1978–83; and many other public activities. Former president of Scottish Mountaineering Club; and several first rock climbs to his credit. Hon D Litt, Heriot-Watt, Hon LLD, Strathclyde, Dr *hc*, Edinburgh.

1970–76 SIR ANDREW GILCHRIST, KCMG. Born 1910, Lanarkshire, and still occupies family house in fruit-growing Clyde Valley, near Lanark. Educated Edinburgh Academy and Exeter College, Oxford. Diplomatic Service 1933–70; latterly ambassador Reykjavik (Iceland), Djakarta (Indonesia), and Dublin. War Service as Major, Force 136 in South East Asia (mentioned in despatches). Books on South East Asia and on Cod War with Iceland; also six novels. To HIDB on retirement from Foreign Office; fruit growing in Lanarkshire since 1976, also frequent writer of letters to editors.

1   Sir Andrew Gilchrist. [HIDB]

2   Professor Sir Kenneth Alexander.
[HIDB]

3   Rear-Admiral David Dunbar-Nasmith.
[HIDB]

4   Sir Robert Cowan. [HIDB]

1976–80 PROFESSOR SIR KENNETH ALEXANDER Born Edinburgh 1922, Educated
George Heriot's School, Edinburgh; School of Economics, Dundee University,
teaching economics, Leeds, Sheffield and Aberdeen 1949–62; Professor of Econ-
omics, Strathclyde University, 1963–80, but on leave while Chairman HIDB
1976–80. Also director Fairfields (shipyard, Glasgow) 1966–8; Upper Clyde
Shipbuilders 1968–71, and Chairman Govan Shipbuilders 1974–6. Various other
public activities, including Economic Consultant to Secretaries of State for
Scotland since 1968, and member of Scottish Development Agency 1975–86.
Principal and Vice-Chancellor, University of Stirling, 1981–86; Chancellor,
University of Aberdeen, since 1986. Hon LLD CNAA; Hon LLD Aberdeen,
Hon LLD Dundee; D Univ Stirling; D Univ Open. Many economics pub-
lications. Lives by by the sea in Pittenweem, Fife, but with flat in Edinburgh
and house in Ardnamurchan (the last being the one where he most likes to be).

1981–2 REAR-ADMIRAL DAVID DUNBAR-NASMITH, CBE, DSC Deputy Chairman,
HIDB, 1972–81; Chairman 1981–82. Born 1921. Educated Lockers Park; RNC
Dartmouth. Royal Navy 1939–72. War service in Atlantic and Mediterranean,
in command of ships from 1943 onwards; 5th Frigate Squadron 1961-3; Commo-
dore, Amphibious Forces, 1966–7; Flag Officer, Scotland and N Ireland 1970–
72. Since 1972 other activities include membership of Countryside Commission
of Scotland, British Waterways Board, N of Scotland Hydro-Electric Board.
Member of Queen's Body Guard for Scotland since 1974; Gentleman Usher of
the Green Rod to the Order of the Thistle since 1979; Vice Lord Lieutenant,
Morayshire, since 1980. Recreations sailing, ski-ing and shooting; and lives on
farm near Rothes, Moray, where he was born. Still looks (1990) like an admiral
in charge of warships.

1982– SIR ROBERT COWAN Born 1932. Educated Edinburgh Academy and Edinburgh University. In business as manager, marketing specialist and consultant,
1958–81. Latterly managing director in Hong Kong for PA Management
Consultants Ltd. With Fison Ltd, 1958–62; Wolsey Ltd, 1962–4; and PA Management, 1965–82. (Among Highland connections, many of his school holidays
were spent in Argyllshire; and his father, a distinguished botanist for many years
at the Royal Botanical Gardens in Edinburgh, lived also for some years at
Inverewe in Wester Ross.) Board member, SDA, from 1982. Hon LLD Aberdeen 1987. Recreations, gardening—and sailing on the rare occasions when he
can. Lives in rural setting in Strathnairn.

Of the five, Bob Grieve was probably the one with the deepest knowledge of
the Highlands when appointed. He had travelled a great deal in the Highlands and
Islands, for work and for pleasure, and in his first three years in the Scottish Office
he had been the planning officer for the North. He had also been involved in a
special study of the problems of Applecross—remote, impoverished, with a declining population but with some good land. He knew also that, to bring prosperity,
he had to develop a few very large projects and a multitude of small ones.
    From the start Grieve judged that the major developments must be in 'trees,

tourists, fishing and industry', with related improvement also in roads and transport. He believed that there had to be two or three centres of population and
industry—Lochaber, with British Aluminium already there and a new pulp mill
(Wiggins Teape) about to open; the Moray Firth, with good weather and all
the space round Inverness and Invergordon, and potential sites for off-shore oil
construction and other industry; and the Dounreay-Thurso-Wick area, with its
recent inflow of scientists and skilled workers for the nuclear fast-breeder reactor
research. Grieve argued that these must be the core round which to build jobs and
prosperity, to stop depopulation and to give a more secure life 'to bright young
crofters' sons'.

The crofting system was a special concern. Although proportionately a small
part of the Highland population, in Grieve's words 'sentimentally and historically
the crofters reflected what the Highlands was about'. It was a different way of life,
close to the soil and with a great deal of mutual help, also with a deep religious
feeling. It was admirable, he said. But it could not last unless the crofters had better
living conditions, with more part-time ancillary work and wider prospects for the
next generation.

Along with crofting, Grieve gave special attention to agriculture—not just
sheep rearing which 'will, as it is practised at present, worsen the depopulation
problem'—but with the richer forms of farming possible mainly on the east coast
and in Orkney. Even there, he said in his first annual report, greater efficiency and
mechanised methods were unlikely to increase population.

His forecasts were controversial. The concept of the Moray Firth development
was new. There was much opposition. Nevertheless, in the 25 years that have
followed, his strategy has been applied—not always with success, but overall
bringing more jobs and greater prosperity.

> The population of the Highlands and Islands has grown from 299,000 in 1966 to
> 353,500 in 1981 (the last census). The Inverness district has grown from 49,500
> people in 1971 to 60,800 in 1986 and is still growing fast; Ross and Cromarty from
> 35,700 to 47,800 (though with increased unemployment), and Lochaber from 17,600
> to 19,400. Employees in jobs were up from 111,600 in 1961 to 150,800 in 1981.
> Unemployment, however, has risen from an average 7.3% in 1960 and 8.6% in
> 1971 to 11.7% in 1981 and 15.6% in 1986. Housing was up from 83,610 in 1961 to
> 113,230 in 1981, with owner occupation far above the Scottish average. Pupils in
> secondary education were up from 16,112 in 1968 to 22,012 in 1985.

Let us look first at the Moray Firth concept, together with Lochaber and Dounreay,
and then in turn at fishing, tourism and forestry: and at how they have developed
under the guidance of the HIDB's successive chairmen. Bob Grieve in 1965
thought that there might be no need for an HIDB beyond about 1985. He
believed that the proposed Regional Councils—actually created in 1974–5—could
eventually carry on the development work which the HIDB would have 'kicked
off'. The Regional and Islands councils in the North have proved strong and
successful. Even so, most people in the Highlands and Islands, I suspect, believe
that the HIDB has a continuing role for many years to come.

Chemicals, smelter, oil and nukes.

In these, the biggest and perhaps most controversial of the Board's activities, it was not always the prime mover. The experimental fast-breeder reactor at Dounreay had been established many years before the HIDB, and it had brought to Caithness many scientists and others, with a spin-off of new activities in the area. That helped to generate a number of new companies, partly funded by the HIDB and employing over 500 people—most notably Osprey Electric, producing underwater television cameras sold worldwide; Norfrost, making compact deep freeze cabinets, high-tech refrigerators, also sold worldwide; and Grampian Recordings, manufacturing high-quality recording tapes. But Dounreay itself, after more than 30 years of successful operation, is now being run down. The loss of jobs has come as a severe shock to Caithness, with a staff reduction by early 1990 from 2100 to 1600, and further cuts to come.

Similarly, the Wiggins Teape pulp mill at Corpach, near Fort William, had been planned and was under construction before the HIDB came. As it turned out, its design was already obsolescent and too costly to compete with other plants in the south; and it was hit by the world recession of 1978–80. It was closed in November 1980, though the related paper mill was kept going. The closing of the pulp mill again meant a grievous loss of jobs in Lochaber, which was not fully regained until 1988–89 with the increase of tourism in that area. The biggest employer in Lochaber is still British Aluminium (now owned by Alcan) with plants in Fort William and Kinlochleven. But there are now a number of smaller new industries there.

Continuing with the catastrophes, mostly initiated pre-HIDB, the most serious was the aluminium smelter at Invergordon. For ten years it was the biggest industrial employer in the Highlands. It was built close to the Cromarty Firth shore, on good farm land close to the town of Invergordon. Planning had begun in 1964 in the Board of Trade and the Ministry of Technology in London, with three major companies as possible owners—RTZ (who eventually went to Anglesey), the Canadian Alcan (who went to Tyneside but were ready to take on Invergordon as well), and British Aluminium, already at Lochaber. Building of the Highland plant was announced by the Government in 1968; partial production began in June of 1970 and full production in May of 1971. The plant was closed down in December of 1981.

That this great development was welcomed by the majority of people in the Dingwall-Alness-Invergordon communities seems not in doubt. Directly or indirectly, some 1500–2000 new jobs were created. It was warmly welcomed by the HIDB. But an aluminium smelter requires a massive supply of electricity and the arranging of this was an intensely political process.

For the Invergordon plant, Alcan were first in the field. They wanted to generate their own power locally, in a coal fired station to be supplied from Northumberland. That was refused by the Labour Government, which wanted to protect the North of Scotland Hydro Electric Board. (The HIDB at that time also wanted a 'ring fence' round the Cromarty Firth within which to generate

5   British Aluminium smelter, Invergordon. [HIDB]

cheap power for new industries, but that too was refused.) Later, British Alu-minium (BACo) came forward as contenders, while Rio Tinto Zinc made its proposals for Anglesey, in Wales.

In the end, the government sanctioned three smelters of equal size. Alcan got their coal powered smelter, but located in Northumberland, while RTZ at Angle-sey and BACo at Invergordon were to be supplied with nuclear power from Britain's new AGR stations. RTZ negotiated exceptionally good terms with the Central Electricity Generating Board, which wanted a bulk buyer for its new North Wales plant. Details were never published. For BACo a complex arrange-ment was devised, with a 21% share of nuclear power from the proposed Hun-terston 'B' station on the Clyde estuary. While the difference in price may have seemed small, it was lethal when the economic recession came in 1978–80.

Immediately after the closure, Admiral Dunbar-Nasmith as chairman of the HIDB wrote to the Secretary of State, George Younger. He set out four immediate requirements for the Highlands:

1.   Transfer the smelter to a new company at a nominal price, not more than £5m; and make electricity available 'at a realistic price, between 1p and 1.2p.'

2. Cheap power from the Hydro Board to be made available for processing forest products in the Highlands instead of exporting timber to Scandinavia.
3. Cheap power also for ferro-alloy plants.
4. Maximum support and assistance to any private operator prepared to build a gas pipeline to the Cromarty Firth. There was, he said, a unique opportunity with oil and gas being landed at Sullom Voe, Flotta and Nigg, for a new petrochemical industry.

It was a bold proposal which could have worked, though it would have required new legislation and a supply of cheap electricity from outside the Highlands. In the eight years following the closure that did not prove possible.

A more detailed account of the rise and fall of the Invergordon smelter can be found in Alf Young's Chapter 7. And, at the time of writing, negotiations are again taking place with Alcan, who took over British Aluminium about a year after the Cromarty Firth closure. The supply of electricity is again an issue. Nevertheless, there is still a slender hope that the smelter may yet be brought back to life.

Meanwhile, after the 1981 closure, the HIDB—with reluctant Scottish Office approval—launched its own remedial action for employment in the Invergordon area. It set up an 'Enterprise Zone' on the Cromarty shore to the west, which over the next four or five years created at least 500 permanent jobs, mostly in small industries. Some were in old companies and some new, but the Board refused any relocation grants from Dingwall or Inverness. Exact estimates of jobs are difficult, because of mobility, but one assessment puts it as growth of 950 direct jobs and 600 indirect.

Was Bob Grieve's concept of a Highland industrial heartland justified? To an extent, yes, though it will always be debated. It is relevant that of those employed at the smelter 90 per cent (apart from craftsmen) came from north of the Great Glen. Of the craftsmen, 60 per cent came from the north; and of the other 40 per cent the great majority came from Inverness or the east coast of the Moray Firth. Nevertheless, with fluctuating numbers at the offshore construction yards, unemployment remains higher than it was before the inflow of families to the Invergordon area in 1968–78. But, a better sign, more recently the growth and prosperity of Inverness and its surroundings have been obvious.

With offshore oil developments from the early 1970s and onwards, three large platform construction yards were opened in the Highlands—at Nigg and Ardersier in the east and Kishorn in the west—while major oil terminals were built at Flotta in Orkney and Sullom Voe in Shetland. A smaller fabrication yard was established also at Arnish, in Lewis. Of these, Nigg and Ardersier remain in business, some-times with full order books, sometimes at a lower level of work. Kishorn has closed, after building the world's biggest concrete structure, and has left an ugly mess in what was once a beautiful bay. By contrast, the two great terminals at Flotta and Sullom Voe, both built with care for the surrounding scene on land and water, have been of substantial economic and social benefit to their island groups. To Shetland especially, offshore oil has meant virtually full employment, great wealth, new roads, improved schools, and public funds on an unprecedented scale. And, in spite of all the oil-related activity, Shetland and Orkney have each retained their own strong character and their extraordinary beauty.

Fish, fishermen and fish farmers.

In 1965 West Coast fishing was at a low ebb, with few boats and these mostly owned by elderly fishermen. The notion of funding new boats was not well received by the Scottish Office, the White Fish Authority or the Herring Industry Board. The West Highlanders were seen as 'lazy'. They would not want to go to sea. They were no match for the 'vigorous' north-east coasters. But that proved utterly wrong. Given the chance, the younger men of Barra, North Uist, Scalpay, Stornoway, Lochinver and Kinlochbervie were as tough and hard-working as any. The HIDB's training and support for them, with new or second-hand boats, was a success. It gave new life to the west coast fishers.

Earlier there had been a pilot scheme, proposed by the Highland Panel. It had not done well. But the new HIDB, irrational as it may have seemed, was determined to prove its commitment to the Western Isles, the west mainland fishers, and to Orkney and Shetland. It launched the fisheries development scheme with visits to the likely areas, in general offering training before the young took over their boats. The usual base was a loan, to be repaid over fifteen years. They had some defaulters, but not many. To the larger places—Scalpay and Stornoway, for example—they offered to finance up to ten boats at first, 50 to 80-footers. Also there were 30-foot boats for combined sea-angling, for tourists and for shell-fishing.

The combination was not always popular—Grieve recalls a North Uist meeting chaired by a minister, convenor of the district council. At the end the minister said he was entirely against tourism but he was for fishing because 'the young men go out to meet danger and adventure and come back and love their wives three times more'. It was, Grieve says, an impressive Old Testament statement. He got the point. But he also had an approach next day, when about to board the ferry to Skye, from two other councillors who 'wanted the tourism, too'.

Sir Andrew Gilchrist, looking back at the development of 'orthodox' fishing, has some reservations. He says that to begin with by far the best return was from Shetland but then the oil came and 'you could make ten times as much by being an oil manager as by fishing'. There were good results also in Orkney and Sutherland; but he is less convinced about the Western Isles, apart from Scalpay. Their production of oysters and their selling abroad were 'excellent' but the return on other sea fishing less certain. In his time the first exploration of deep water fishing for blue whiting was begun, with two trawlers working for the HIDB. He believed that it could become a very large business, if developed on a national scale, and plans were prepared for the fish-drying plant at Breasclete on the west coast of Lewis. He also pays tribute to the work of the Campbeltown and Orkney boatbuilding yards, 'one of Bob Grieve's big successes'.

The Breasclete factory opened in Sir Kenneth Alexander's time, in October of

1978. After the research it looked a strong development, with blue whiting and ling in the Atlantic waters to the west. The research, however, had failed to take account of the fishermen's preference for more than one buyer. At Breasclete there was only one purchaser at the harbour, the Norway-owned company who would process the fish drying. The fishermen preferred either to fish for conventional catches nearer home or to sail to mainland ports, in hope of higher payment. Too late it was realised that the Norwegian management had done too little to gain the confidence of the fishermen. Too late also, it occurred to the HIDB that the selling problem could probably have been overcome by electronic estimates of what mainland prices would be, and by discounting that price by 10 or 15% as the equivalent of the sailing time which skippers would have saved. An agreement on that basis might have been achieved. But sadly the factory closed after about three years. Later it reopened with a plant turning fish oil into pharmaceutical and health food products.

By the mid 1970s, uncontrolled sea fishing and the lack of an EEC policy brought a reduction in catches. Since then quotas have been introduced, but overfishing continues, aggravated in the western seas by disregard of the quotas by east coast boats. Nevertheless, the Fisheries Development Scheme stands out as probably the HIDB's biggest achievement. As Rear Admiral Dunbar-Nasmith said in a report to Parliament after his retirement, 'successful fishing has rejuvenated many a small island such as Eriskay and Scalpay' and he went on to recommend a 'controlled development' of fishing for the benefit of the Highlands and Islands and of the rest of the country. That there are now twice as many boats based in the west and in the northern isles as there were in 1965 speaks for itself.

What of the newcomer, fish farming? Little was known of it in 1965, whereas now there are more than 320 fish farms in the HIDB's area. It is an industry that has grown from nothing. Two-thirds of the production is for salmon, with shellfish and rainbow trout making up the rest. Fish farming, however, has drawbacks—the intrusion of its cages on otherwise beautiful lochs, the pollution of water below the cages, and the on-shore buildings that are needed.

Commercial breeding of trout and salmon had begun in Norway, Iceland and Ireland some time before it came to Scotland. In the late 1960s the first experimental farms were working, one at Lochailort (east of Arisaig), one at Otter Ferry (Loch Fyne) and one at Ardtoe in Ardnamurchan. Much money is needed, since for salmon it is a five year process—one or two years in fresh water, two years in the salt water cages, then the sales and payment. Lochailort was the only one to survive (though more recently new companies have come to Otter Ferry and Ardnamurchan). It was owned by Unilever's subsidiary, Marine Harvest, and by 1970 they were producing five to ten tons a year. They asked for, and got, a small grant from the HIDB, which had an unforeseen importance. Having proved that their system worked, Marine Harvest wanted to register a patent. The Board opposed this because it would have stopped small-scale fish farming and given Unilever a monopoly. It was 'quite a fight', Andrew Gilchrist says, and to Dunbar-Nasmith it was memorable too. It went to court, and the HIDB won by showing that it was *ultra vires* to seek a patent if public money had contributed to the enterprise. Unilever persisted, thinking of going to appeal, but was eventually persuaded not to. Since then relations have been good.

A year or two later Andrew Gilchrist gave a dinner in Inverness, with the Secretary of State for Scotland present, at which he served two salmon and asked his guests to say which was wild and which farmed. He did so because the farmed salmon was said to be inferior. His guests could not tell the difference—but the debate continues (and for a critical view read Alison Johnson in Chapter 2).

The great growth of fish farming followed, directed by Dunbar-Nasmith (deputy chairman from 1972) and strongly supported by Sir Kenneth Alexander, with rapid growth from 1976. Alexander points to its value both in providing food sold throughout the UK and in generating jobs in remote northern places, including some for crofters. Alexander regards fish farming as one of the prime achievements of his time (others being clear recognition of the need for plural jobs for crofters, the starting of community co-operatives, and the opening of the Craft Centre at Beauly, of which more later).

The Scottish west coast and the islands offer good sites for fish farming. Ideally, you need plenty of clear fresh water close to the shore for the first stage, and then clean sea water for the cages at the second stage. Ease of transfer from land to sea is important; and for the cages the ideal is a strong tidal flow, but protection from storms. Disease is likely if there is insufficient movement of the water, though in this Scotland seems to have had less trouble than Norway or Iceland.

The conflict between commerce and the environment remains. Fish farming has been a major success, thanks to help from the HIDB, but may be overstretching itself. It has brought full-time work for many and part-time work for crofters. But it has also marred the beauty of sensitive places—Loch Sunart, the Summer Isles and the first view of the sea as you approach Lochailort among them.

Land, landowners and life.

Long before the Board was created—indeed going back to the pre-war and post-war research of Fraser Darling—there had been debate about the use of land in the Highlands and Islands. Systematic work was done by the land division of the Board over many years, and in Sir Kenneth Alexander's time it came close to fruition. It was a bitter blow when, at the last stage, the new Government in 1979 put it into cold storage.

By that time, after years of study, the HIDB had arrived at what it saw as a fair and practicable way to deal with those landowners—a small minority—who were frustrating development of valuable land. In Alexander's words, its scheme had 'every conceivable safeguard against bureaucratic misuse by the Board or by the Secretary of State'. First, a case had to be made that there was genuine blockage of development; that had to be examined by a technical committee representative of all the skills, drawn from agricultural colleges and others; that committee had to produce a forward plan, with the landowner being part of the process and having the opportunity to agree with that plan. Failing that, the method would be to apply compulsory tenancies rather than take over the land. (The Board was well aware of a number of cases where tenants had abandoned possible improvements because their landlords did not want them.) In the last resort, however, land could be taken over—but then only after referring the whole process of consultation to the Secretary of State for Scotland.

The case for action would have had to show that development would bring more employment and create more prosperity. Sir Kenneth Alexander believes that if this approach had been applied it would have led to no more than four or five major estates being examined over a five-year period. The Board had specific cases in mind, but it knew it must work within a strict legal framework, testing counter arguments. He also believes that application of the process would have produced 'dramatic results' among other landowners not directly involved, not least where tenants had been reluctant to press for reform or development when the landowner was likely to be unsympathetic.

Before the 1979 election there had been informal talks with senior Conservatives in Scotland, who had shown interest in the HIDB proposal. After the election it became clear that no action could be expected. The Board's proposal was never tested, and indeed there was never any formal response from the Scottish Office. Had there been more pressure from within the Highlands, it might have been a different story.

Tourists, climbers, hotels and B & Bs.

More than three million visitors a year, spending about £460 million. Some 17–18,000 full-time tourist-related jobs, or above one-sixth of all full-time employed people in the Highlands and Islands. One-fifth of the visitors from overseas (with cars from as far away as Spain, Italy, Austria, Sweden and Norway to be seen on our roads), and higher than average spending in the Highlands by the overseas travellers. Not bad—a remarkable increase compared with the 1950s.

Among the reasons for the gain: roll-on, roll-off ferries, first coming into service on the Clyde in 1954 and for the Western Isles from 1964; greatly improved roads, especially the major routes such as Perth-Inverness-Cromarty Firth and Glasgow-Fort William-Kyle and Inverness-Ullapool; higher standards in hotels, better B & Bs, and organised camping sites; and, in winter, more ski-ing centres—though still inadequate to meet demand. In all of these, from 1965 onwards, the HIDB has played a significant role, along with the Scottish Office and local authorities..

Yes, but is there another side? Personally, I look back with some nostalgia to the days when the road to Skye was quiet, when you could pick your own peaceful camping site almost anywhere in Glen Garry or Glen Sheil on the way north or south (though the midges could be murder), when there were no caravans at the Glen Brittle camp site (but some good food at the little hotel) and when you could count on crossing Sgurr Dearg, Sgurr Alasdair and Sgurr Squmain without meeting anyone else. Selfish, of course, but those were great days, even if it did rain. Today many thousands more find their way to Glen Coe and the Cairngorms and the Cuillin every year—and that is right and good—but some of the peace and private regeneration has gone.

Back, though, to the very real achievements of the past 25 years, both through Government subsidies for ferries, trains and buses, and through grants, loans, training and publicity by the HIDB. The publicity has proved rewarding both at home and abroad. Visits were and are arranged for tourist and holiday writers (though Judith Chalmers was somewhat reserved about one of the trains and one hotel that she encountered); and groups of Highland hoteliers have gone, partly paying their own fares, on HIDB publicity campaigns in North America, France, Germany, Sweden and other places, with apparent success. At the same time, at home, the Board has established tourist organisations in each district with some 50 information centres, some open all year and some in summer only. An example: the little tourist office at Lochranza in Arran, established in the summer of 1989 mainly to service people coming or going by ferry from Kintyre, was astonished to find by the end of the season that it had served over 10,000 customers. (Source, the *Arran Banner*; and having seen the office at work I am not too surprised.)

As to hotels, grants and loans have been given quite generously to those with improvement plans, subject always to inspection. In the Outer Isles in particular the hotel standards were poor, partly because, until the ro-ro ferry came, holiday visitors were few. At an early stage, too, the HIDB decided to build five new hotels in the remoter areas then just beginning to attract more visitors. In the end only two were built—on Barra and in Mull—and a third (Raasay) was created by adaptation of a house. Of the Isle of Barra Hotel Derek Cooper, in his admirable book *The Road to Mingulay*, is blisteringly critical—saying that as planned by the HIDB it was too big, too costly to heat (facing the Atlantic), and never likely to pay. I stayed there twice in its early days and greatly enjoyed it, with comfortable rooms, a good view, and good food. It was nearly full on both occasions. But Cooper may well have been right, for it was eventually sold at a knock-down price to a local hotelier. The Mull hotel, too, has had its problems but seems to have fared better.

B & Bs similarly could apply for grants to improve facilities. As with hotels, there was a requirement that annual accounts should be submitted, but there were also cases where an applicant received money to add an extra room or two and then did not take visitors. Not much could be done about that, other than blacklisting. More often, people who had had a grant to put in a second bathroom have come back, wanting baths or showers for each of their visitors' rooms. They knew they were subject to supervision; and, as both Gilchrist and Fasken say, gentle pressure has paid off. Is the HIDB's assessment too optimistic? An article in the *Scotsman* in the autumn of 1989 spoke of 'mediocre breakfasts', outrageous prices and 'no feeling of welcome or warmth or homeliness'. The experience of my wife and myself at about the same time was quite different: good breakfasts, comfortable rooms, friendly hostesses and prices generally in line with £9 per person per night, give or take the odd pound or two. Keeping an eye open for B & Bs in new or well-kept houses—most probably in receipt of HIDB grants—is a guide to a good night.

One other useful innovation was imported from Ireland by Andrew Gilchrist. While ambassador there he had seen Guinness put much money into cabin cruisers up and down the River Shannon. When he came to Inverness he was horrified to find that there were no boats on hire on Loch Ness. Now there are plenty.

Trees, skis, co-ops and many others.

Much more ought to be said, but it will come in later chapters. Forestry was one of Bob Grieve's top four—not so much the planting, a matter for the well-established Forestry Commission, but the need to extend the 'value added' side which was, and still is, a high priority. As Dunbar-Nasmith said in his 1982 letter to the Secretary of State, instead of exporting timber to Scandinavia we needed modern timber processing plants in the Highlands. Though much progress has been made, that remains a prime concern for Sir Robert Cowan and the Board today. The major plants at Dalcross (near Inverness), Kilmallie, Fort William and Argyll are now producing valuable sawn timber, for use among other purposes in framed house-building, roof trusses, sheds, and pallettes. And the Board is making progress in persuading architects and builders to accept home-grown timber. It is, though, an area for further action.

Another activity on which Bob Cowan has concentrated is marketing, with particular concern to help the smaller businesses. As he says, in a four or five man business in Glasgow one can 'nip out' to call on customers for an hour or two and be back in the afternoon. In Skye or Sutherland that is not possible. The Board has therefore 'cross fertilised' its own marketing and it has sought to persuade buyers to come from the south. In livestock marketing, for example, it has induced auction companies to get more buyers to come from as far south as Penrith, and it has helped crofters to combine and group their sheep and cattle for the sales. It has also offered tourist packages to buyers—'come and bring your wife and have a weekend and do a deal'.

It is vital to the Highlands and Islands, Cowan says, that there should be numerous small businesses and diversity of productions. That is both healthy for each community and a safeguard when one of the bigger developments fails. As an example he cites the closure of the fish processing plant at Ardveenish in Barra in the summer of 1989. Unlike the Breasclete closure, it provoked little comment in national or local newspapers because so many other developments had taken place in Barra, with its bakery, its abattoir, its fish farming, its hotels and the co-operative. As in many HIDB areas, the fish farming had improved the viability of crofters, a big increase in tourists had helped the hotels, and there were other jobs available. Similarly, as mentioned earlier, there was the example of Wick-Thurso and its many successful enterprises—with Norfrost improbably making deep freeze refrigerators for world-wide export (crazy by normal industrial standards, but a success, with 300 employees); Osprey Electronics, with its underwater cameras, high tech and with 150 employees: Caithness Glass employing 120 people

1   Sir Robert Grieve, first Chairman of the Highlands and Islands Development Board,
Torridon 1986. Photograph by John Foster.

2 Scarista Beach, Harris. Photograph by Richard Ardern.

3 Highland Cattle, Luib. Photograph by Peter Davenport.

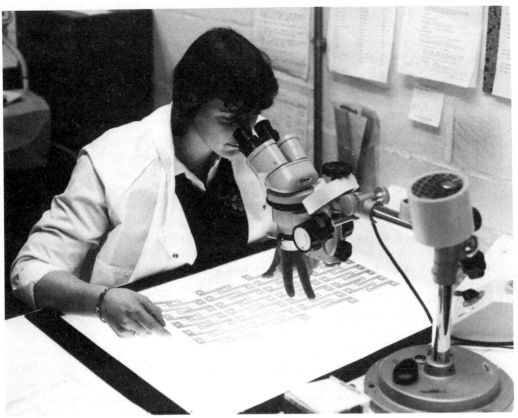

6   Flexible Technology, Rothesay. [HIDB]

in Wick; Mark Templeman making industrial gloves, and others. These were small businesses grown larger and with diversity of production.

The number of small businesses launched or sustained with HIDB grants or loans now runs into many thousands. A proportion, of course, have failed. The HIDB has had to endure much criticism over money lost in failures. Yet the 1984–5 Commons Scottish Affairs Committee's inquiry came to the conclusion that, far from being spendthrift, the Board had been too cautious. Sir Robert Grieve, early in the Board's life, drew attention to the fact that losses were not one-sided. He cited among early casualties a goldsmith, an optical technician, a business in Campbeltown and another in Strathpeffer—'fine men', he said, and while the Board had lost about 6 per cent of its investments 'they lost everything'.

Community co-operatives were one safeguard and a source of extra jobs. They were first generated by Sir Kenneth Alexander, following a study in 1976 of the Irish experience. They provided, as their name implies, for part-time work to the mutual benefit of a community. They were first launched in the Western Isles—in Ness, Park, Eriskay and Vatersay—and in Papa Westray in Orkney. They determined their own activities, from growing and selling vegetables when none were available to providing a local bus service. They were at low cost to the Board in launching, and eventually self-supporting. By 1988–9 there were 24, from Yell in the north to Campbeltown in the south, but mostly in small, remote communities. Only two of the originals had been wound up. Meanwhile the co-ops had set up their own communal movement, 'Ace HI' (the Association of Community Enterprises, Highlands and Islands) with an office in Dingwall and Sir Kenneth Alexander as president.

Another small but socially important HIDB service is in supporting village halls. *Why*, the city dweller may ask. Because it is one way to help in keeping people—especially the young—in the remoter places: they provide for dances, debates, gymnastics, parties, wedding receptions, the mobile cinema, flower shows, Gaelic classes and so on. A well kept and warm village hall is a real asset, and a little help from the HIDB can keep it cleaner and warmer. Consider also community contributions such as the new (1988–9) secondary school at Liniclete in North Uist—a spectacular £12m development, with full community facilities including a library, swimming pool, cafeteria and a radio studio that can feed directly into the BBC in Stornoway, Inverness, Glasgow or London. The prime reason for the school, of course, is to save children from the more southerly of the Western Isles (North Uist to Barra) from having to go to secondary school in Stornoway, living in hostels or boarding houses far from home during term-time.

In recent years the Board has been trying to make itself more accessible, especially for small businesses or enterprises. This was a particular concern of Admiral Dunbar-Nasmith and it has been further extended by Sir Robert Cowan. In all there are some 24 area offices, stretching from Arran to Lerwick and from Grantown to Tiree. To take the Scourie (Sutherland) office as an example: its territory runs from Ullapool northward to Durness and eastwards to Melvich, and it is run by an energetic young man, George Campbell, a graduate of Aberdeen University with some experience of land management, woodlands, fish farming and the requirements of tourism. Within his area there are 860 crofts, of which about 300 are actively worked. He is there to advise on development plans and the possibility of grants or loans, and to put people in touch with the relevant HIDB departments. An interesting job, rewarding to clients as to the Board.

Finally, ski-ing. Soon after being established, the Board took over the Cairngorm estate where the new downhill ski runs were being developed by the Cairngorm Chairlift Company. In a good year—such as the extraordinary 1979—it can provide for up to 6–7000 people a day from New Year to early May. In other years, such as 1988 or 1989, it may have good snow for no more than two months. It has been and will continue to be controversial because many more people want to ski there, but extension of the tows and runs must mean breaking into the corries below Cairn Lochan, which naturalists and others regard as sacrosanct. The pressure may be reduced by the opening of the new ski runs at Aonach Mhor, east of Fort William (a splendid site, but with some dangerous edges—which I say having seen some of the test ski-ing there). There are proposals also for new runs near Dalwhinnie, and there is capacity for more at the White

Corries, above Rannoch Moor. The demand for ski-ing is certain to increase, unless the 'greenhouse effect' diminishes Scottish snow; but in the Cairngorms the preservationists' case must count.

A tale of two peninsulas

Early in 1980 I was asked to report on two remote communities in Wester Ross— one self-supporting, the other in deep decline. One had a new road, linking it to inland villages, and built at a cost of £750,000 in 1974–6. The other in 1979 had refused a road offered by Highland Region at a projected cost of £480,000, because its people preferred their peaceful isolation. The thriving community was at Scoraig, on the north side of Little Loch Broom, and it was the one without a road or motor cars. The other was North Applecross, to the west of Torridon, and there the road had come too late to stop depopulation.

Returning to the two peninsulas in the summer of 1989, we found that North Applecross was no longer in decline, while Scoraig had doubled its population (from nine or ten families to 20—including 11 primary school children and 11 secondary, with a new secondary school built with funds which the families themselves had raised). The main reason for the recovery of North Applecross was the arrival of fish farming, with HIDB support. Scoraig's growth was of its own making, thanks to the strong character and creative determination of its people, nearly all incomers from Lowland Scotland or from England.

The core of the Scoraig success lies in five or six families or individuals, mostly knowing each other, who moved to the peninsula in the 1960s. They came to a barren land without trees, no longer able to support crofting and devoid of other occupation. The last of the old Highland crofters were about to leave. The new arrivals intended to make their livings mainly from other activities—one as a boatbuilder, one making violins, one by knitting and weaving, one by making wind generators (low power electricity), and one making spinning wheels. They keep sheep, in the old crofting style, and one is also part-time postman and ferryman.

Walking in to Scoraig by the six-mile path or looking from across the water, the scene is transformed. There are clumps of trees (pine, spruce, rowan, birch), shelter belts, vegetable gardens (broccoli, potatoes, lettuce, turnip) and a variety of growing fruit. The houses have been rebuilt or extended or are new—one a round, low-level structure facing the open sea. The primary school has been at work since 1970, with a fully trained teacher who had come with her husband among the first incomers. (He, a refugee from Hungary in 1956, is one of the master gardeners of Scoraig and also teaches part-time in the school). The secondary school opened in 1989, with a teacher from Easter Ross paid by funds raised by the Scoraig people themselves, and with unpaid, part-time teaching by parents with scientific, language and musical qualifications. The secondary building itself has been constructed from the remains of a ruined church, by the Scoraig people— an extraordinary achievement. Again, there has been a small grant from the HIDB and some funding from Highland Region. If the school satisfies the Scottish Office inspectors in each of four years, then the Regional Council will take over the full costs from 1993.

Life in Scoraig is not easy. It requires constant work to maintain frugal standards and it depends on harmony within a small community. For some who came to live there it proved too stark: but for those who have stayed it is a good life, and their children have done well. The range of achievement among those whose primary schooling was in Scoraig may be judged by this listing from a single family (that of the primary teacher): one, the oldest, is a prawn fisherman based at Ullapool and Little Loch Broom; one is in Hull, working for a PhD in potato disease; one is making and restoring violins in Germany; one is at the Royal Northern College of Music in Manchester; and twins are training as teachers at Moray House in Edinburgh. These were their occupations in the autumn of 1989.

One other important aspect: the people of Scoraig have been blessed with benign landowners—brothers from London, with an estate inland from Scoraig, but sympathetic to what the Scoraigers have done.

North Applecross is a different story. In 1980 it seemed on the way to total depopulation. Most of those with houses there were old—too old to work their crofts effectively—or absentees working at the Kishorn construction yard or away all week in Easter Ross or as far off as Glasgow. Driving by the new road one saw that at least half the crofts were derelict and even the sheep were few. On the same route in 1989 we counted three new houses and eight restored croft houses—some said to be occupied by fish farmers and some holiday homes, which at least provide economic value in building work and in shopping trade.

Just one hopeful sign in 1980 was a youngish family, the Kilbrides, incomers from the south, who were trying to set up as crofters with a weaving and spinning workshop. Even with their energy, though, the prospect was poor. The old crofters, too old to work the land, were blocking access to land by the newcomers and even preventing them from re-building their house; and the Crofters Commission, a timid body, was unwilling to intervene. But the Kilbrides took their case to the Land Court and won the right to their share of the ground, access to their house, and a fenced 'apportionment' of land in which to keep their tup (the breeding ram). They were able also to establish their weaving shop beside the new road.

Now they have some 70 breeding ewes, a 'registered flock' of a rare breed, the Shetland-Gotland, of Swedish origin, producing wool which is both soft and strong. The wool can be sold as such, but much of it goes into knitted jerseys or sweaters; and in the summer seasons of 1987, 1988 and 1989, the whole of their output was sold through Lesley Kilbride's shop. As they say, there is nowhere else for visitors to stop in the 22 miles from Applecross village (in South Applecross) to Sheildaig on the road to Torridon—apart, that is, from pausing to admire the splendid views of Skye, Raasay, the Torridon hills and, on a clear day, Lewis and Harris.

The Kilbrides are among the first to admit that relations with the old crofters were 'testy' for some years, though not now, and they are also among the first to defend some aspects of the old system. When there were a number of active crofters within a township, it made sense to divide the land so that each had some good patches and some poor plots, on the old runrig system. It was essential also to have a 'righ' or leader, usually the grazing committee's clerk. But when only one family was working the land the old restrictions made no sense; and, as an outsider, I find it extraordinary that the Kilbrides had to wait six or seven years after buying a share before they could properly use their land or rebuild their house. Today only three or four crofts in the whole length of North Applecross are still working crofts, and each is run by a single family. It is said, however, that the recent (1985) creation of the Scottish Crofters Union is at last achieving some of the reforms that the Crofters Commission had failed to bring about.

For my wife and myself, going back to Scoraig and to North Applecross was a cheering experience. For both communities, life is better than it was. Long may they prosper.

Past and future

Along almost all of the mainland west coast there are jobs for all who want them. Fish farming, tourism, small industries, crafts and forestry have brought this about. Again taking Applecross, North Applecross and Torridon as a test, it is estimated that in recent years some 200 people have returned from the oil construction yards or other jobs, or from further south, to work in their home area. The north coast is less fortunate, lacking the shelter of lochs and bays that permit the breeding of fish. Crofting is no alternative, except in the broad straths of Halladale and Naver. But overall—west and east and in the islands—there can be little doubt that recent years have seen a great increase in prosperity, living standards, education and self-confidence.

That must be to the benefit of Britain as a whole. The Highlands and Islands are providing food, holidays, timber and craft products for the whole of the UK, as well as strategic bases for offshore oil and for the Royal Navy, Army and RAF. There is no call for 'chucking buns' across the Great Glen.

Looking back at the question with which this chapter started—*would it matter if Northern Scotland became depopulated?*—my reply is clear. Even clearer, indeed, in 1990 than it was eleven years earlier. The Highlands and Islands are of immense value to the UK and to Europe. Northern Scotland needs and deserves the help it has had.

ALASTAIR HETHERINGTON—Oxford University (MA, English). Army 1940–46, Royal Armoured Corps, Normandy and beyond. *Glasgow Herald* 1946–50. *Manchester Guardian* 1950–75; Editor 1956–75. (*The Guardian* from 1959, and printed also in London from 1961). With BBC Scotland 1976–80. Research professor of Media Studies, Stirling University 1982–87; Emeritus since then.

For a detailed account of the HIDB's grants and loans, see Appendix

Chapter 2

Four Personal Perspectives

2a   An Absurd Sense of Optimism

Anne Lorne Gillies

I composed a song on the way from Stirling to Ballachulish. Pretended it was Gaelic, and sang it to the bus's whining drone. My brother whined 'shurrup'. What should I care. I was four and going to visit the land of my waking dreams— my father's stories—his big books with gold letters and tissue paper between pictures. James Stuart of the Glens. The Red Fox. Cluny MacPherson. Prince Charles Edward. Glencoe. Forty years later the names still stir.

When I was born my father had held me up to see the Campsies. From that moment I had learned that one day I would live far beyond them. Far beyond the world. And the world itself (a space bounded only by burns and dykes and hillsides, noisy with peewits and a clocking hen) did little to disturb the dreamer. I would live in the Highlands—somewhere; I would speak Gaelic—soon: the bus trip was some kind of rehearsal. I was still too young to understand my father's own history. The nervous excitement of his youth in London during the birth of modern Scottish nationalism; his belief in the inseparability of cultural and economic regeneration; theory put to the test in a slate quarry in Ballachulish and the storms that beached him on the limestone of Stirling—a man more powerful with pen than pick-axe; the endless search for a way back North and, for his children, the gift of his own father's preferred language.

A year later, in welly boots, I arrived: Rockfield School, Oban. I can still smell the disappointment. Wet coats hung on iron pegs, the cat sat on its mat, the plasticine on its board. And the big girls snarled 'What are you gaping at?' as I clung to the railing. In hot weather Dunstaffnage—ancient stamping ground of King Robert the Bruce—sent its post-war children to school with tar in their hair from melting pre-fabricated roofs. In bad weather the cripple's legs turned purple under their calipers and the tinks slunk down from the hill. There was no Gaelic in Rockfield, though much later I would discover how many of the teachers kept it hidden in their closets—even the infant mistress, with her studied 'Dreenk up your meelk, Enne Gillies'. A truculent Englishman came down from the High School once a week to teach *taffy tiffy taffy tiffy taah taah* and 'When daisies pied'.

(At least in Stirling the heidie called us bairns, the jannie gied us aipples and Miss Flett learned us 'Will ye buy my sybies' and 'Queen Mary Queen Mary'). Och well, what difference. I doubt I would have spoken Gaelic in any case: talking was not on the curriculum, even before the teacher belted me for asking the girl beside me what page we were on.

Things took a turn for the better the year sweets came off the ration. Our class was taken by the new Headmaster: he had been away at sea while the landlubbers were sterilising their classrooms, and his priorities were different. I skipped up the road to the strains of the waulking song he taught us: *he mo leannan ho mo leannan*— the sun shone from his bald head. I joined his Gaelic choir and went to the Mod to discover the wonder of Woolworths and the horror of sleeping two in a bed.

Even better, a dignified lady from South Uist hoisted her considerable frame over our fence to offer my mother 'assistance with the beasts'. For years she echoed through the house, a seamless flow of laughter and tears, piety and bawdry, Gaelic and English: my brother and I entered the secondary school well prepared for the delights of the Gaelic class.

I soon realised why the Gaelic classroom was so small. Everyone else went to learn French, far away in the Languages Corridor. Some of them proceeded to German—while we were working backwards through the eighteenth century to Mairi Nighean Alasdair Ruaidh and a smidgeen of ancient Irish.

The Gaelic lesson was conducted in English. There were girls from Mull and Morvern, and boys from Ardnamurchan, but their native bilingualism helped them little in learning lists of prepositions or the declension of irregular nouns. To me it was all as easy as 'mensa mensa mensam'. I left school with a complete set of An Comunn Gaidhealach prize-books on my shelf and a mean way with a prose passage still as tentative in the art of ordinary Gaelic conversation as I had been six years previously. Gaelic lessons yielded a little local history—a slight realignment of Leaving Certificate perspectives, where the Scots appeared and disappeared like seasonal clegs around royal English heads. But without the seal of Education Department approval Highland history stuck in the imagination as definitely unimportant and probably untrue: Alasdair Mac Colla, the Lordship of the Isles, the Battles of Carinish and Harlaw, Inverlochy and Falkirk, all barely distinguishable from tourist-guide legends of Fingal and his seven-league boots.

A girl in my brother's class went to elocution lessons: the Rector of the school said we should all aspire to speak like her ... hail to thee blithe spirit ... Yet those were halcyon days. The Rector was a Gaelic scholar, poet, piper and source of most of the traditional songs I have treasured and shared to this day; he taught Greek while rehearsing '*The Lament for the Children*' on his twelve-inch ruler. The Head of the Gaelic Department was President of An Comunn Gaidhealach, kenspeckle Provost of the town in an otter-skin sporran. English lessons were punctuated by the hilarious insights of a Lewis-born poet—much published Prometheus still bound to his blackboard. The maths teacher's brother, douce man, was the Customs Officer in Barra when the *Politician* went down. The Domestic Science teacher had the voice (and legs) of a Drimnin *banarach*. Oban High School Gaelic Choir competed—and often won—against the Nicholson

Institute and Portree. Even Govan could muster enough Gaelic-speaking juniors to join the Mod élite in those days.

(*Am I that old?* Nowadays you will travel far before you will find a native Gaelic-speaking child in Mull or Lismore, Morvern or Ardnamurchan, Jura or Islay or Tiree—'Argyll ... from which Gaelic spread like snowdrops' as my famous English teacher has described his adopted habitat. But the snowdrop is a plant of peculiar—if not miraculous—insistence: absurd green shoots sprouting through ground too hard to till. And today Gaelic is beginning to push its way upwards to create its own unlikely springtime, not only in Argyll but in parts of Scotland where the winter has been much longer, the ground even more forbidding.)

Twenty-five years ago I made a monster and called it English. Its nostrils flared, its eyes bulged, its mouth yawned, its body was a length of rope I begged from a man on the pier at Leith. The University Highland Society carried it through the streets of Edinburgh on Charities Day, its symbolic coils strangling our Gaelic-speaking throats, and the children of Tynecastle almost realising the metaphor (at least for the girl on the end) by jumping on its English tail. We gave it away to a man in a car who wanted it for his Christmas party, and took ourselves off to an establishment renowned for the elasticity of its licensing hours and the fervour of its Gaelic choruses.

That was the year I wrote an allegory for the Highland Soc Year Book—priceless treasures mouldering under lock and key in a miserly castle while the world outside grew uniformly grey. Symbolism was the stuff of our adolescence. Obsessive heroes in the School of Scottish Studies collected the remnants of Gaelic culture before the last tradition-bearer escaped to Tir nan Og. Stony villains stared southwards from their offices in St Andrew's House. The man who would carry the jewels of Gaelic-medium education into the primary school classrooms of the Western Isles was still composing concrete Gaelic poems in desultory free periods at an Edinburgh secondary. At the University a scholarly Englishman delivered formal lectures on comparative philology to a solitary Honours Celtic student.

About this time I discover myself wearing white lipstick on the pages of a Gaelic magazine, declaring my ambition to do well in life and raise a family of Gaelic-speaking children. But in the Gaidhealtachd concerned parents were busy weaning their children off the language to prepare them for the schools where teachers hastened to complete the process. Education was a prescription for departure. Gaelic broadcasting was *da cheathramh agus fonn*. A political blow for Gaelic was altering the flight-path of Concorde during the Mod Gold Medal Finals. After graduation the Highland Soc went its several ways—teachers, lawyers, ministers, doctors—to Dingwall, Dunfermline, Oxford, Hong Kong, Kuwait. And when I finally settled down to raise a family my carefully nurtured son took a unilateral decision and stopped speaking Gaelic after six months in an English-medium nursery school.

(*Am I really that old?* Nowadays Gaelic promotion has leapt out of the poetry-book and into the filofax. Students have graduated, via nocturnal road-sign writing, to daylight political lobbying. Education authorities and the media compete to lure Gaelic-speaking graduates back to the Gaidhealtachd. Concerned bilingual parents run playgroups to prepare their children for Gaelic-medium primary education. Monolinguals attend language classes in time to help with their children's homework. Regional councillors and civil servants smile with apparent benevolence upon the increasing demand for Gaelic education and co-operate to anticipate its every implication. And my daughters learn to read and write and think and talk through the medium of Gaelic in a Glasgow school in the shadow of high-rise council flats.)

Almost thirty years ago I spent holidays in Tiree: lived with a school-friend, shared her Gaelic-speaking granny for a while, envied her casual birthright, and recognised for the first time the extent to which I lived daily between two disparate communities—aspired to one, belonged to neither. Almost thirty years later I was invited back to the island as Education Officer of Comunn na Gaidhlig—to address parents on the benefits of Gaelic-medium education. Irony sat with me on the plane from Glasgow, met me again on the tarmac, awaited me in the shiny new school.

'The meeting will need to be in English' I was told. 'Not many of the parents

7   Gaelic as a medium of instruction: Carnish, North Uist.
Photograph by Sam Maynard/Eolas.

have Gaelic nowadays. Some were born in the city and have come back to the family home; some were born here but haven't kept up the language; some are incomers but want their children to be part of a Gaelic community. They queue up to enrol their children in the Gaelic playgroup, but it's back to square one when they go to the primary ...'

A crowded classroom, parents perched on undersized seats, faces like a sea of snowdrops. A generation reaching out to find a way back to the future; willing me to convince them that through their children they can restore what had seemed irrevocably lost. A year later the memory still stirs. Strathclyde Regional Council has happily acceded to the establishment of Gaelic-medium Primary Unit in Cornaigmore, to wrest a new bilingual generation from the monster's jaws. As I write the parents wait while officials scour the county for a teacher to staff the Unit: the effect of wintry policies, scattering Gaelic-speaking teachers to the four winds, do not disappear at the first glimpse of sunshine. But the climate is changing fast.

I go my ways around the islands. Read posters advertising last week's open forum with HIDB officials, next week's meeting to discuss school boards. The children go to Gaelic summer camps, on north-south educational exchanges—use the expertise of local history societies to research their school projects. In Breasclete the teacher observes with wonderment that her infants seem immune to English. In Liniclete the French teacher takes me round the new community school, describing its potential in rich idiomatic Gaelic. In Sleat I talk to Gaelic College students about their local work-related research projects, watch the data-base grow. In Portree, listen as eight-year olds discuss the dialectal idiosyncracies of computer software instructions—their own speech echoing the North End twang of the infant teacher who gave them the gift of bilingualism.

Cultural revival, economic regeneration, and everywhere the acknowledgement of the importance of the community in shaping its own future. I sing a Gaelic song under my breath. Feel a sense of belonging—to an expanding, outward-looking Gaidhealtachd that spills across old divides, defies yesterday's frost. I am filled with an absurd sense of optimism. What a life—and only half completed.

Dr Anne Lorne Gillies— Singer, broadcaster and, since 1988, Education Officer with Comunn na Gaidhlig (CNAG), the National Gaelic language promotion agency, funded through the HIDB and Scottish Education Department.

2b   Conversions at Scarista

Alison Johnson

When I was asked to contribute to this book I was slightly alarmed by its scope: 25 years of the Highlands. I've been in Harris long enough to forget exactly how long, but surely not *that* long! But here I am, a veteran, an established settler ready to give advice to recent arrivals or to curious visitors: never drink the water unboiled, always carry a loaded revolver in your puttees, that sort of thing.

There's something reassuring about a good dollop of time, it seems. When my first book, *A House by the Shore* came out, it was subtitled by the publisher *12 Years in the Hebrides.* The title was a lie anyway, as it's five minutes rough walk to high tide mark, nevertheless the reading public expects Hebridean houses to be by the shore, and I was told 'near the sea' wouldn't do at all; but the subtitle, if anything, seemed even wider of the mark. Twelve years of personal monoculture wasn't how I had thought of it. It included three years schoolteaching, seven years dog ownership, eight years self-employment, five years parenthood. There were fractions of years (which all add up) spent in the ferry queue at Kyleakin, and at motorway service areas between Aberdeen and Plymouth.

But if I didn't notice life rearranging itself into a twelve year glob of Hebridean homogeneity, did the Hebrides notice *me*? What has twelve years—more than twelve years now—of me, or at least of me and him, done to alter the face of Harris?

Well, we did paint the house white. (It takes about 0.1 of a year every three years, subtitle *A Third of a Year in Sandtex*, quite a thought.) We can see its gleaming walls from Amhuinnsuidhe, fifteen miles away, from the summits of Ben Luskentyre and Roneval, from the remote offshore islands of Taransay and Scarp, even from North Uist. Khaki would be more environmentally discreet, but there's no denying the primitive satisfaction afforded by that white blot on the landscape. After all these years, it's still a pledge of transformation, of something achieved through our own hard physical slog.

We were unused to hard labour when we first came to the island: that's what made it such a rewarding experience. Newly married, penniless, rendered unemployable by too much education, we had a dream of restoring a large old house by our own efforts, just for the fun of doing something we hadn't done before. Turning the restored gem into a country house hotel seemed an obvious consequence, since even at that optimistic stage of life we realised we would need to earn some money to keep the wolf from strolling in through the hole in the wall. Indeed, earning money couldn't wait much longer if we were to purchase even an unrestored gem; so we taught for a few years in Tarbert, not really doubting that the meagre savings from our salaries would conjure up the required derelict mansion. Astonishingly, it happened. We bought the old manse at Scarista in 1975.

It had been empty for a decade, broken and battered by the fierce Atlantic weather which scours the treeless slope behind the dunes of Scarista Bay. There were coils of barbed wire in the kitchen, seed potatoes in the dining room, bales of hay in the minister's study. Water poured through all the skylights, leaving joists and floorboards oozy with rot down to ground level. Windows were broken, doors hung askew. The only sign of cultivation in the extensive walled gardens was a stunted elder bush by the broken front gate. The rest was piled with rubbish, fertiliser sacks and fencing wire on top, then a layer of broken bedsteads, bits of fireplaces and smashed slates, indicating past renovations; underneath that, a litter of bottles which had mostly contained either champagne or syrup of figs, an unlikely cocktail for some vanished minister; and beneath all the bulky soph- isticated detritus of post-war Britain, the undateable rubbish of the past, red layers of peat ash and black layers of muck, the tipped loads of generations of hardworked servant-girls.

At that time, country house hotels were not yet to be found behind every crumbling wall and down every potholed track. By now, the Good Hotel Guide and Basil Fawlty have turned them into a familiar national institution; but back in the mid 1970s our scheme to turn a filthy old ruin on a windswept outpost somewhere near Rockall into a civilised hostelry sounded like madness. Our relatives were distressed, our friends embarrassed. The men from the HIDB fingered their chins and looked pitying, but came up with a grant. If ever they thought they were backing a project doomed to failure, they must have felt it was Scarista House. We had no training, no money, could only hope to let four bedrooms because building regulations forbade use of the attics, and couldn't serve our prospective clients with so much as a glass of wine because the Church of Scotland, which controlled the conditions of our title, had dug its hypocritical heels in. Yet there we were insisting we could first of all complete an ambitious conversion job between the two of us, and then aim for the top of the market and high ratings in the prestige guides.

Somehow it worked. Faith moved mountains of timber and plasterboard, sand and cement. It failed, though, to move the Church of Scotland: it took three years and the threat of legal proceedings to achieve a reluctant relaxation of our feu disposition. By that time we had indeed made distinguished progress in all the major restaurant and hotel guides. Satisfied customers had seen to that. They didn't seem to care about the hardboard ceiling in the drawing room, the squeaky floorboards in the dining room, the weeds ramping through the over-ambitious gardens we were too busy to maintain. They loved the food, the fresh shellfish and sweet island mutton and venison; they loved the view, the two miles of sandy beach pounded by Atlantic surf; they loved the peat fires, the wall of books in the library, the local girls we employed, the hens in the car park, the smell of fresh-baked bread in the hall. 'This place is *special!*' people often say.

They're right, but the credit isn't ours. The house was always like that. Filthy, gaunt and grey as it was when we first walked up to it, once in through that collapsing front door we forgot the squalor and delapidation and basked in its grace and serenity. Who or what built that into this severe bastion of Presbyterianism I don't know, but there it is, warming and twinkling, bringing out the best in people. That magic made it easy for us to survive the renovation period, sleeping in a damp, gritty bed and waking to damp, gritty clothes, eating mostly what we could grow, washed down with the occasional luxury of homebrew. We still look back to that year and a half of massive physical labour as one of the happiest times of our lives; the old house deserved it—and gave so much in return.

Hotel keeping wasn't so much fun. We were ambitious for a reputation and succeeded in gaining one. By our fifth season we had spectacular ratings in the *Good Food* and *Good Hotel Guides* and other guides were following along nicely. The result was ghastly: a nauseating influx of Foodies. They jetted up from London for the weekend with a new secretary or someone else's wife, Harris one trip, Dijon or Vienna next: wherever there was a new blot on the Foody atlas. They scribbled notes on the menus and talked to each other in intense and unmannerly whispers. They got agoraphobia on the beach and were too intent on their plates to hear the laughing soul of the old house. Suddenly, I hated cooking. Why should I waste time making them lunch when they had been too hung over to get up for our excellent breakfast? How dare they fix greedy eyes on that plate of prawns when a turn of the head would show them the sun setting into the Atlantic? Why, for that matter, should they eat the poor prawns at all, rather than *vice versa*?

It was that last question and others related which gave us terminal indigestion. For years we had been butchering sheep, gutting fish, murdering lobsters. It became uncomfortably clear, both that these creatures would rather have escaped our attentions and that we had more fellow-feeling for lobsters than for Foodies. These were not happy discoveries for hoteliers at the peak of their careers.

If we had allied clean hands to contrite hearts, we would have chucked it there and then; given them nothing but beans till the end of that season and closed the doors after it. But a little exercise of worldly wisdom revealed a tolerable compromise. Our customers should live, if not on beans, at least on creatures which had led a relatively natural life—no factory farmed produce, in other words. No poultry (we have hens who supply eggs, but they protest at being eaten themselves) no veal, no bacon—hang on! Just try bearding uncertain first-thing-in-the-morning tempers with a bacon embargo. But again, think of the average British baconer, reared indoors on bare concrete, son of a mother who spends virtually her whole life in a pen too small for her to turn round. We discovered Heal Farm in Devon in the nick of time, and since then all our pig-meat has come unpatriotically from the West Country, by Datapost. (I just hope people like me, whose sausages require a special four-hour round trip with a postie on overtime from Stornoway, don't make Datapost so uneconomic that they axe it.)

Absolutely no farmed fish. At that time, everyone still thought fish farming was wonderful news—employment, cheap protein, no undesirable environmental consequences. Scarista Against Fish Farming stood alone. We hated it on humane grounds, and suspected its effects on marine life. Now, of course, all that and much more is causing official concern, but probably too late. The frustration we felt in trying to get people to listen to our arguments against this filthy habit was very potent in turning me into a serious conservationist; because, bluntly, if something—indeed anything—looks good for our own species, however short-term, we are generally unmoved by the most glaring harm it may do to other species, however long-term.

We took to spending a lot of time in the boat, negotiating the tricky reefs and tiderips of the Sound of Harris, pondering on birds and seals and sandeels. Hotel-keeping became a less and less probable mode of existence, but the guests didn't fade away: far from it. Scarista House had become *something*, worth a detour, 'a special place'. We thought of closing our doors to guests and merely living there—after all, it was our home. But in the end we couldn't do it, not here; because everything is more precarious out here, low employment, poor communications, dodgy supply lines (though we actually *do* drink the water unboiled). We have wonderful local staff, and our well-heeled customers spread a bit around to local retailers; and people like to have the place there, not because it's an amenity, but because it's been heard of on the other side of the world, because it's a success where success is hard. It has, after all, become a landmark in more than its white walls.

This year we are selling up and people are asking 'How can you bear to leave it?' It isn't difficult. The old house is too generous to be treated merely as a possession. We gave it a leg up when it was needed: now it's running and will run on without us, offering the same gracious welcome as it did when we first squeezed in through the collapsing front door.

ALISON JOHNSON lives on Harris. She and her husband, Andrew, restored the old manse at Scarista and have run it for twelve seasons as a highly-acclaimed hotel. As well as non-fiction under her usual name, she writes novels under the name A Findlay Johnson. Her interests are wildlife and sailing.

2c   A New Confidence?

James Hunter

In the autumn of 1965, when the Highlands and Islands Development Board began work in Inverness, I was at the start of my fifth year in Oban High School. The new agency, I am afraid, was not one of my constant preoccupations. Nor was I peculiar in this. The HIDB's aspirations for us, the first Highland generation whose careers and prospects the Board's members and officials might have hoped to influence, featured scarcely at all in Oban High School conversation, as far at least as I can now recall. It was not that we were taken up entirely with our imminent examinations. Nor was it that we gave no thought to matters other than the sporting achievements of Celtic Football Club or the music of Lennon and McCartney. These things were important to us. But so were political issues.

The Conservative Party, which had been in power for as long as any of us could remember, had been displaced in 1964 by Labour. We had keenly followed the election. And we took at least an intermittent interest in Mr Harold Wilson's endeavours, the overall thrust of which we mostly supported, to modernise the British economy. Like Mr Wilson, we believed our country to be in urgent need of change.

We read newspapers, we talked politics; British politics; international politics. We were particularly passionate, I remember, on the subject of Rhodesia, where the resident white minority, under the leadership of Mr Ian Smith, were then embarking on their supremacist experiment. But we were not greatly exercised by the inauguration, much nearer home, of the Highland Board; nor even by the Parliamentary battles surrounding the passage of its founding Act.

Most of us, I think, either knew or suspected that such plans as the HIDB chairman Professor Robert Grieve might have been making for the Highlands and Islands were unlikely to impinge greatly upon us. If questioned about our future, we should have predicted, quite correctly for the most part, that our lives would be lived well beyond the area for which Professor Grieve and his colleagues had been made responsible. And this, we should probably have added if pressed, was not necessarily a bad thing.

31

We might have been one more set of Highland emigrants in the making, but we were not, in any sense, refugees. We had not fallen victim to famine, war or eviction. And although we were told repeatedly that we were not properly appreciative of our good fortune, we were well aware that many more opportunities were open to us than had ever been available to our parents.

We were the products of a welfare state. And that did not mean simply that we had been among the first babies to be born under the beneficent aegis of the National Health Service. It meant also that our rights of access to education, including higher education, were virtually unlimited. And so there was nothing to prevent those of us with the necessary academic abilities acquiring qualifications which would ensure that we got good jobs.

Most such jobs, of course, were located far away. A few newly-trained teachers, doctors, ministers and the like might find employment in the Highlands and Islands. But any other young people who chose to remain in their own localities were automatically deemed less successful, possibly even by themselves, than those of their contemporaries who had moved south or who had gone overseas. The son who stayed at home to work the family croft was not unappreciated by his parents. But the other son, whose graduation photograph was prominently displayed on the kitchen dresser and who was invariably said to be 'doing very well for himself' in Glasgow or Vancouver was, in many instances, a greater source of family pride.

Almost a century earlier, John Murdoch, the pioneer land reformer who did so much to foment the crofting revolt of the 1880s, had pressed the education authorities to provide a school syllabus more closely tailored to Highland circumstances. Not only were the schools wholly neglectful of Gaelic culture, Murdoch pointed out; they were doing little or nothing to enhance the Highland population's chances of making better use of Northern Scotland's natural resources. 'Husbandry is not taught' he complained. 'There is nothing done to fit the people along the coasts to turning the wealth of the sea to account.' That remained the case in the 1960s. In Oban, as in other parts of the Highlands and Islands, the school curriculum was concerned much more with the wider world than with our own communities.

Unlike John Murdoch, of whom we had never heard, we did not quarrel with this state of affairs. Indeed it did not seem at all odd to me then, though it does now, that the school subject in which I came to take most interest, history, was concerned exclusively with events in England and on the Continent. From members of my own family, of course, I had heard something about the past of my own place and people. But not until I chanced to read John Prebble's book about the Battle of Culloden and its aftermath did it begin to occur to me that Highland happenings and Highland personages were as much a part of history as the Corn Laws and the foreign policy of Good Queen Bess.

This devaluing of our heritage was inherent in our situation. School belonged much more to the urban and industrial world for which we were being equipped than it did to the quite distinct social setting in which we were brought up. And because the life to which we were being directed was almost universally thought better than the one we were leaving behind, so the knowledge we acquired in school seemed not only different from, but superior to, the quite different bits of information we picked up at home. The latter, which had to do with matters as diverse as stalking, stock management and Gaelic tradition, might be of some sentimental significance. But it was not going to help us to 'get on'. And so we were not encouraged to rate it very highly.

In contemplating the Highland exodus of which we were a part and in pondering how to stem it, I suspect, Professor Grieve and his newly-appointed Board dealt in not dissimilar categories. Talk of Gaelic and crofting and land reform was all very well. But practical men—and Board Members considered themselves nothing if not practical—knew, or at least believed strongly, that the principal cause of the continuing depopulation of Northern Scotland was to be found in the region's failure to participate adequately in the post-war expansion of the British economy. And once the Highland disease had been thus diagnosed, the remedy was obvious: to establish in the north big businesses of the sort which had made the south so successful.

'Manufacturing industry is very poorly represented in the Highlands and Islands' Professor Grieve wrote in the HIDB's first annual report. 'Without it, the region will continue to lack any real possibility of a substantial enough rise in numbers to give credibility to Highland regeneration ... Modern industrial enterprises are absolutely essential in providing more of the kind of skills and initiative which will breed new enterprise and broaden the range of social and cultural leadership.'

Such an approach was understandable. Unfortunately, however, it could all too easily result in its proponents becoming somewhat dismissive of more indigenous economic activity which tended, of course, to be much smaller in scale than the 'manufacturing enterprises' which the HIDB hoped to locate in the 'linear city' which its more optimistic members were planning for the Eastern Highlands. 'It would be daft,' one of these Board Members was reported to have commented caustically, 'to try and catch sprats when we could catch a whale.'

And there were whales to be caught. The largest was landed in the summer of 1968 when it was announced in the House of Commons that British Aluminium were to construct a massive smelter at Invergordon.

The HIDB's initial efforts to industrialise the flat lands surrounding the Cromarty Firth had ended in controversy. The Board had become enmeshed in the affairs of Invergordon Chemical Enterprises, the first of a long series of ultimately abortive and often wildly speculative ventures founded on the proposition that Easter Ross had a glittering future as a prime petrochemicals centre. And since Invergordon Chemical Enterprises was the brainchild of one of the Highland Board's own members, Mr Frank Thomson, the HIDB's strong links with the company were incautious to say the least.

In the course of the political furore which followed press inquiries into the Thomson-HIDB-Chemical Enterprises triangle, the two-year-old Board's reputation had been badly dented and its chairman had contemplated resignation. Hence the note of self-justification to be detected in Professor Grieve's response to the smelter announcement: 'When you get an undertaking of this size coming to the Highlands, so decisively bringing the whole centre of gravity further north, there are no criticisms, no disappointment, only thankfulness. It ought to be regarded by everyone as a superb prize.' And so it was. But only for a time.

Today the rate of unemployment in Easter Ross, much of which suffers from many of the social and economic problems associated with industrial dereliction is, as it has been for several years, a good deal higher than it was when news of British Aluminium's imminent arrival was first released. The smelter stands lifeless on a site that was once one of the most fertile tracts of farmland in the Highlands. And its empty shell, sadly, is by no means the only monument to the failure of the industrial promotion policy on which so many hopes were founded.

The pulp mill at Fort William, another creation of the 1960s, has long since been shut down. At Arnish in Lewis, Kishorn in Wester Ross, and in several other localities across the northern half of Scotland, the platform yards and other facilities brought into existence in the early 1970s to meet the needs of the offshore oil industry have all too evidently been abandoned by their owners. And even the Atomic Energy Authority's experimental centre at Dounreay, which antedated the HIDB by several years, but to which the Board's first chairman helped direct Britain's prototype fast reactor in 1966, now faces closure.

On New Year's Day 1982, when working as a journalist on the staff of a Sunday newspaper, I travelled north to record the human consequences of the Invergordon smelter's precipitate demise. In the little Easter Ross town of Alness an unseasonably warm sun was highlighting the trim lines of the housing estates which had been built to accommodate the British Aluminium workforce. Women were crying in homes still hung with Christmas decorations. 'They told us we would have work here for a lifetime' said one man of British Aluminium, the HIDB and all the other organisations which he claimed had combined to entice him to a job at Invergordon. 'It was just another of their bloody lies.'

They were not liars really. There were occasions when the people in charge of the Highland Board could be distressingly susceptible to the charms of a self-proclaimed entrepreneur armed with not much more than an off-the-peg company and a nice line in headed notepaper. But Board Members and their officials, for the most part, were entirely honest folk who, being wholeheartedly committed to the cause of Highland development, naturally chose to serve that cause by the means which made most sense in the context of the time. And if they selected the wrong means they were in good, or at least prestigious, company.

Though Ministers were eagerly egged on by the HIDB, it was Government, not the Board, which was ultimately responsible for projects such as the pulp mill and the smelter. And Government, in those days when Mrs Margaret Thatcher was an obscure Opposition backbencher, was wholly identified with the notion that economically underprivileged regions could be readily regenerated by growth centres of the type planned for Invergordon.

Small was not beautiful then; neither in business nor anything else. 'There is a tendency in certain planning minds to think in terms of concentrations of populations around existing towns or large centres ... with a view to factory development.' So wrote the engineer and businessman John Rollo in February 1965, nine months prior to the HIDB's inauguration. 'This will be fatal for the Highlands because it will result in the complete destruction of the agricultural crofting population. Far more effective would be concentration on the fostering and development of small factories located where the people are and have their homes and so allow them to have wage-earning work and work their crofts as an ancillary to give increased income.' But Rollo, although he had long had a key role in locally-initiated development of the sort financed by the Highland Fund, and although he was to become the Highland Board's first deputy chairman, was simply spitting in the wind.

In an era when UK agricultural policy was committed to the expansion of domestic food production by way of a complex and generously-funded set of supports and incentives designed to promote the emergence of a highly-capitalised and highly-mechanised farming industry, crofting itself was generally reckoned a poor prospect. Indeed the part-time crofter, so central to John Rollo's 1965 vision of the Highland future, sometimes seemed destined to vanish entirely from the scene.

In the early 1960s many hundreds of smaller crofts lay vacant for lack of any interest on the part of prospective tenants and, at the commencement of the decade, the Crofters Commission, established 10 years before the HIDB and then, as now, charged with the task of administering crofting legislation, had gone so far as to propose the elimination of the part-time holding.

The security of tenure which crofters had obtained in 1886, the Commission proposed, should be widely curtailed and at least two-thirds of the crofting population persuaded to abandon holdings characterised by the Commission as hopelessly uneconomic. The land thus made available, the Commission continued, should be used to create more substantial units. And from the Commission's description of the type of holding its members had in mind, it was quite clear that the men responsible for crofting policy were inclined to favour a course diametrically opposed to that advocated by John Rollo: 'First, such a unit should not fall short of the type of unit which is regarded as viable in other parts of the country; second, it should be capable of carrying sufficient stock to yield an attactive income; and third, the tenant should be required to devote his whole energy to working it.'

Crofters simply refused to have anything to do with such a policy on the grounds that the wholesale amalgamations favoured by the Crofters Commission would lead to still more depopulation. But in rejecting the Commission's approach crofters, not for the first time, were wholly at odds with expert opinion, which considered the part-time holding to be as obsolescent as the sickle or *cas-chrom*. And it was to expert opinion, rather than crofters, that the HIDB was more inclined to listen. The Board was ready to back agricultural improvement, stated Professor Grieve. But the result, he warned, 'would be more food from the Highlands for the rest of the country rather than more people for the Highlands.'

Crofting, it appeared, had as little meaning for 1960s development planners as Gaelic—which the HIDB's first chairman thought to have no future—had for 1960s educationalists. Nor was this similarity in outlook purely coincidental. The

8   Sheep-farming, Bragleenmore, near Kilninver, Argyll. [HIDB]

people responsible for our schooling were at one with the Highland Board in their beliefs as to what was best for Highlanders. Well aware that our circumstances differed markedly from those of the rest of Britain and well aware, too, that we were materially disadvantaged in comparison with most of our fellow-citizens to the south, both development practitioners and pedagogues sought to redress the balance by means of a strategy best described as assimilationist.

Hence the neglect of our Highland heritage in Highland schools. Hence the failure of those schools to provide instruction in subjects such as agriculture, fishing and forestry. Hence the widespread conviction that crofting must inevitably give way to farming. Hence the central role in development policy of measures intended to promote the industrialisation of the Highland economy.

Most of us, as I have mentioned, accepted most such thinking then. But the years since 1965 have shown that we were wrong to do so; not merely because so much of what was intended to transform the Highlands for the better has had, in the end, an opposite result; but also because there is mounting evidence to the effect that those very features of Highland life which we were implicitly encouraged to ignore, even despise, might after all be capable of contributing substantially to our region's regeneration.

Contrary to my expectations of 25 years ago, I did not leave the Highlands permanently on leaving school. Today I work for an organisation, the Scottish

9   Reindeer farming in the Cairngorms. Photograph by Oscar Marzaroli.

Crofters Union, which is itself symbolic of a new confidence and assertiveness on the part of the crofting community. And my family and I live in Skye, an island where, for the first time for well over a century, the population is rising, not falling, and where there is no longer an all-pervasive sense, as there seemed to be in so much of the Highlands and Islands in the 1960s, that economic opportunity is something which must always be sought in other places.

Now that farmers are being urged daily to diversify out of agriculture, and now that the creation of a more varied economy in the countryside is the major objective of both UK and EEC rural policy, the part-time crofter no longer seems an anachronism. Indeed modern crofting problems are often the reverse of those which characterised the 1960s, with the demand for crofts far outstripping the supply and with holdings changing hands at prices beyond the reach of young, local people who, in contrast to my own generation, are no longer unanimously convinced that crofting has nothing to offer.

More employment is still needed. But new jobs are becoming available. And not the least encouraging aspect of many recent developments—of which fish farming is the most obvious example—is that they are taking place in the High-lands and Islands in order to capitalise upon our natural advantages rather than in order to benefit from an artifically provided set of financial incentives.

Nor are our resources purely physical. One of Skye's biggest private sector employers, the Clan Donald Centre, owes both its existence and its success to the heritage our schools so persistently disregarded. And in many other less tangible but even more important ways our long-neglected cultural background is beginning to receive the attention it deserves. Children are taught today through the medium of Gaelic. Teenagers attend a Skye business college where Gaelic is the language of instruction in subjects such as computing and accountancy. And in Lewis even crofting figures in a technical college course.

Between such educational changes and the hard-headed business of economic development there may, at first sight, seem little connection. But the link, to my mind, is fundamental. It has to do with that most critical of all the elements that go into the provision of new economic opportunities, self-confidence.

That this was a commodity in short supply in Northern Scotland in the past was not unrelated to Highlanders and Islanders having been given to understand, over several generations, that their culture was essentially inferior, their collective historical experience of no real interest, their language intrinsically second-rate. A people accustomed to think thus of themselves were bound to lack faith in their own abilities and bound also to accept that their communities had no very worthwhile future other than that which could be provided by the injection of industry, capital and expertise from outside.

Now we are at last beginning to glimpse that this need not be so; that we have much here in the Highlands and Islands that is of great intrinsic value; and that we have, above all, the capacity to provide better prospects for ourselves. The HIDB, though associated initially with a very different approach, has had the courage and the insight to assist those novel trends. And although it remains to be seen how the Highlands and Islands will fare at the hands of the Local Enterprise Companies to which HIDB functions will be devolved in the 1990s, these companies will at least be able to draw on one invaluable resource: the growing number of people who believe that the Highlands and Islands of Scotland can now offer opportunities every bit as attractive as those available elsewhere.

DR JAMES HUNTER was born and brought up in North Argyll. He went to Oban High School and to Aberdeen and Edinburgh Universities. He is the author of *The Making of the Crofting Community* and several other publications about the Highlands. He was till recently Director of the Scottish Crofters Union. He is to be a Board Member of Highlands and Islands Enterprise.

2d The Intangible Values

Derek Cooper

What was it W B Yeats said? 'Wherever men have tried to imagine a perfect life they have imagined a place where men plough and sow and reap, not a place where there are great wheels turning and great chimneys vomiting smoke'.

No great wheels turn in the Highlands and Islands; no great chimneys vomit smoke. There are still a few residual golden eagles in the hills and most of the glens are as silent as the grave. Visually this might well be the perfect place. Where else would you find all that particular beauty; such seascapes, such emptiness? It actually lives up to the cliches—all that stuff about 'the last great unexploited lung of Europe' and the Beloved Wilderness.

There's a very powerful myth going about that if you could only get yourself a slice of this inactive action your Quality of Life would be immeasurably improved overnight. In the last 25 years a steady stream of refugees from the urban industrial south has fanned out north of Inverness seeking the good life.

For some it's been a little white crofthouse in the west; usually damp and uncomfortable and vacated with alacrity by the local owners in favour of a new home bright with Dulux and wall-to-wall luxi-pile carpeting. Others have trudged to the islands with a symbolic goat and staked out their future in a boutique selling tourist trivia, a cafe specialising in herbal teas and tofu or one of those potteries where all the artefacts look slightly misshapen.

These incomers seeking spiritual relief from what they call the Rat Race are immediately distinguishable not so much by their alien clothing but from their highly articulate expectations. Used to urban amenities, it is they who will often lead a community's pressure for better hospital facilities, a new road, an extra teacher in the local school. Not always but egregiously often it is they who will get up a campaign to oppose a defence development or some nuclear encroachment on their carefully chosen Highland haven.

Not always, but again quite conspicuously often, they will be running the little good food restaurant that gets in the national guides, the award-winning hotel, the lucrative outlet that none of the locals had thought of. Nothing wrong with that. Thousands of highlanders and islanders have left to make their mark down south and further afield, why shouldn't it work the other way round?

The sporting estate run by the man from Switzerland, the tearoom owned by a German, the leisure centres and country house hotels firmly in the hands of English couples should arouse no hackles—we're all part of the great European community, aren't we?

The Board's massive commitment to tourism has certainly changed the traditional face of the region. The essential supplies of life in a crofting community like barbed wire and sheep dip have been extended to include a vast range of products which had never been thought of as essential before.

The descent of incomers and summer visitors has redesigned the shelves of a hundred stores. Where humble basics like tinned baked beans and bottles of Camp coffee stood you'll now find olive oil, garlic, arabic coffee beans and pitta bread.

In such centres as Lerwick and Kirkwall the visitor can buy consumer durables which were once found only in Aberdeen or Inverness. Consumerism is as buoyant here as it is in the south. Indeed the region has in the last quarter of a century taken on a pronounced urban aspect. It's been a material revolution centred, the cynic might say, on the television set firmly anchored in every sitting room from Vatersay in the west to the ultimate croft on Unst.

Paradoxically, the new affluence has in a way robbed many a small township of the individuality it once possessed. The standardised fixtures and fittings, the identical cars and vans outside every house, the same programme on every TV set, often the same processed food on every table, has a dispiriting effect on the visitor looking for the soul of the Shetlands or the deep inner heart of the Gaidhealtachd.

The mass-produced and unlovely mobile homes anchored on crofts for summer visitors, the identical packet of cornflakes on every breakfast table, the same awful sliced white bread are, I suppose, the price that has to be paid for being a part of the consumer society. But the prosperous uniformity of it all doesn't present much joy to the romantic in search of the vibrant vestiges of an ancient way of life. All too often the only manifestation of culture the tourist is vouchsafed is a ceilidh complete with electronic keyboards and quadrophonic sound—a plasticised Saturday night vision of a tartan past which doesn't appear to be around any longer and one which, who knows, may never have existed.

Subsidies and grants have produced an amorphous blight of roadside development which often appears to have little to do with sensitive planning and nothing at all to suggest that anybody gives a damn about the resulting insult to the landscape. Peat-fired townships have been swept into the age of all-electric-fitted-kitchen-kit-bungalow conformity with little thought for the critical eye. Every pebble-dashed, pre-assembled home, the arrival of every new caravan-to-let, adds to the suburbanising of the Highlands and Islands.

So what? Why should a little bit of unaesthetic blight put anyone off? Beneath the formica, behind the smart new net curtains, the heart is surely still Highland, the old values remain unchanged? Sadly, development all too often means a degradation of the environment. Fish cages in the sea lochs, prefabricated sheds

10 Improved croft house, Doune, Lewis. Photograph by Sam Maynard/Eolas.

on the shore, abandoned rubbish on the skyline—that's the price that has to be paid for creating more jobs. If there are no jobs there will be no people.

The pity is that quite a lot of the high-risk schemes of the last two decades have left only a blot on the landscape and the jobs they were expected to provide have vanished. It must have seemed at the time a perfectly viable wheeze to have a precision engraving works on a moor in the middle of Skye or a spectacle-making factory in Barra. The defunct £4 million fish-drying plant in Breasclete and the doomed £2 million fishmeal factory at Ardveenish bring to mind that one-man HIDB of the 1920s, Lord Leverhulme.

The people of Lewis found his aspirations inimical and eventually he retired defeated. His Grand Design was all very commercially rational and visionary. Stornoway was to become the greatest fishing port in Europe—there were to be canning factories and jobs for all. Nothing is left today. It makes one wonder whether ambitious industrial transplants and infusions of capital in these remote parts of Britain are really what is called for. The small-scale community co-operative stands a better chance of surviving, but even there setbacks have been experienced.

Leverhulme was not defeated by the climate or the hostility of the landscape.

It was much more elemental. What he wished to achieve was not something which the people of Lewis or Harris valued highly. Jobs are vital, but the pursuit of increased production at any price is a sterile philosophy. Much of the development of the last 25 years has been based on the Leverhulme principle that More is Better. Leverhulme was a developer with a developer's tunnel vision. He saw Lewis solely as a building brick in his business empire. If more fish could be caught there would be more work for idle hands, more products to sell, more profit at the end of the financial year. The Leverhulme view of life is still alive and well. One fish cage is good, two fish cages are better. The fallacy that the happiness and moral health of a community increases in proportion to its ability to create more goods and services is seldom questioned.

Environmentalists who question the wisdom of filling every sea loch with cages or every hill with conifers are regarded with suspicion. Tourism is seen not as a potentially destructive force but as a benign influence, even though the rest of Europe offers tragic examples of the way in which the visitor industry has destroyed the very areas it was supposed to assist and preserve. The Costa Brava is one of the most obvious examples of the ravages of mass tourism—scores of fishing villages have been vandalised to create short-term wealth.

In the Highlands and Islands, catering for holidaymakers often turns traditional values on their head. The erosion of the Calvinist Sabbath could, of course, be seen as a liberating and life-enhancing development. It's only a minority of people who want the children's swings chained on Sunday and the golf club kept shut. How nice it would be if the boats and buses and planes could be put on a seven day schedule as they are in the rest of Britain. How convenient if all the shops could be open too. It would be good for tourism and good for business.

But anybody who has visited the Highlands and Islands in the depths of January when there are no tourists around will realise the price that has been paid for all those crowded roads in summer and the bed and breakfast signs swinging outside every other croft. Half the region seems to be permanently shut down. Hotels are closed, shops shuttered, visitor centres locked. 'It's like living in an evacuated depressed area', an incomer complained, 'it really reminds me of one of those awful seaside towns on the south coast that only comes to life in the summer and then life is unbearable because nobody's got a minute to pass the time of day with you'.

Maybe it isn't as bad as that everywhere, but drive from Inverness to Durness in the depths of winter and it really does seem as if whole stretches of countryside have gone into hibernation. Perhaps the same kind of thing happens in other parts of Europe which lean heavily for survival on tourism; perhaps it is inevitable.

Promoting the Highlands as a seasonal theme park is not a particularly attractive prospect, but the rich have always regarded it as a pleasure playground. The Bulloughs of Accrington bought the island of Rum as a private summer home; Lord Strathcona on Colonsay, the Woods of Raasay, Matheson on Lewis were in their own way the first of the tourists. They did it in great style, of course, with a retinue of servants and yachts standing by with steam up, ready to sail hither and thither at their slightest whim.

Even as I write, the island of Gigha has been bought for sums in excess of £2 million. 'Some people yearn for a train set', the new owner, Malcolm Potier, told a journalist, 'but for years I have dreamed of owning a Scottish island.' He claimed he wouldn't change anything—but should an island's future be left to private decisions made for private reasons?

Many of us hoped that when the Board was set up in 1965 it would have powers to restrict the unfettered land-thirst of the rich. I doubt if there is another part of Europe which has been as screwed up by private landlords as the Highlands and Islands. But nothing has happened in the last two decades to prevent whole communities from being bought and sold on the open market as if their well-being was of no importance.

Several estate agents in London and Edinburgh have departments which specialise in selling topographical playgrounds to the highest bidder.

We are talking not about showbiz celebrities investing their fairy gold in flow country forests, but hardfaced businessmen buying vast tracts of real estate; land that can be blighted permanently by proprietors who have no ambition other than to sell it at a profit and use it in the meantime to satisfy personal ambitions. It is often difficult to find out who does really own an island or a peninusula. It may be a syndicate of stockbrokers who use the land for fishing and shooting; occasionally it is a maverick with a jackdaw complex—someone who collects land titles because land is the one investment that always increases in value.

The classic instance of an individual holding a community to ransom was Dr John Green, who like many before him behaved in his Hebridean kingdom in a manner which would not be tolerated in the South of England, where he had his permanent home. The story is worth retelling because it illustrates how defenceless the Board has been when confronted by an arrogant predator.

In 1922 the Scottish Board of Agriculture bought the island of Raasay for about £37,000. When in the early 1960s it became government policy for the Board to dispose of its assets, Raasay House Hotel, the home farm and several houses on the island were put up for grabs. Strangely, few people were interested. But perhaps that was not strange. There was no car ferry to Raasay and its inaccessibility would have deterred the casual investor.

One man did, however, present himself as a potential purchaser. Dr Green's debut in the Inner Hebrides as a property-fancier was in March 1957, when his wife bought the 6100 acres of Scalpay, 125 acres of Longay and the 8-acre island of Guillamon off Skye for £11,000—less than the price of their own suburban home in the Sussex retirement resort of Cooden. These three islands were sold four years later for more than double that sum to a London banker. Green had realised that buying up bits of the Highlands and Islands was a far better investment than the stock market. He had the taste of profit in his nostrils. When Raasay House, complete with the gardener's house, the kennels, the old fort, the boathouse and Borrodale House and its land was put out to tender, Green got the lot for the derisory sum of £4000. During the next five years the Department of Agriculture sold him a further twelve plots of ground; 1014 acres in total for £3688. Green took great pleasure in outbidding the locals for every acre.

Only twice during the long period that he owned his Raasay assets did Green set foot on the island. He allowed the historic Raasay House to fall into decay and his other properties were left empty and boarded up. When the islanders pleaded for a car ferry he refused to sell the one-fifth of an acre which would have provided a site for the slip. It took many years for the HIDB to negotiate a buy-out price with Dr Green and by then you might say that the heart had gone out of Raasay.

An even more disastrous stewardship than Dr Green's turned Eigg into one of the most demoralised islands of all. The island was bought in 1972 by the Anglyn Trust, a self-styled non-profitmaking charity with ambitious proposals to help handicapped children. The 'principal' of the trust's school was a 19-stone cockney who called himself 'Commander' Farnham-Smith. In his brief lairdship Smith applied for permission to sell most of the trees on the island, failed to pay wages, put families out of their houses and generally spread a social dry rot over his domain.

The local MP (Russell Johnston) was as dismayed with the posturing of Smith on Eigg as he was with Green on Raasay, but nothing, it seemed, could be done. At the end of 1974 the HIDB, conscious of the threat that Smith presented to the survival of Eigg, offered him a handsome £250,000 to leave. Although Smith had paid only £89,000 for his 5000 acres, he regarded this as inadequate and sold the island (some would say out of spite) to a character called Schellenberg for a marginally higher price. In August 1989 the *West Highland Free Press* examined Schellenberg's thirteen year reign. They did not enthuse. Despite the £230,000 invested by the HIDB, Eigg did not seem to be in good fettle at all.

There are many other parts of the region suffering from the *rigor mortis* of private ownership. The tension created by alien and almost always absentee landlords doesn't make for harmony and unity of purpose. There is local frustration and natural resentment at the way in which land can be sold and resold to provide profits for people who are often never seen. Conflict often smoulders for years, surfacing sometimes as a confrontation between local poachers and an estate's water bailiffs. When land use is reserved for German or Brazilian sportsmen and KEEP OUT notices are on every gate, how can you blame the natives for getting restless? In October 1989, two Wester Ross men were indicted at Dingwall Sheriff court for sinking a £500,000 boat belonging to the owner of Inverinate Estate, Sheikh Mohamed el Shahid bin Makoutm. It was, the fiscal revealed, a reprisal for wrong, real or imagined, inflicted on the community by the estate. The men were sent to prison for nine months and three months respectively.

Nobody who seeks to understand the heritage of landlordism should under-estimate its debilitating effect on generation after generation. There is nothing new about this stranglehold of private ownership. It has always been there. A hundred years ago the anger of the people at their exploitation and victimisation was graphically documented in the evidence presented by township after township to the members of the Commission of Enquiry who travelled round the Highlands and Islands in the summer of 1883 listening to the grievances of the crofters and cottars. Those who owned the land regarded the peasantry as a nuisance and a drain on the purse. On many estates there were ruthless evictions. Evictions are no longer possible, but an estate still has the power to inhibit local enterprise, even act against the public interest.

There are those, and I number myself among them, who believe that had the Board been equipped with power to curb the excesses of private ownership the spirit of the region would have been considerably strengthened. To this day the Board has neither the financial resources nor the political authority to assume the role of landlord. In a decade when the wilder excesses of free enterprise have been elevated into an economic philosophy, the dilemma of a public body armed only with good intentions and the passive power of friendly persuasion is there for all to see.

What often disgusts the local population is the way in which the speculator invariably claims that he has only bought his chunk of the Highlands to provide himself with a little peace and quiet. One such was a property developer called David Lewis, who at the end of 1973 bought the 15,000 acre sporting estate of Strathaird in Skye for—yes of course—'peace and quiet'. A few weeks before snapping up his big lump of south Skye he had paid £2 million for a 2345 acre estate in Hertfordshire. Unfortunately for Lewis, the property market promptly collapsed. Within eight months Strathaird was on the market again—during that time Lewis had managed to spend 90 minutes touring his £750,000 worth of peace and quiet. By the end of the year the only offer he had received was £100,000 and, with fingers badly burnt, he was eventually forced to sell to Iain Anderson, the flute-player and star of the rock band Jethro Tull.

Anderson has turned out to be a benign landlord. He has a rock star's income and with the Board's assistance has set up the biggest salmon-farming operation in the island. People speak highly of him and he appears to be exercising his power with great consideration for local opinion.

Much the same can be said of the merchant banker Iain Noble, an Old Etonian with a gift for making money. In 1973 he bought 22,000 acres of Skye for the knockdown price of £5 an acre. Inside the highly efficient businessman there lurked a romantic visionary determined to revitalise Gaelic culture. Noble taught himself Gaelic, set up a Gaelic college and cultural centre and proceeded to inject enthusiasm and cash into his estate. Over the years he has started a knitwear industry, a whisky business, a small fishing fleet and ostentatiously embraced the Gaelic ethos. Some of his actions, designed to make his estate more financially efficient, have disquieted crofting tenants used to the easy-going paternalism of his predecessor, Lord Macdonald. Even his fight to have road signs erected in both Gaelic and English has been construed by some as an attempt to challenge the authority of democratically-elected councillors. He is not universally popular.

The landlord's lot is not a happy one. But should there be such a class of people at all? In Nigeria they have a much more intelligent attitude. 'Land', runs a tribal saying, 'belongs to a vast family, of which many are dead, a few are living and countless numbers still unborn.'

Allowing huge areas of land to be 'owned' by individuals has over the years proved to be the very worst form of social contract. In the nineteenth century it led to the mass migration of Highland communities and the impoverishment of hundreds of thousands of acres. The profligate misuse of land and the appropriation of common resources into the hands of a few has imparted to parts of the region an air of neglect and ecological vandalism.

I am reminded frequently on my travels of the words of the late Sir Frank Fraser Darling, who in 1944 established what came to be known as the West Highland Survey. His conclusion was unequivocal: 'The Highlands and Islands are largely a devastated terrain ... any policy which ignores this fact cannot hope to achieve rehabilitation.'

A lot of money has been spent in the last 25 years, but in 1990 we are still waiting for radical solutions. All we are promised is a businessman's vision of the future—a Highlands and Islands Enterprise which will no doubt generate lots of entrepreneurial activity. But rehabilitation ought to mean more than the creation of commercial opportunities for the enterprising to make money.

DEREK COOPER is the author of several books on the Highlands and Islands, including *Skye, Hebridean Connection, The Road to Mingulay, Skye Remembered and The Whisky Roads of Scotland. Road to the Isles* won him a Scottish Arts Council Award.

Chapter 3

A Long Term Assessment

James Shaw Grant

It is dangerous to make general statements about the Highlands and Islands.

Over the past 25 years the area has presented a bewildering series of variations on the theme of decay and regeneration. It has been, in effect, a working laboratory of social, economic and political problems and attempts to resolve them, some successful, some failed, many still to be proved. The numbers involved have been so small it is possible to see the interplay of forces down almost to the personal level.

The history of the period, however, is not local, parochial and unimportant: it illustrates truths which are of universal significance and gives warning signals about some of the mistakes now being made, with the best of intentions, in many of the developing countries of the world. Above all, it illustrates the close relationship, the reciprocity, between social and economic problems: the blindness and bluntness of political instruments in dealing with them.

Within the area and the period there have been—and still are—isolated townships which seem to have reached the point of no return: the evacuation of the islands of Stroma and Scarp lie just outwith the time scale. On the other hand there have been areas like Shetland which struggled to sustain indigenous, and relatively stable, industries against the onrush of an extravagant but short-lived prosperity resulting from the discovery of North Sea Oil.

In the Western Isles the principal industry both at the beginning and end of the period was the production of Harris Tweed, surviving despite the fact that the weaving process, for social reasons enshrined in an 80-year-old trade mark, is carried out at the homes of the crofters in scores of widely scattered villages. The high-tech fabrication work for the oil industry at Arnish, which overshadowed it for a few years, was then mothballed, but may yet be reviewed.

Against all the normal criteria of economics and geography, Caithness now exports freezers from a rural environment to cities and countries renowned for their manufacturing skills, while nearby Dounreay, an eminently successful project working at the frontiers of human knowledge, will shortly suffer, as Invergordon and Fort William already do, an entirely new problem for the Highlands—large scale industrial unemployment, imported into the area by the abandonment of grandiose development projects of central government in which political rather than commercial considerations prevailed both at the birth and the death.

The political decisions in regard to Dounreay were deliberate: determined by national policy with little regard to the local effect. The political decisions which doomed the Invergordon aluminium smelter were taken long before the event and without any intention of bringing it about. For what seemed good reasons at the time, mainly to protect the North of Scotland Hydro Electric Board, the Labour Government refused to allow the Invergordon plant to generate its own electricity. The complicated formula devised to price supplies drawn from the national grid left Invergordon with the short straw when the aluminium industry in Britain had to contract. The closure was the result of political decisions. It was, however, not planned or foreseen. It was purely inadvertent.

Dounreay has had a permanent beneficial effect on the social and economic life of Caithness, although that was not the reason why the site was chosen. At Invergordon the net benefit (or disbenefit) of the short-lived development, which was intended as a contribution to regional regeneration, is more difficult to gauge, and no serious attempt has been made to establish the facts despite their relevance in a situation in which even the most market-orientated government is necessarily involved in social engineering in some areas and to some extent.

An equally wide range of *conservationist issues* is illustrated by the Highland experience.

There have been emotive clashes over the age-old custom in the Ness district of Lewis of using the young of the solan goose as food (once a necessity, now a locally esteemed luxury); the culling of seals in Orkney; the use of a wild fowl habitat in Islay to provide peat for the distilleries; the depredations of geese on the grasslands of Uist; and the afforestation of the 'flow country' in Caithness. Each has raised different issues in the relationship between conservation and development: between the indigenous population and outside pressures.

Haunting these controversies are the ghosts of Highland history. If the Clearances had not been imposed on the crofters by 'improvers' in the nineteenth century, the intervention of conservationists, some of them exercising a similar arbitrary authority, might not be quite so widely resented in the twentieth.

Other, more important, conservationist issues are raised by the effect of the fall-out from Chernobyl on sheep and deer farming; fears of coastal pollution from both Sellafield and Dounreay; and the almost complete destruction of the herring stock by over-fishing, mainly by vessels from outside the area—a calamity averted by a Draconian ban, sustained for several years, which inflicted great loss on the fishermen who had not been guilty of over-fishing as well as those who had. The economies of Shetland, Lewis, Scalpay and other areas, in effect, were made to bear the cost of a short-sighted system of plunder from which they had derived no benefit and from which they would have been protected if local views had been listened to by central government.

Behind the conservationist issue in fishing lies a complicated *political struggle* between local fishermen, asserting a special right to the seas adjacent to their homes, and central government, making token concessions to these demands while

4   Building sheep fanks, Lewis. Photograph Sam Maynard/Eolas.

5   Sheep from Uig being unloaded at Lochmaddy. (HIDB)

6   Decks of fishing boats in Oban Harbour, Argyll. Photograph by Peter Davenport.

7   Barguillean, Argyll. (HIDB)

substantially insisting on the freedom of the seas for all British nationals. That long-running controversy is now complicated by Britain's membership of the European Community, adding a new layer of conflicting interests to the old.

It is idle to speculate whether, if Britain had pursued a *policy* of regional protection for fishermen in the past, we would have a more convincing case for generous quotas than we have when arguing on a basis of state against state; but it is still important to trace back the effect on remote communities like Out Skerries of games of political poker, played by politicians in Brussels often motivated by considerations far removed from the welfare of those affected by their decisions.

The Highland scene also provides us with a case study of a revolution in the fishing industry almost as far-reaching in its potential as the replacement of hunting by farming in the pre-historic past. The full effects of the revolution will not be felt until the farming of white fish and shell fish has become commercially viable, as the farming of salmon and trout has done in the period under review. Already, however, conflicts of interest have arisen between farmers and 'hunters', between commerce and recreation, together with new problems of conservation and new risks of pollution. The haphazard way in which these problems are resolved (or left unresolved) raises important administrative, and perhaps constitutional, issues.

Fish farming would have developed in the Highlands and Islands even if the HIDB had not existed, but the pace and the effect on the local economy would have been very different. The Board has given encouragement (critics say not enough encouragement) to local firms whose profits, as well as wages, remain within the area. More significantly, the Board was able to resist, through the Courts, an attempt by a multi-national company based in England to register a restrictive patent which could have given it a virtual monopoly over the farming of salmon.

The Board is now addressing itself to an even more important revolution in communications technology. It is contributing nearly £5 million to a £16 million programme for the replacement by British Telecom of 43 telephone exchanges, between Shetland and Kintyre, within three years, and the introduction of other facilities which will place the Highlands on an equal footing with Glasgow, Manchester and London in competing for jobs in a wide range of computer-based industries.

Without the Board's initiative, the gap between the Highlands and the rest of the country in job prospects would have widened dramatically because purely commercial considerations put the area at the bottom of British Telecom's priority list. The effect of this interference with the free play of market forces, in the provision of essential industrial infrastructure, will be closely monitored far beyond the Highland area. It is not only the Board's biggest single investment, it is the most imaginative project of the kind so far undertaken in any rural area in the world.

The extent to which the Board's initiative succeeds will be determined not only by its own effort but by the local response, and that will be affected to some extent by a legacy of *social problems* inherited from the past. These are now, fortunately, passing away but are not wholly dissipated and still have to be taken into account.

The relationship between these intertwined social and economic problems stands out with exceptional clarity in the small commmunities on the periphery of the Highland area.

For instance, the age structure in a township has a bearing on the availability of peat as fuel, the management of common grazings, the abandonment of small islands or remote areas, the maintenance of communications whether by public transport or private car, the retention or closure of schools, the existence and use of village halls, and, even in larger communities, although less obviously, it affects the response to development opportunities.

In a study of inbreeding on St Kilda, Professor E J Clegg of Aberdeen University suggests that 'many potential marriages did not occur because of their known consanguineous nature' and that 'the increasing restriction on choice of mates within the island population could have been a significant factor in the emigration which occurred in the later period of occupation.' St Kilda is clearly a special case and it was evacuated well before the period we are concerned with, but similar pressures must have arisen less dramatically in other closed communities and may still be reflected to some extent in social attitudes and economic responses.

Another study by Professor Clegg illustrates the sort of problem that arose in a relatively large community (Lewis and Harris) as a result of a long sustained process of selective out-migration deliberately encouraged, and sometimes assisted, by central government as the only remedy for an island which was, perversely, regarded as congested although it was one of the most sparsely populated parts of Britain.

Professor Clegg's attention was attracted by the anomaly that 'as the population of the two islands increased during the latter part of the nineteenth century, the number of marriages contracted in the islands decreased both relatively and absolutely' until by 1951 the proportion of women over 55 who had never married was far removed from the Scottish norm and 'possibly more extreme' than in Ireland.

Over the last quarter of a century the situation has changed considerably for the better and the islands are now quite close to the Scottish norm in the proportion of women of marriageable age who do marry, but the old problem is still with us in another form. There is a serious social hangover in the plight of many elderly people in remote villages without families around them to provide the comfort they are entitled to and for whom the state, which was largely instrumental in creating the problem, still fails to make adequate provision.

This social problem of our period, costly to the welfare services and even more costly in human suffering, is largely the result of excessive and selective emigration, encouraged by the state in a relatively remote past. Those who know the islands intimately would also argue that the social problem was itself reflected, in economic terms, in a certain reluctance to take up the opportunities offered by the Highland Board during the early years of its existence. A population dominated by the elderly is not readily receptive to new ideas. Until comparatively recently the islander tended to show initiative only when he had first *escaped* from his own environment.

This is a situation which has wide implications.

It should be of interest to social historians in Scotland to investigate the circumstances in which a hundred years of ostensibly paternalistic government, in what was for much of the period the richest country in the world, resulted only in converting the problem of finding work for a young, vigorous and expanding population into an even more intractable problem of geriatric dereliction and economic decay. Even more importantly, the conjunction of market forces and political ostentation which is creating modern cities in the developing countries, without regard to the effect on the hinterland, may well be replicating the British mistake on a vastly greater scale; recreating the 'Highland problem' in the African bush or in the rural areas which provide the teeming hordes for Mexico City.

Against this background the Highland experience, and the efforts of the Highland Board to undo the errors of the past, acquire *international significance*.

The situation in the Highlands and Islands has been transformed for the better in the last 25 years. The change is due, in large measure, to the activities of the Board, but it is important to know what other influences have been at work, and whether the Board was denied even greater success by government restraint, extraneous circumstances, or mistakes in its own policies or administration.

The very wide powers given to the Board by the Act of 1965, and subsequent amendments, match the complexity of the problem with which the Board has had to deal. Just as we can see on the ground every variety of developmental problem, so we can trace, in the records of the Board, the effectiveness—or ineffectiveness—of almost every conceivable remedy. The Board itself has, in effect, been engaged in a learning process. As a result it has made many changes in its approach and, perhaps most importantly, has moved much closer to the people and communities with which it has to deal.

When it was set up there was a strong lobby in St Andrew's House to locate the Board's headquarters in Edinburgh. Those who took this view missed the essential fact that the Board itself was an important contribution to Highland development: its mere existence took into the Highland capital a considerable amount of hard cash in the monthly pay cheques, and a great many skilled professionals whose presence enriched the social and intellectual life of the town.

It also missed the point that there is a geographical perspective which alters the appearance of problems as we view them from different environments. The Board has found by experience that Inverness itself is too remote in some respects: there has been a steady, if perhaps tardy, recognition of the need for a Board presence in all the different areas it serves.

There must also be some significance in the fact that, the more intractable the area, the more the Board relies on community spirit rather than individual commercial initiative. If loyalty to one's neighbours and voluntary effort provide the last toe-hold for a community on the point of disintegration, has that got a message for the wealthier parts of the country where the forces that really motivate society are concealed by the scurrying multitude of individuals intent on personal gain?

Apart from the interplay of social and economic factors, one can trace in the Highlands some important political truths.

The first demand for a Highland Development Board came from within the Highlands, principally from the Highland Development League. The Chairman of the League was Dr Lachlan Grant, a GP in Fort William, and the Vice-chairman, Rev T M Murchison, a native of Glenelg and a future Moderator of the Church of Scotland.

The League's activities were so resented in some quarters that a letter to MPs by the Chairman, Vice-chairman and Secretary, protesting against the proposed allocation of Highland water power for private exploitation by the Grampian Electricity Company while the young men of the Highlands were on military service and could not make their voices heard, was reported to the Committee of Privileges as a *prima facie* contempt of the House of Commons. This trivial issue engaged the attention of senior members of the Government on five separate occasions in the middle of the war—in fact in the month in which Russia was invaded. The Committee eventually decided there had been no contempt, and the House of Commons unanimously rejected the private legislation against which the Highland Development League had protested.

The outcome of the 'contempt' proceedings was a victory for the League, but the Highland agitation for a Development Board got nowhere until the STUC added its political clout nearly twenty years later. Valuable though the intervention of the STUC was, there was another reason for setting up the Highlands and Islands Development Board which was even more important, although it is generally overlooked: in 1965 the Labour Government had a very slender majority, and there were nine Liberals in the House of Commons, several of them representing Highland constituencies.

An examination of the record shows that all the legislation over the past century which has effectively changed the situation in the Highlands has been passed by governments clinging precariously to power. The legislation for the Highlands passed by governments with secure majorities has been bland and ineffective.

This highlights the plight of geographically defined minorities in a democracy where political power is determined by the counting of heads. Ideological minorities can exercise influence in every marginal constituency in the country. Geographical minorities can exercise real power only in a hung parliament, and then very modestly.

The Highland experience also illustrates the extent to which legislation to ameliorate conditions in peripheral areas is often undermined inadvertently by general legislation applied to the country as a whole.

For example, the Community Charge or Poll Tax bears particularly heavily on the more remote areas, which have lost the protection of low rateable values, and may bear even more heavily on them in future as political pressures arise—as they inevitably will—for a uniform rate throughout the whole country.

The Crown Estate Commissioners are taking steps to defuse the criticism that they are undemocratic and unrepresentative, but, however well they succeed, the fact remains that, as a result of a deal struck between the Crown and Parliament in the remote past, more money will be siphoned out of the fish farming industry in the Highlands on behalf of the Treasury than the Treasury, through the Highland Board, has put into its development.

The *language problem* in the Highlands, although different in many ways from the language problems facing emerging nations, also raises issues from which lessons of general value can be drawn. When the Board was set up, the received wisdom was that, if the economic problems were resolved, Gaelic could largely be left to look after itself; in fact some Board members doubted whether language was important, and whether there was, in reality, any such thing as a local culture and way of life. It was later, well into our period, before it became fairly generally accepted that the nourishing of the language might be a useful development tool: one aspect of the restoration of morale in the more difficult areas.

Although it lies well in the past, it is essential to the understanding of our period to explore the love-hate relationship between the Lowlands and Gaelic which has existed at least since Walter Scott softened (with a somewhat sickly romanticism) the old unbridled hostility expressed in the Statutes of Iona in 1609 and the Disarming Acts which followed the rebellion of 1745. It is also necessary to explore the changing attitudes within Gaeldom itself, where at one time it was considered progressive to promote English as the language of social and economic advancement, and it is now considered progressive to promote Gaelic almost in the same terms. The Church helped to keep Gaelic alive when it was being suppressed in the schools, but now, when educationists are recognising their past mistakes, some church leaders seem prepared to jettison Gaelic as unimportant.

Quite apart from the renewed interest in Gaelic, there are some exciting *cultural developments* taking place in the area and the Highland Board is increasingly supporting them as a key element in the process of rehabilitation. A great many diverse factors, both from within and from outside the Highlands, have contributed to this, but perhaps the most important has been free access to tertiary education which has brought into the arena many whose talents would otherwise have been wasted. On the other hand, the very high proportion of Highland school leavers who train for the professions increases selective out-migration and the difficulty of retaining people of high ability on whom the future of the area depends. One of the Board's greatest difficulties is in creating jobs commensurate with the abilities available—or, alternatively, persuading people within the area to train for the jobs that could be provided if a qualified pool of labour existed first.

A great deal of worldly wisdom has been acquired by the Highland Board in the handling of development problems, but, so far as I know, its experience has not been analysed and codified in any way that might provide guidance for others, or even for itself. Moreover the Board's experience, even if it were readily accessible, covers only its own functions, and leaves out of account many of the factors that bear on the social and economic well-being of the area it serves.

The intervention of governments to help under-developed or distressed areas is generally based on ideology, on political pressure, or on someone's hunch. We need a much more scientific approach to these matters, based on practical experience in the field.

The value of the Highlands as a potential laboratory where cause and effect can be examined on the ground is greatly enhanced as we move towards a unified Europe in which the inevitable concentration of political and economic power is offset by a desire—genuine, but often ill-informed and ill-directed—to try to restore some balance between the periphery and the centre.

The multi-disciplinary team—or permanent institution—which would be required to carry out the investigative programme I have sketched would itself be a contribution to Highland Development, as the location of the Board's head-quarters at Inverness has been, quite apart from any insights into the process of good government which might emerge from its work.

And, as I indicated at the start, the benefit would not be confined to the Highlands or even to Europe, as many of the emerging nations, following in Europe's footsteps, seem determined to repeat Europe's mistakes.

DR JAMES SHAW GRANT, born Stornoway, educated Nicolson Institute and Glasgow University. Editor *Stornoway Gazette* 1932–63. Chairman Crofters Commission 1963–78. Member HIDB 1970–82. Director Grampian TV 1969–80. Chairman Pitlochry Festival Theatre 1971–83. Deputy Chairman Eden Court Theatre. (CBE, MA, LLD, FRSE, FRAgS)

11 Hebridean Post Office, 1971.
The photographer Oscar Marzaroli, who died in 1988, made a number of films in the Highlands and Islands and produced a wide range of photographic studies of Highland people: many of these studies have appeared in exhibitions and have been included in published collections of his work. In addition to the photographs on this and the following two pages, Plates 9, 40, 44 and 45 are also by Marzaroli. Copyright holder of all Oscar Marzaroli photographs is Anne Marzaroli.

12   Ardveenish Fish Factory, Barra, 1981.

13   Calum MacLeod, Raasay, 1981.

14   Salmon Fishermen, Staffin, Skye.

15   Market day, West Loch Tarbet, Harris, 1983.

Chapter 4

The Land

GEORGE HOUSTON

Whoever and whatever has left the Highlands in the past, the land question has never moved far away. From the early nineteenth century of Donald MacLeod's 'Gloomy Memories' till more recent years of tax-based tree planting and large sporting complexes, the Highlands have never failed to generate arguments about the origins, merits and demerits of different forms of land ownership, control and use. The persistence of large private estates, often retained for their valuable sporting assets, provokes periodic criticism, while the unique crofting system, with around 12,000 participants, has not only survived but, for its size, has the highest profile of any land-based community in Europe and has been one of the most successful in attracting special EEC support.

In the immediate post-war years Highland depopulation was widely deplored and the economic development of the region, including land development, was acknowledged as desirable, but proved of limited political interest at a UK level. My first encounter with the idea of a regional development authority came during the preparation in the 1940s of a research paper for the Fabian Society on Roosevelt's Tennessee Valley Authority, whose aims and activities seemed relevant to the Highlands. Twenty years later, shortly before the election of the Labour Government of 1964, I joined a group of mainly urban Scots which prepared proposals for a Highland Development Authority subsequently reflected in the Labour election manifesto and eventually in the 1965 Act setting up the Board. None of us had any doubt that influencing the use of land would be an important aspect of the work of the authority. This view was reinforced by government statements during the parliamentary debate on the Bill, especially by William Ross, Secretary of State, who declared that any plan for economic and social development would be meaningless if proper use of the land were not part of it, and added that one of the main limitations on land development in the Highlands was 'the existing rights of possession and occupation in regard to all land capable of agricultural use in any form'. Removing these limitations was 'the purpose of the powers in relation to land which the Board will have'. These powers were wide-ranging and included the right of access to land to prepare development proposals, the right of compulsory purchase and the right to hold, manage, or dispose of land.

In early 1967, about a year after the Board was established, I received a phone call from Prophet Smith, a full-time member of the Board, inviting me to Inverness to discuss with him and the chairman, Bob Grieve, the way in which the Board might prepare and carry out measures to assist the development of agriculture, horticulture and forestry. The Board had not yet appointed any senior member of staff with experience in this area and had at first given responsibility for land-based development to another full-time member, John Robertson, a farmer from Easter Ross, who did not hold out much hope for Highland agriculture outside Easter Ross and who had already antagonised some of the farming community by arguing the case for forestry rather than livestock farming—a view reflected in the initial strategy of the Board set out in its first report. The Board was also under attack from farmers' organisations because of its support for large-scale industrial development on good arable land around the Moray Firth, while in the House of Lords a few large Highland landowners who had strongly opposed some of the Board's land powers were now criticising the Board for its lack of help to farming. Responsibility for land policy was transferred from John Robertson to Prophet Smith, who already had the fisheries portfolio and who had been active in the agricultural co-operative movement. A new initiative was planned.

During the next twenty years, when I remained an adviser to the Board on agricultural matters, the acquisition of land by voluntary or compulsory means was seen as a measure of last resort to achieve development objectives rather than as a desirable end in itself. On several occasions the Board entered into negotiations to buy land, including at least one case where the purchase was prevented by ministerial veto, and eventually bought the estate of Rahoy in Morvern. Consideration was given to using compulsory powers of purchase on at least two occasions, but as a general rule the Board sought to influence land use by all means short of acquiring the land itself.

This cautious approach disappointed some of the Board's strongest supporters, who felt that a few large landowners still hindered, rather than helped, the 'social well-being and development' of the Highlands which the Board was expected to promote. Board members like Prophet Smith and Tom Fraser, who considered that land acquisition could be a useful policy lever, were also well aware that the extension of public ownership of land in the Highlands, particularly by the use of compulsory powers, would lead to a political row. In such a situation the Board must be certain of vigorous and public ministerial support for its policy.

In the late 1960s the Board had come under strong media attack which caused the Labour administration unwelcome embarrassment, and two members of the Board, including John Robertson, resigned. Around this time I met William Ross at Heathrow airport. He was very angry and urged me to go and see Prophet and ask him 'What the hell are you up to?' It was a Thursday and I suppose the Secretary of State had just left a Cabinet meeting where he had been given a rough time for the bad press the Board was receiving. I doubt if he would have welcomed an announcement the next week that the Board was proposing to act on his suggestion to remove the limitations on land development arising from 'existing rights of possession and occupation in regard to all land capable of agricultural use'.

Political factors were not the only influence on the Board's approach to land acquisition. Before deciding to take over land by voluntary or compulsory means, the Board had to be satisfied that all legal and administrative obstacles could be overcome and that the estate or estates to be affected could be shown to be examples of the misuse or serious underuse of land and capable of development in ways which would have beneficial effect on incomes and jobs. When the Board addressed the issue of land acquisition in the later 1970s it was advised that under the 1965 Act it was in the same position as a local authority seeking the compulsory purchase of land for industrial or housing development and would have to follow procedures which were inappropriate for the acquisition of large tracts of land for agriculture or forestry. Alternative procedures must be available and these required new legislation. After many months of discussions proposals were agreed which had the support of local authorities, the Highland N.F.U. and Board's Consultative Council. By then, however, the Labour Government was near the end of its term of office; had it won the next election the new administration would presumably have been more willing to make the legislative changes than subsequent Conservative governments. After the 1979 election no one was surprised when the land question was first placed on the back-burner and then removed to a more remote part of the Scottish Office kitchen.

Agricultural Policy

Reluctance to become involved in land acquisition did not mean that the Board was powerless to influence the use of land for traditional or other agricultural purposes. But the Board was slower to approve a programme of agricultural development than to take the initiative in encouraging industry, tourism and even forestry. For years the Highland Problem, which the Board had been set up to overcome, was perceived as depopulation, closely linked to the lack of job opportunities. Land-based activities, especially farming, had been shedding labour for decades; forestry expansion seemed the most likely to increase rural employment. By 1965 agriculture, which had benefited from state-aided investment programmes in the post-war years, provided about 10 per cent of the region's income and occupied less than 15 per cent of the working population. The improvement of agricultural production and incomes throughout the country was invariably associated with a trend towards larger units and labour-saving technologies and could be seen as a main cause of rural depopulation. For a regional agency to encourage further agricultural development and improvement might seem like reinforcing a demographic trend the Board was attempting to reverse; to overcome this problem increased output of existing or new land-based products would be essential. Even then it was unlikely that the decline in the farm workforce would be halted, far less reversed; at best it could be slowed down.

In March 1968, two and a half years after its formation, the Board formally adopted an agricultural programme indicating the three main ways it intended to use its statutory powers to promote and encourage agricultural development: firstly, by the preparation and implementation of proposals for the comprehensive development of selected areas; secondly, by setting up non-traditional development projects under its own control or in co-operation with others; and thirdly, by the provision of loans and grants on favourable terms to private individuals or organisations undertaking approved investment in farming, horticulture or related enterprises. These activities would complement the work of existing public bodies.

The first policy approach involved land development surveys, a suggestion inherited from the Advisory Panel on the Highlands and Islands which was dissolved when the Board was established but whose recommendation that such surveys should be carried out for Mull and the Strath of Kildonan the Board was committed to implement. The prospect of such surveys caused alarm among the owners of a few private estates to whom they represented the first step towards state control of land use and even, perish the thought, of land nationalisation. Their worries proved ill-founded. Implementation of most of the modest proposals of the Kildonan survey, including forestry and agricultural development, depended on the co-operation or coercion of several landowners. Their enthusiasm for development was not overwhelming and the Board was not convinced that coercion was likely to succeed, or would indeed prove worthwhile. Thus the Strath of Kildonan, despite its emotive role in the history of the Sutherland Clearances, did not become the site of the Board's first attempt at an area comprehensive development scheme; subsequent changes in land use in the Strath were marginal.

The Mull survey yielded more substantial results based on an attempt to win the co-operation of all those on the island who were interested in development. A local committee was formed, a development officer appointed and various proposals for forestry and farm-based as well as other projects were put into effect. The existence of publicly owned land facilitated some of these developments and many individual farmers also responded by carrying out investment projects approved and partly financed by the Board, although ambitious proposals for the development of Killiechronan estate were not implemented.

In another mainland area, North Argyll, an agricultural development programme was also initiated and met a good response from farmers, but the attempt to prepare comprehensive development schemes for selected areas was not successful enough to persuade the Board that this was the best way to proceed throughout the Highlands. The attitudes and motivation of the owners or occupiers of land were obviously crucial to land development. Since compulsory purchase was not considered a policy option and attitudes were very difficult to change, the emphasis must be on finding those occupiers of land who were anxious to make better use of it, identifying the barriers to their doing so and providing the appropriate technical and financial help. The Board's strength lay in its ability to provide additional funds to farmers and others considering land development projects, but the fulfilment of its role also required, to quote its policy statement, 'the exercise of its duties to co-operate with and if necessary co-ordinate, the efforts of the other bodies working in Highland agriculture'.

The idea that a regional development agency should have such a co-ordinating role might seem self-evident to the innocent, but it was by no means so obvious to those who feared they might be affected by such co-ordination. The number of public and private bodies interested in some aspect of land-based development in the Highlands has never been low and tends to rise at a more rapid rate than the area's population declined in the nineteenth century. The growth and sometimes even the survival of such bodies seems to depend on their emphasising their unique contribution to a highly laudable cause, not in the extent to which they allow that contribution to become part of a much wider objective. Everyone agrees in principle with the need for a balanced approach to land use, but everyone also wants to use their own weighing machine. A high media profile is not achieved through compromise, and the accolade of colleagues is reserved for those representatives who defend their corner till everyone else has gone home exhausted. In recent years this war of the quangos has been seen by some as the best means of reaching the ideal outcome, so that, in the slightly amended immortal words of Adam Smith, public agencies, by pursuing their own institutional interests, will be led, as if by an invisible hand, to promote an end which is no part of their intention.

The Board, although always stressing the desirablility of co-operation among public bodies, has been as reluctant to claim it has a co-ordinating role as it has been to acquire land. Any advance towards a common agreed programme was often achieved by stealth, involving other bodies in a consultative way so that they were locked in the decision-making process rather than standing outside waiting to criticise any proposals they had not helped to formulate. More recently, as discussed later, co-operation has grown around specific measures and new influences have helped to strengthen the case for public bodies reaching agreement on a strategy for land-based development, although the Board has not acquired, nor apparently sought, the formal co-ordinating role that once seemed the logical consequence of its status as a regional development agency.

The second arm of the Board's agricultural policy was to initiate special development projects, particularly in new forms of land use, which would remain under the general control or guidance of the Board, at least in the early years. By 1967 the Board had already begun to examine the feasibility of a major development proposal for the Western Isles, the reclamation of the Vallay Strand in North Uist for a comprehensive bulb project. Investigations lasted five years, during which Dutch consultants costed the project at £1.4m and experiments at growing bulbs on machair croft land produced yields which suggested poor rates of return on such an investment. The Board abandoned the project in 1971—as it did a much smaller subsequent scheme to introduce blueberries as an alternative crop in Easter Ross.

A more successful initiative was taken in 1970 with the establishment of a pilot shrub project in the Kintyre peninsula. By the mid 1970s the evidence from the scheme suggested that it was technically and economically feasible to grow and sell hardy nursery stock in favoured areas of the West Highlands. Since then several experienced and some not-so-experienced growers have, with Board assistance,

built up flourishing nurseries in the area and are now an important source of
heathers, rhododendrons and other shrubs for garden centres all over Britain. The
success of this development depended not only on the skill and hard work of the
growers but on the willingness of the Board to finance the pilot scheme and to
continue to support the commercial nurseries in their early, difficult years as well
as to help finance their efforts to work together in promoting their products. Most
of the growers had the wisdom to encourage others to come to the area, so that
Argyll now offers a commercial supply of a range of plants. The advisory service
of the agricultural colleges has also helped the expansion of horticultural enterprises
throughout the Highlands, so that by 1988 their total turnover approached £5
million and the industry provided employment for around 500 people.

Another project which illustrates the need for the Board to take a long-term
view of such initiatives is the red deer farm at Rahoy, in Morvern. Following
research at two Scottish agricultural institutes, the Board decided to acquire an
estate on which to test the commercial viability of deer farming in the West
Highlands. The decision met fierce criticism—including the contradictory views
that Rahoy was 'too good a sheep farm to go to deer', and that it was 'more
suitable as a sporting estate than for any kind of livestock farming'. The Board
took possession of Rahoy in 1977 (by which time the sheep had been removed)
and for the next seven years built up a herd of around 500 hinds, mainly by
purchasing calves from other estates. During this period of development unex-
pected disease problems arose, a change of management was necessary and the
agreed technical preconditions for a reasonably viable enterprise were not met.

In the year before the project was due to end, the Board came under pressure
from the government, committed to privatisation, to sell its assets and, despite
opposition from the deer farm's own advisory committee, supported by a Par
liamentary Committee, both of which felt that a further period of development
was justified, Rahoy estate, including the deer farm, was put on the market. An
acceptable offer for the deer farm was not received however, and the Board
reversed its decision and decided to retain ownership for a further period. An
arrangement was made with the Hill Farming Research Organisation (HFRO),
which had become involved in an advisory way, to take over the direct management of the farm.

By 1989, 12 years after the first deer calves were introduced, very satisfactory
technical targets had been reached on calving percentages, weight gains and disease
control. Feeding and veterinary regimes had been established and, perhaps most
significant of all, it had proved possible to increase the size of the herd to over 700
hinds—nearly double the limit which had seemed likely at the outset. These
technical achievements took place in a period in which market prices, especially
for hinds, had risen substantially, possibly higher than will be maintained. But the
Rahoy project suggests that, given the necessary technical skill, deer farming may
well be a practical alternative to sheep and cattle on Scottish hills, at least if all
these enterprises receive similar levels of direct support. At present deer farming
does not qualify for the hill subsidies available for sheep and cattle.

The third of the Board's policy measures, which soon became its main financial involvement in Highland agriculture, was not introduced without difficulty. Soon after I became involved as an adviser I presented a paper to the Board suggesting that it should set up a 'land bank' offering loans at preferential rates to farmers willing to undertake approved projects which would help to maintain employment and raise farm incomes. The Secretary to the Board, Bob Fasken, an experienced civil servant, had a better idea. The Board already had a financial understanding, approved by Treasury, which allowed it to offer grants and loan assistance under Section B of the 1965 Act for industrial projects up to a certain financial ceiling. It had not by then (1968) requested that this be extended to farming, but by doing so the same purpose as a land bank could be served with much less bother.

The case was prepared and presented to the Department of Agriculture and farmers' organisations. I, naively, expected an enthusiastic welcome from both, but it was not quite like that. The Agricultural Department pointed out that it already provided a range of production aids to Highland farmers and claimed, quite correctly, that it had been actively and successfully encouraging agricultural development in the Board's area for many years. 'Highland farmers', an official remarked, were 'our customers'—did the Board really want to get involved in this area? Off we went to enlist the support of the Scottish NFU. They liked the idea of subsidised loans, but were unhappy at the prospect of these being available only to Highland farmers. Could the Board please not publicise the scheme too widely, so that the NFU was not inundated by protests from its Lowland members? The Edinburgh establishment was haunted by the spectre of a new kind of Highland poacher, a regional development agency which might offer special help to the people who actually worked the land in its area.

The Board, led by Bob Grieve and Prophet Smith, was determined to pursue the scheme and it was finally agreed in 1969. During the next 20 years it paid out a total of over £30m, mostly in loans at preferential terms or grants to reduce interest charges. Bad debts in the agricultural sector have averaged around 2%, the lowest of any sector and less than a third of the overall average. The Board also carried out and published periodic evaluations of this aspect of its activity, at the time a rare instance of what is now a Treasury requirement for all new policy measures. Some Board members were afraid these evaluations would bring bad news; in the event they were sufficiently favourable to repel the challenges of the men in dark suits from the Treasury who did not like the idea of special loans to farmers—wherever they lived.

In this programme of assistance to traditional farming enterprise in the Highlands, the Board, while concentrating on production methods, was aware that problems of marketing livestock, particularly from outlying areas, were holding back livestock improvement. Before the Board was set up various co-operative marketing organisations had been established in the Highlands, several of them involving a system of contract feeding to Lowland farmers, and in 1967 the Board agreed to provide finance for such marketing projects in the Uists, Mull and Islay, mainly for calves, but also for sheep. By 1975 most of these schemes had run into financial difficulties, three had gone into liquidation and the Board had to write off £27,000 in bad debts—or nearly 10% of the total amounts advanced.

A new approach was adopted in the late 1970s, with the emphasis on direct selling to lowland farms rather than contract feeding the young stock. Since 1978 the Board has assisted the establishment of 15 livestock marketing organisations, mostly on the islands off the West Coast, but also in Shetland, Wester Ross and around the Moray Firth. From a few thousand sheep and a few hundred calves in the early years, sales through supplying groups exceeded 100,000 sheep and about 2000 cattle in 1988, most of the stock passing through a co-operative federal organisation (HILL) which became a limited company in 1986 and which has extended its purchases beyond the original producer groups. About 3500 farmers or crofters—one-third of all livestock producers in the Highlands—now belong to co-operative marketing groups. Other changes in livestock marketing have taken place during the past ten years and auction markets, slaughter houses and wholesalers have all participated in the improvements, many with Board help. The more favourable economic climate, particularly for sheep farming in the early 1980s, has helped these marketing developments and there is also evidence that, relatively speaking, Highland livestock prices in this period rose more rapidly than in Scotland as a whole.

Three of the special development initiatives of the Board which have had the most obvious positive results—the Argyll nursery project, the Rahoy deer farm and the marketing schemes—illustrate two general points. Without public support maintained over difficult early years, none would have succeeded; and in any programme of development unforeseen problems are bound to arise, requiring a high level of technical and managerial skill to overcome them. Another development of the 1980s, machinery groups, organised with the help of the farm co-operative movement, suggests that co-operation among small producers can be successful under certain circumstances.

The Board has on several occasions attempted to influence government and EEC policies as they affect Highland agriculture. In the early 1970s, when the UK was negotiating terms of entry to the Common Market, Dr Mansholt, the agricultural commissioner, announced his wish to visit Scotland. One of the main 'sticking points' about UK entry was the system of hill subsidies for sheep and cattle, which the UK had adopted but which was absent on the continent. The Scottish civil servant involved in negotiations with Brussels and responsible for Dr Mansholt's itinerary was John Gibson, in his spare time a writer of Scottish historical novels. He arranged an RAF plane to fly Mansholt to Lossiemouth and then took him directly to Culloden Moor. It was a bleak, wet and stormy winter morning. John Gibson described to his guest the scene of battle (though not its outcome) and then swept his arm across the moor. 'Dr Mansholt' he said 'we have had our Highland Clearances, we don't want any more'. The Commissioner, no doubt uncertain of Scottish history, was then taken to meet the chairman of the Board, Sir Andrew Gilchrist, a former diplomat, who presented in what can only be called his own inimitable fashion the case for special help for the Scottish hill farmers, including, of course, the famous crofters and their way of life. Thus was the task of the UK negotiators lightened and the case for Hill Livestock Compensatory Allowances (HLCAs) strengthened.

Once entry to Europe had taken place and the Common Agricultural Policy had embraced structural changes as well as market support measures, the Board, along with other bodies, began to explore ways in which finance from Brussels could be directed towards the Highlands; the Irish, it was agreed, should not be left to pursue such an objective on their own. Eventually the EEC agreed to sponsor an Integrated Development Programme for the Western Isles, covering land and livestock development as well as fish farming and infrastuctural invest-ment. Although the term 'integrated' was misleading, since in EEC terms it referred to financial sources rather than the nature of the programme, Brussels offered to reimburse the Exchequer by 40% of the public expenditure, which no doubt persuaded the UK Treasury to meet the balance, assuming it did not realise that under the Fontainebleau agreement the IDP reimbursement would be deducted from the UK rebate. After the IDP was completed an agricultural development programme for the rest of the Scottish islands was approved and is also partly financed from Brussels. The adoption of such programmes was actively supported by many bodies, public and private, but the Board had special reasons for welcoming such a development, for it confirmed the view that the concept of regional aid was applicable to agriculture and that the Highlands and Islands exemplified a rural area where preferential assistance was justified for land-based as well as other economic development.

Agricultural Trends

An obvious question—*has the Board made a significant and measurable impact on farming or related activities?*—is impossible to answer convincingly, for no-one knows what would have happened in the absence of the Board's influence. Several of the Board's special initiatives, such as the Uist bulb scheme, have left no permanent effect. Others, like the Argyll nursery project, the deer farm and livestock marketing schemes, have produced more lasting results. But the effect of the Board's most important intervention measure, its grants and loans assistance under Section B of the 1965 Act, taken up by 40% of Highland farmers, cannot be assessed separately from the related public expenditure by DAFS and other bodies. The only practical way of reaching a judgement on this measure is to compare what has happened on Board-assisted farms with the rest of Highland agriculture. Two detailed studies made in the 1970s provided evidence that, in terms of output, income and jobs, Board-assisted farms showed much more favourable trends; a causal relationship between Board help and this difference in trends cannot be identified, far less proved, and the earlier studies have not yet been up-dated.

Whatever influence the Board may have had was much less powerful than the economic forces, including national policy measures, which have affected agriculture and land use over the past 25 years. No regional policy could over-come the tendency for the agricultural population (especially the number of hired workers) to decline. No aids to investment could prevent the sharp decline in the real price of agricultural products (after allowing for inflation) or the rise in interest rates. In the latter years of the 1980s British agriculture has been in serious economic depression and Highland farming has not escaped.

To measure trends in farm output, farm incomes and farm population is not a straightforward exercise at a national level and is even more complicated when attempted for a region. Until the early 1970s official estimates were published of the agricultural output of the seven crofting counties and these suggested that the Highlands' share of Scottish agricultural output was then around 11% and had declined slowly for some time. Comparable data for more recent years are not available and the evidence is much cruder. From 1970 to 1985 total cattle numbers in the Board area remained close to 350,000, while total sheep numbers fluctuated around 2.5 million; pig and poultry production continued to fall. The area of crops declined by around 3% and the most significant changes were a shift from oats to barley and a decline in the area of potatoes and fodder crops. In this period the average 'real' price of cattle and sheep, the Highlands' main output, had fallen by about 20%, so that their numbers were maintained in difficult economic circumstances. The main contrast with the rest of Scotland was that outside the Highlands total sheep numbers rose by 5% and the crop area rose by 14%, mainly because of an increase in cereals. There is little doubt that the Highlands' share of Scottish farm output has continued its decline.

Over the same period the aggregate income of all those working the land in the Highlands (farmers and farm workers) has certainly fallen in real terms, but the sharp decline in the employed labour force, now roughly half the level of the mid 1960s, and the much smaller fall in the number of farmers, has meant that the income per head in agriculture has not declined so much. Farm businesses in the Board's area are on average smaller than in the rest of Scotland and the total number of non-family workers (full-time and part-time) on Highland farms is now less than one-fifth of the total number of farmers and family workers. In the early 1960s hired non-family workers were a much larger part of agriculture's working population.

The trend in the social structure of the farm population towards family businesses and part-time farming has not halted the tendency for a higher proportion of farm output to come from a smaller number of enterprises. More than two-thirds of the Highland ewe flock is now in 1000 of the largest flocks, or one-sixth of the total. Similarly, two-thirds of the cattle are in less than 900 herds, or one-fifth the total. Highland agriculture is a two-sector economy, with over two-thirds of holdings classified as part-time or spare-time and less than 3000 as full-time farms.

The crofting community has for a long time obtained only a small part of its income from the land. There are now about 600 crofts classified as full-time and probably another 3–4000 where the income from agriculture is a significant part of the household income.

In the 1980s a widespread assumption about European agriculture has been that the output of most farm products should be decreased, not increased. This view has been based on the existence of much higher than usual stocks of farm commodities, particularly of cereals and dairy products, and the common though not unanimous belief that European surpluses of food can not, in the long run, be used to make up for shortages elsewhere. Agriculture policies were thus modified so as to lower real agricultural prices, while milk quotas and structural measures were introduced with the aim of reducing output and taking substantial areas of land out of food production. As these policy changes were being introduced, the farming community also became the main soft target of a section of the environmental movement, who found the media hungry for any news that farmers were ruining the countryside, uprooting hedgerows, destroying the soil structure and generally wasting public money by producing food no one wanted—or, rather, had the money to pay for. More recently the EEC food stocks have come down towards a more acceptable level and farmers' net incomes have been declining at a rate which, if continued, could bring a fall in output and a rise in market prices that consumers would not welcome.

The Highlands have not been immune from the influence of European farm policy, nor from the high public profile sought by critics of modern farming practices and land development measures. Although the chief end products of Highland agriculture, beef and lamb, have not been in persistent surplus and the typical farming system is based on low industrial inputs and extensive hill and upland grazing, the EEC Commission disapproves of improvement programmes which might lead to increased output on individual farms, even when this is the most sensible way for a particular farmer to survive and may, as in the Highlands, be associated with maintaining rather than increasing the general level of production.

Conflicts between those who work the land and those who want more emphasis on wildlife protection and conservation have mainly arisen around the designation of Sites of Special Scientific Interest (SSSIs) and attempts by some conservationists to prevent or restrict programmes of agricultural development designed to improve or maintain the incomes of those working the land, especially in more remote areas. The Integrated Development Programme for the Western Isles, which the Board and other bodies had spent years in promoting, was held up for several months because of widely publicised claims that it would seriously damage the natural environment of the islands. In the event the media soon lost interest and although conservation staff were sent to the islands to investigate over 1200 projects the only conservation problem that actually arose in implementing the IDP concerned a single drain.

Throughout the 1980s conservation bodies have urged government to redirect resources away from agriculture improvement to nature conservation and the UK government has responded by replacing measures to assist farm improvement by schemes for farm diversification, farm woodlands and modifying farm methods in Environmentally Sensitive Areas (ESAs). By the autumn of 1989 these measures had made very little impact in the Highlands. Those interested in diversification found the HIDB schemes of more relevance: the farm woodlands scheme, following political pressure from conservation bodies, was made less attractive to stock-rearing farmers and was aimed at areas of arable land; and so far only one ESA has been established in the Highlands. Despite the serious economic pressures now affecting many Scottish farmers and the popular expectation that a 'new agricultural revolution' is on its way, Highland farming (including crofting) shows no obvious sign of deviating from the main secular trends discussed earlier and which have been apparent during the past 25 years. This picture could change rapidly if the regional aids given to farming in less favoured areas were abandoned. HLCAs, or subsidies on hill cows and ewes, came to about £18m in 1989 in the Board area; their removal would have a devastating effect on the economics of Highland livestock farming.

The Highland Board, while continuing to stress the importance of agriculture to the region's economy, has recently adopted a new land sector strategy, under which the majority of its land expenditure 'will be channelled through projects and marketing with less being spent as Section B investment'. In responding to individual farm applicants, priority will be given to those in fragile areas, to new entrants and those undertaking non-traditional livestock enterprises. This shift in emphasis is partly in line with national policies, but also takes into account the sharp fall in the land sector demand for Section B assistance—from over £3m in 1985 to £1.3m in 1988. The Board also gives support to the intensive area approach, especially for remote areas, which it claims could have considerable development impact through a series of initiatives. This bears a family resemblance to the comprehensive development schemes of the Board's early years, and the hope is expressed that in present circumstances such an approach, currently illustrated in the Board's North-West Development Programme, will receive support from the EEC and central government. The old land question (*under what circumstances will land acquisition take place?*) has disappeared without trace and at the time of writing the strategic role of the Board when it becomes 'Highlands and Islands Enterprise' is not clearly defined.

Other Land Uses—Sport and Forestry

The Highlands are fortunate in that they have always provided facilities for a wide range of leisure and sporting activities complementary to each other and to other land uses. Most of the conflicts which have arisen in recent years have their origin in the much greater number of people now able to visit the countryside and the new types of country-based sports available. One enduring aspect of sport in the Highlands is the social division between the traditional minority pursuits of the very rich and the less costly recreations enjoyed by a much larger number of the less wealthy. In recent years Highland estates with access to salmon rivers, grouse moors and most of all stags, have doubled or even trebled their market value. The right to shoot one stag and acquire its antlers (but not its venison) can now cost the same as buying 20 blackface lambs. As the agricultural use of land brings in lower net returns, its sporting use has become much more profitable. And while disagreements between shepherds and gamekeepers were always common, sheep are being removed from some estates so as to concentrate on their sporting use;

farming, forestry and sport are no longer considered mutually compatible land-uses by all estate owners.

The most important change in land use in the Highlands over the past 25 years has been the increase in forestry. In 1988 over 460,000 hectares, or 12%, of the Board's total area, was under trees; of this, more than half had been planted during the Board's lifetime, at first mainly by the Forestry Commission, but in recent years predominantly (over 80%) by the private sector. Since its formation the Board has consistently supported forestry expansion, but has had no powers to influence the area or location of new afforestation and is not involved in the consultative process; it has, however, provided financial assistance for downstream activities and approved a pilot scheme for farm forestry which was intended to introduce private investors to farmers. This aroused little interest and was closed after the new farm woodland scheme was announced.

Before the Budget changes of 1988 new planting in the Board's area was around 12,000 hectares a year, or 55% of new planting in Britain. About 3000 man-year equivalents were employed in establishing and harvesting operations and a further 500 in downstream activities. It now seems likely that unless government policy changes the rate of forestry expansion in the Highlands will decline to less than half the recent rate. The financial restraints on the Forestry Commission, the uncertainties affecting potential private investors and political pressures from conservation bodies will all contribute towards this trend.

The Board's declared policy is for an increase of forestry area by around 200,000 hectares or just under half the present area. But the Board's success in helping to achieve this target depends on winning allies in the Quango War. The Forestry Commission and local authorities with planning powers, such as Highland Regional Council, tend to favour forestry expansion in the Highlands, where the area of suitable land substantially exceeds the Board's target. But conservation bodies, including the Nature Conservancy Council, with statutory obligations, consider that there is 'a continuing conflict between forestry and nature conservation' and have identified large areas of Caithness and Sutherland as a typical battleground. Military metaphors appear appropriate as a local taskforce is formed and then reinforced to speed up the process of designating SSSIs in areas suitable for forestry.

Fortunately, there are signs that a peace movement based on a multilateral understanding may gain strength. In 1989 a working party set up by Highland Regional Council produced a report, agreed by all the participating agencies, including the Forestry Commission and the NCC, which makes recommendations taking into account both conservation and forestry interests and which would enable planting in Caithness and Sutherland to expand to a level consistent with 'a viable forestry industry'. The proposed land use change would affect less than 6% of the total area of the two counties. The next few years will show whether all agencies co-operate in implementing these proposals, although the desired rate of expansion is unlikely to be achieved if the Forestry Commission is unable to adapt its planting programme to make up for a decline in the private sector.

Another welcome development is the general support from all agencies, including the Board and local planning authorities, for what is now called 'an indicative forestry strategy' for the Highlands which would suggest the extent, location and nature of new afforestation in the Board area. Should this happen, and it will depend on government approval and be assisted by EEC interest, then an important step will have been taken, after 25 years, towards the adoption of a land use strategy which the early supporters of the Board had expected would be achieved in a rather shorter period.

Looking back over this quarter century, one unforeseen change in attitude towards land use in the Highlands has certainly taken place. Whereas in the past the under-use of land was a common reason for criticising those who owned or occupied it, some landowners are now compensated for not being allowed to undertake certain developments and an articulate body of opinion counterposes the productive use of land to its conservation; it questions the wisdom of encouraging the more efficient and intensive use of land for food and timber production or for leisure activities. While few unashamedly embrace the extreme concept of the Beloved Wilderness, priority is given to preserving the countryside and the wild life of a particular time period. The concept and achievements of economic growth and efficiency, from which modern standards of living have developed, are considered inappropriate to the present and future use of land, particularly in areas such as the Highlands.

For those like myself, who have long shared the view that the people who live in the Highlands are as entitled as the rest of us to try to improve their incomes and standard of life and who, if necessary, should receive appropriate economic support to bring about such developments, the argument that these aspirations are in conflict with maintaining what is manifestly, for us, the Beloved Highlands is certainly novel; that of course does not prove it wrong.

Like many other city-born Scots, my early contact with the Highlands arose from my parents' rural upbringing. Annual visits to my father's family croft on the Shetland island of Yell left their idyllic childhood memories, but also a less comfortable appreciation of why virtually all my uncles and aunts had left for the mainland or North America. Returning to Shetland in recent years I have never been in any doubt about which time period and environment my father's generation would have chosen—had they been given the chance.

GEORGE HOUSTON, who retired in 1988 as Professor of Agricultural Economics at the University of Glasgow, was agricultural consultant to the Highlands and Islands Development Board from 1967 to 1987, an independent member of the British Wool Marketing Board for 15 years and economic adviser to several national and international organisations. He is co-author of *Agrarian Change in the Highlands*, published in 1976.

Chapter 5

Crofters and Crofting

Iain Thomson

'A sad day we left the croft' was a phrase once in common usage. My grandmother resorted to it from time to time, for it fitted well the weariness of old age in an upstairs Inverness flat when the day had gone wrong. For her the youthful crofting days had become a state of mind. They spoke of kinships in the land of her forebears, gave a heartfelt peace and a sense of belonging. They spelled out the humanitarian values found in shared hardship and poverty. They whispered a love of native glens and the fulfilment to be found in simple work harnessed to the seasons.

Were these sentiments merely the play of senile nostalgia, or did crofting people possess a definable ethos? Was crofting really the 'good life', with the suffocating midges in a sultry hayfield conveniently forgotten? Well, 25 years ago the Highlands and Islands Development Board was certainly not given to such whimsical speculation on the meaning of the quality of life or an elucidation of the Highlanders' character. They properly addressed themselves to the main issue of the time, a falling population in economic decline.

Not altogether unexpectedly, when handed an anaemic patient as large as a sixth of the United Kingdom and called the Crofting Counties, the Board set up a Land Division. It promptly thought of rural resettlement with a cash transfusion as a means of restoring colour to the face of the glens. With a crusading zeal which may now seem a little naive, the Board espoused some of the more radical views of its first Consultative Council. The purchase and subdividing of certain extensive Highland estates into crofts or holdings was considered a practical exercise in repopulation. I well remember young shepherds at the time becoming quite excited by the prospect of a heft of sheep on the hill and a rejuvenated croft in some remote glen. Nor was it surprising that an attempt to realise such schemes should be thought feasible and desirable when one considers the Board's opening team...

Roddy MacDonald, a Gaelic speaking Skyeman, became the first head of the Land Division. Though urbanely city-suited, his roots drove deep into crofting; he was 'one of them' and naturally mirrored Highlanders' aspirations. Moving from the Department of Agriculture in Inverness came Gordon Elliot. There his

16   Old croft house, Shetland. [HIDB]

responsibilities had been for crofting affairs and he well understood the problems of smallholdings when he became the Board's senior lands officer. Add to these sympathetic views Board member Prophet Smith, a retired Shetland crofter, and the egalitarian visions of Chairman Bob Grieve and it is easy to see why repopulating the straths to roll back the ravages of the Clearances should be considered.

It was not to be: lack of finance or political influence intervened. Many would-be young crofters felt let down. Land nationalisation, for such it would have been, retreated into the land-use surveys of Kildonan Strath and the Northern Isles. The Board concentrated rather on helping individual applicants in their private schemes and that first heady vision of homes in the hills became, for some, a bitter hangover.

In those days, however, many Highland shepherds enjoyed the use of a croft as a 'perk' of their job, and such an arrangement had been my own good fortune. Each August I scythed the croft's two acres of meadow hay and hung it green on a fence to cure. The winter feed for my two cows and followers secured, I scythed a few acres of rashes for their bedding. Transport to the stone-built barn was simple, either a sheet on my back or pulling the all-purpose 'hurly'. Hard work all through the year. A round of drinks on a temperate night out in today's money was my wage. Nevertheless, given a little saving and the sale of my stock, I left the glen with over £1000 in the bank.

Crofting was viable in the 1950s and 1960s and Department of Agriculture cropping grants kept the land in a desirable rotation as the support levels covered planting costs. It was profitable to grow your own tatties and sell the surplus to the local shop to help with the groceries. An acre or two of oats cut green for feeding in the sheaf was balanced with neeps and the traditional Shorthorn cross Highland cows put to an Angus sire provided succulent beef from this system. Sadly such beef, with its higher fat content, is largely unwanted today by a nation sheltering behind double glazing.

My neighbours in Kilmorack were crofters set in this mould. Each sheaf was carefully tended and turned to dry at the fence. 'Number 34 is still a little wet in the head', I used to tease them when strolling across on a damp September morning for a 'news'. Their hens knowingly awaited the fresh grain and gathered conversationally at the stackyard where newly-cut shellach branches were laid on the stone founds to prevent the bottom sheaves from rotting in the season's new stacks. Eggs were exchanged each week for groceries at the travelling van and now and then a sack of oats for the 'extras' would be bartered.

Old MacRae placed particular emphasis on his potato crop. 'When the birch is out it's time the tatties are down', he would repeat every spring. With dung from his eight cows the tatties throve, and then as purple October evenings hinted at frost his agitation to secure the crop became just as insistent. In childhood he remembered a week's November frost which ruined the family's main winter diet. Hungry mouths for himself and his eight brothers taught him a lesson which he carried into his eighties. Not least, his carefully pitted tatties paid the rent.

Such was the style of crofting in the years prior to the birth of the Board. Healthy frugal living with employment for the menfolk at the ghillying or perhaps drainage and fencing. Low input, low output, plus a varied cropping style provided habitat for a wide range of wildlife. Symbiotic living, with the land held in religious reverence. Much was to change—and at a surprising rate.

'Of like crofting status' was the official designation of the first holding which I tenanted at the beginning of the 1960s. This phrase indicated that whilst the farm had failed to be registered legally as a croft, it still qualified for some sections of aid available to crofting due to its size and location. I paid a rent of £51 a year for a house, 60 acres of kindly arable and 220 acres of rough ground. This rate had been fixed by an astute solicitor and agreed by my predecessor on his entry in 1914. No holding could be regarded as a croft if its rental exceeded £50; hence Cluanie remained unregistered. I was thus debarred from some securities justly given under successive Crofting Acts—most notably the right of assignation, that is the naming of one's successor to the tenancy, and the advantageous housing grants. The right to purchase the croft was not even a dream in those days.

Struggling as an ex-shepherd with a foot on the first rung of the ladder to eventual owner-occupancy, my keenest lack was the collateral with which to borrow from the banks. Security for an overdraft, it seemed in those simpler years, was a luxury enjoyed by the already wealthy in order to reduce their tax burden. Few if any crofters ventured such extravagance and so during the expanding years of the 1960s and early 1970s many indigenous people were to fall behind and witness the slow beginning of an encroachment over their land and interests which is well under way today.

The 'swinging sixties' for the crofter meant re-seeding. Generous government assistance for lime, slag, grass-seed and labour turned bogs green, hillsides lush and confettied tired croftland with white clover. From Shetland to Barra lime was spread by every conceivable means and with an unaccustomed enthusiasm. One South Harris crofter worked a precipitously steep croft and solved his liming requirements with an ingenuity of which Heath Robinson might have boasted. A contraption resembling a medieval siege machine was constructed. A tea tray nailed stoutly to a long wooden cantilever served to carry the charge of lime. Its propulsion unit was provided by a length of rope tied to the back of a battered Ford van. Several downhill dashes, a suddenly tautening rope, and lime dust engulfed the hillside, to the amazement of his neighbours and the excitement of an assortment of otherwise idling dogs. Casting reason aside, the charge was doubled and the power unit careered downhill. A fatal glance behind brought a splintering crash and the hissing expiry of a green Ford van amidst a shedful of squawking hens.

Lacking such imagination, I deep-ploughed 20 acres of rashes and set about transforming 60 acres of heather. Old MacRae watched across the march fence. 'Well boy' he drew wisdom from the distant hills 'the rashes saved many's the lamb in an April storm and the heather fed plenty of ewes through a winter's snow.' By the late 1970s liming mania had become uneconomic and the rashes marched back in force throughout the Crofting Counties. Once-bright reseeds showed signs of too many sheep and too few cattle.

A swing away from house cow, cropping and the suckler herd became a stampede in the 1970s. People followed as smallish holdings were amalgamated to produce that dearly beloved topic of college lecturers 'the viable unit'. Crofting could no longer drift along as a way of life; economic reality stepped into the byre and punctured the wheelbarrow. So began the irrelevance of crofting to food production in national terms.

Fortunately the industry's declining agricultural importance was offset by a boom in rural housing and road improvement. In the 1950s an extension 'out the back' replaced a wooden lean-to. Rayburn cookers, imitation tiles and twin tub sinks were the housewife's pride—and that was before you saw the seaweed wallpaper in the new bathroom. Dormer windows winked across the machair and tarmacadam mysteriously reached back doors when road widening happened to be going on in the district. Loitering hens were finally banished from their age-old sun trap for the sake of the smart sittingroom carpet.

This first phase in raising housing standards served well to train the crofter and his son in the skills of the building trade. When the next stage came along—a splendid bungalow for the croft—the labour force was at hand and some outlying communities throve by building each other's houses. A JCB digger was available at weekends when not on hire to the 'County'. Concrete block work? No problem. A joiner? Well Willie John over at Dunmore would be free next weekend.

Crofting's community spirit was ideally suited for the task of providing sound houses in remote and difficult areas, where outside contractors would have been financially out of the question. In any case townships had been working together since the days of re-roofing granny's 'black house'. Siting the space-heated update, however, sometimes caused comments from an older generation whose forefathers had built on the poorest land and preserved anything that would take a spade. Through his telescope old MacRae watched a young progressive crofting neighbour take an acre of land out of a 'deep field' to site his concrete block steading and bay-windowed bungalow. MacRae made it plain to the district that no good could come from such profligacy with the sacred resource.

Co-operating in local house improvements, I offered to build the septic tank for a crofting friend who had decided to get married and add on a bathroom at the same time. Sunday was my day for 'quiet' jobs and he being of an indeterminate faith offered no objection other than to indicate that discretion might be called for in view of the considerably stricter views of some of his neighbours. I finished the block work on the first Sunday and daundered over the following week to do the plastering. The tank brimmed with water. I baled out the hole and taking down a couple of pails of cement began the tricky task of making the plaster stick to the wall. Voices drifted down to me. I looked out cautiously. The most devout Sabbatarian of the district was leaning on the gable talking to my friend. I hastily withdrew to the bottom of the tank, a wet site. The water began to rise. It became a race between the length of their conversation and the height of my wellingtons. I stood miserably, head down, as the plaster plopped off the walls. The wellies won and I hauled out for a dram. Tolerance and humour once bound together a Highland community.

Only slowly did the HIDB come to grips with crofting and its problems. John Bryden, who succeeded Roddy MacDonald as Chief Lands Officer, was a pipe-smoking theorist with an understanding of European politics. On behalf of the Board and alongside other organisations, he helped to persuade the European Commission that assistance to maintain the social fabric of remote and economically fragile areas was an integral part of the overall well-being of member states. Ultimately the parturition of much paperwork presented us with the Integrated Development Programme. Though it only covered the Western Isles and was considered a pilot scheme, it became the test case for possible implementation of wider arrangements throughout the EEC.

Well you can't spend £20 million over five years in sparsely peopled islands without seeing some dramatic results. Never slow to spot which side the jam is spread, the islanders soon had the Stornoway HQ of their Island Development Plan wading in applications. Perhaps the area of livestock improvement and fencing gave the widest spread of the 'loot' and few crofters missed the chance to keep out their neighbours' sheep. The islands gleamed with new wire and grew smart green fenceposts by the mile.

Coupled with this resurgence of interest in livestock came the IDP's help to build new auction marts at Lochmaddy and Lochboisdale. These centres provided infrastructure for marketing initiatives set up by the Board. At last came official recognition that cattle and sheep from the crofts could do better than come at the tail end of mainland sales. The grading and batching of store stock for mart presentation or private sale has helped to change the image of west coast animals. This, together with a move by the Department of Agriculture to supply continental bulls and Cheviot tups through their hiring scheme, has brought about a product more in keeping with current market demands and crofter returns have duly benefited.

I have to tell you that the story of a mechanic who was called out to a grey tractor in Glenelg which stubbornly refused to start, only to find its diesel tank stuffed with bruised oats, is apocryphal. Nevertheless as the second-hand grey Ferguson tractor became obsolete on prosperous east coast farms its rapid import-ation to the north and west put the Highland garron out to grass and for twenty years they became the quaint mode of power for all small units.

The great machinery cycle from large to small farm encompassed all forms of implements, including the ingenious binder. This machine above all others could communicate its wishes to a human operator and one felt humbled by its cleverness. I bought my first binder for £30 and contracted it around the crofting Braes of Kilmorack for £1 an acre—at which useful rate, I may say, the machine soon clattered its way out of debt. Its knotter mechanism, however, had the cunning trick of throwing a loose sheaf whenever the apparatus felt in need of a rest. Late one evening, as the dew began to fall, a succession of loose sheaves prompted a halt. A group of 'experts' gathered about the watchful binder as it stood thinking behind my grey 'Fergie'. I was fiddling with its knotter when up flashed the stripper arms, hooked under my belt and threw me on top of the red lid. The malicious contraption was about to lunge again—which must surely have opened my entrails—when a quick-witted crofter switched off the tractor power drive. Two days later I waved it goodbye on a lorry to Skye.

Not before time, the IDP solved the problem of spare parts for these dating tractors as machinery once again began to trundle out west on CalMac ferries. This time though, much was shining new and *en route* to crofters' machinery syndicates or the progressive individual. The peace of the islands was punctuated by the cough of 80-horsepower engines. Yet those backward crofters who didn't consign their 'old grey friend' to slow burial below the shifting Atlantic sands now have a valuable antique on their hands instead of a dubious overdraft.

Greater agricultural activity as a result of the IDP scheme—or at least a prospect of such in outlandish areas which were slowly reverting to a natural state—brought about a sharp division between the crofting fraternity and awakening conservation interests. Ploughing up the machair, draining neglected wetlands and the effect of intensive practices on the hard-pressed corncrake created a debate as grating as the call of the bird itself. Seemingly with scant reference to crofting opinion, the Nature Conservancy Council had crept up on the Highlands and planted its Special Scientific Interest designation overnight. Worse still, the official representatives of that agency were frequently not of Highland extraction. One

Harris crofter expressed a widely-held feeling: 'The English have destroyed their own countryside and now they've come to tell us how to run ours.'

This acrimonious confrontation between various powerful Government bodies has only now become somewhat blunted by the inclusion within recent schemes of conditions from which the crofter may benefit financially by turning over part of his holding to 'wildlife production'.

The undoubted success of the IDP at the beginning of the 1980s led the Board towards a vigorous policy on rural revitalisation and similar development schemes have been launched in Skye and the north west. For this enterprise the Board's charismatic Vice-chairman Ronnie Cramond must take great credit. Crofters have shared fully in these benefits—particularly, once again, through livestock grants and those providing straight cash incentives for the retention of improved breeding stock. Hugh MacLean, as last head of the Land Division before this section became Natural Resources, did much of the groundwork for these schemes and now carries his experience to the position of Chairman of the Crofters' Commission.

Nobody, however, foresaw a spectacular change of fortune for the discarded cattle of the Highlands. Relegated to romantic painting of droving days or a tourist trap below a hotel window, the stately Highland breed had been put 'down the road' by all but the most reactionary crofter. Imagine his astonishment when the value of fourteen-year-old Morag's last heifer calf quadrupled overnight. A hairy crock of gold arrived at the bottom of the bog as continental cattle buyers plundered the Highlands, paying unheard-of prices for the native breeds. Cattle and conservation have become the latest wheeze across in Germany and our picturesque breeds suit the job admirably.

Closely allied to improvements in stock has been the Board's lead in marketing initiatives, though the slogan 'Big Stock Country' has yet to see crofters round a mart ring in stetson hats. The encouragement to producers selling groups of store stock has been successful in achieving higher returns for participants. Of equal importance, their sponsorship of a scheme to eradicate the scourge of sheep enzootic abortion has led to a real premium in the auction ring for healthy ewes. To a lesser exent diversification into more exotic livestock such as mohair goats, milking sheep and angora rabbits has left crofters unimpressed. (Could the memory of living on rabbits during hard times be slow to fade?)

'The biggest social, environmental and economic rip-off in the history of the Highlands' was the way fish farming was described to me by one Achiltibuie crofter. Yet it is seen by many as the Board's greatest single success. Its rapid spread into almost every suitable river and sea loch in the Highlands took many by surprise, and not least the crofter who found the bay below his window suddenly agleam with leaping salmon. Few crofters seemed aware that the sea-bed rights for such operations were only dispensible by an obscure but powerful body, the Crown Estate Commissioners.

Fewer crofters had the financial resources, know-how or influence to participate in the ensuing salmon boom. The emergent industry swam into being with the Board's full backing and a rising tide of high prices in its tail. A labour force was also at hand— as one propaganda leaflet put it 'most locals are used to handling small boats'. Wage rates and conditions often left something to be desired as 'the boat people' contented themselves and indeed were grateful for a job opportunity on the doorstep. Yet deep down some felt that another valuable resource had been plucked from under their noses by entrepreneurial outsiders enjoying privileged contacts and considerable support from the taxpayer.

The view that an industry with such potential should have been more carefully planned and more gradually expanded to contain the possibilities for greater financial participation by local people was often expressed. Crofter co-operatives similar in arrangement to sheep stock clubs were suggested. Little happened and even adequate compensation to crofters over loss of shore access had to be fought out in court by an Ullapool sheep club co-operative.

So be it. By and large the natives, with generations of bonding between the sea's bounty and the land's harvest, sat on their gunwhales and watched. Now that the ebb tide of over supply and prices below the cost of production threaten to carry some salmon cages towards the rocks of insolvency, perhaps crofters should consider that they are indeed, after all, the chosen race.

Overshadowing all other facets of crofting these past years has been an exceptional right to be granted within a democracy. A purchaser is empowered in law with the right to buy without necessarily having the willing consent of the owner. Every crofter now has the singular right to buy his house and land from his landlord at fifteen times the annual rent.

Outsiders are perplexed that there has been no rush to acquire such valuable assets. At the turn of the century Lord Leverhulme was even forced to give away his Bernera crofts and the reluctant owner-occupiers became known as the 'free gifters'. One snag is, of course, that as a proud owner you are debarred from many areas of crofting support, in particular the vital housing grants which have meant so much since the days of tin roofs. Memory fades slowly in a land of oral tradition and the total security currently enjoyed may be seen as sufficient.

There is now considerable pressure from the south to obtain a few acres, a house with a view and relief from the moving escalator of London life. For how long crofters will ignore rocketing prices and fend off this southern invasion remains to be seen. A man whose childhood home looks out on the Summer Isles said to me 'My father had to sell the old house after the war for £40. Today £40,000 wouldn't buy it.' The Highlands face an English take-over, for which the bridge-head is now well established. Mixing the vastly different races is not always easy or pleasant, for the resentment of a defeated people simmers below the surface.

It could be that in helping new entrants to crofting the Board is doing some of its most valuable work. The first rung of the ladder is the hardest and it is paramount that young Highland blood has a chance against the economic pressure from outside. Again in backing the recently-formed Crofters' Union the Board has shown that it values not only the rural dimension but also the Highland culture and its aspirations.

Should crofters take it as a compliment that they can now sell holidays in their homes? Holidaymakers enjoy paying to play at the work of a croft: dig peats, milk the house cow or struggle to clip sheep—activities that were a dire necessity for past generations are now attractive to people frustrated by computer print-outs and motorway mania. A crofting lifestyle still has much to commend it as an antidote for today's sick society.

By bending his back, by bending the rules, by flexing with each season's whim, the crofter has survived. The challenge for the future of crofting will be to bend and not break the old values which gave my grandmother so many happy memories.

>IAIN THOMSON shepherded in Wester Ross in the 1950s, gaining experience of a croft when allowed a few acres of land at the head of Loch Monar. Those early years are portrayed in his book *Isolation Shepherd*. Tenanting a holding near Beauly, Inverness-shire, designated 'of like crofting status' gave him insight on crofting law. Amalgamations gave him the unit of Tighnaleac of Breakachy, which he was later able to purchase; that gave him 20 years of farming experience in the Braes of Kilmorack. Surrounded by crofters, he watched the gradual break-up of their system and the arrival of 'holiday homes' and 'white settlers'. In six years as Convenor of the Scottish NFU's Highlands and Islands committee, he was at the heart of the successful campaign in Brussels and London which established the Agricultural Development Programmes, helpful to many crofters.

Crofters are to be found mainly in the North-West and North of the Scottish mainland, in the Outer Isles, and in Skye and Mull.

They have small landholdings, either owned or rented at low cost, and their position has been protected by law since 1886. For most it is a hard life, in remote areas with much rain. To survive, many combine part-time farming with other part-time work, such as fishing or weaving or sometimes running a B & B. Some take industrical jobs in the East Highlands for much of the year.

Above all, the resident crofter values his independence and his relations with other crofters in his vicinity.

(A.H.)

8   Ullapool, with East European fish factory ships (klondykers) in Loch Broom. (HIDB)

9   Fish farming in Harris. Photograph by Sam Maynard/Eloas.

10   Blar Mhor Industrial Estate, Fort William. (HIDB)

11   Cromarty Firth. Queen's Dock, Invergordon (under construction) (HIDB)

Chapter 6

The Sea

JAMES NICOLSON

Fishing has long been important to the Highlands and Islands of Scotland, where land and sea, worked together, provided a living and there emerged the crofter-fishermen, a race which was never really understood by the rest of the country. Traditionally the herring was the most important fish in this area, caught in driftnets from the scaffies, Zulus and Fifies of the crofter-fishermen and from the more efficient steam drifters of other parts of the country, where men made fishing their full-time occupation. Such towns as Stornoway, Wick and Lerwick saw their population double during the herring season, as hundreds of boats arrived and thousands of gutter lasses assembled to gut and pack the herrings in barrels with salt.

Two world wars and the loss of markets in Russia and Germany brought the great days of the herring fishery to an end and its decline was sorely felt throughout the Highlands and Islands. There were other species to be caught, such as haddock and whiting and several kinds of shellfish; but these could not be salted, and in the absence of processing plants marketing was a problem and transport costs were high. Besides, the boats were small and part-time fishermen were no match for the full-time seine net men from Peterhead and Lossiemouth and a dozen ports in between.

There were exceptions, of course, communities where men—and women—devoted their full attention to the fishing industry, following the herring in its season and fishing with seine net or creels the rest of the year. Shetlanders began to invest in new dual-purpose vessels soon after the Second World War, taking advantage of the grants and loans available under the Herring Industry Board and White Fish Authority schemes. Increased mechanisation on Orkney farms led to an expansion of the fishing industry there, especially in the island of Westray. Caithness, too, had a sizeable fleet of seine netters operating out of Wick and Scrabster.

On the West Coast, ring netters operated successfully from islands such as Scalpay and Eriskay. Special attention had been given to Stornoway where, between 1959 and 1963, the Outer Isles Fisheries Training Scheme had helped to provide eight new vessels. Nevertheless the rich stocks of fish around the north and west coasts of Scotland were exploited mainly by fishermen from the East

Coast and, in spite of an extension of Britain's fishing limits to twelve miles in 1964, a large proportion was taken by foreign vessels.

The first report of the HIDB, published in 1967, stated: 'Fishing is very important where it really counts, and that is largely in certain islands and other communities, where the tradition is still strong and where processing of the fish can be the basis of a land-rooted industry.' Prophet Smith, a Shetlander and a full-time member of the Board, was given the fishing portfolio because of his knowledge of the industry. The man who had to implement the Board's policy was James Lindsay, Head of the Board's Fisheries Division.

The Board wasted no time in getting to grips with the problem and on 7 February 1966 submitted to the Secretary of State for Scotland its plans for the development of the fishing industry in its area. Twenty-five new vessels would be built at a cost of £750,000 as part of a five-year plan to encourage new entrants to the industry. Suitable training arrangements would be made by the Board. The Board anticipated that its assistance would be in the form of loans, the grant element being provided by the normal fisheries authorities. It was stated that special attention would be given to the Outer Isles.

17   Boatbuilding, Burray. [HIDB]

Applications were accepted from the summer of 1966 and by the end of that year 26 applications had been received, of which nine had been approved. The first vessel to be built under the scheme, the Stornoway-registered *Alpha*, was ready on 22 June 1967 and a year later ten vessels were fishing.

The new scheme proved so successful that in August 1967 the Board decided to increase the number of new vessels to be built to 35, the additional ten being intended for Orkney and the Pentland Firth area. It was also realised that the scheme's benefits could be greatly extended by supporting the purchase of good second-hand boats from other parts of the country. By the end of 1970 the Board had approved 92 applications for new boats, of which 79 were fishing.

Having set the lower limit of assistance at 40 feet, the Board then realised that there was a demand, unmet by the statutory authorities, for small boats suitable for shell fishing and sea angling. The Board decided to give grants and loans for this class of vessel and the response was immediate. By the end of 1970, 66 applications had been approved, 30 boats were already fishing and nine more were under construction.

In order to maximise the benefits to the Highlands and Islands, the Board decided that as many boats as possible should be built within its area. There was already a long tradition of boat building in the region, mainly in small yards and sheds, the builders desperately short of capital to improve their facilities. Within a few years 29 boatbuilders were involved in the HIDB scheme, from Unst in the north to Campbeltown in the south.

While most builders continued to produce wooden vessels to traditional hull designs, new firms were encouraged to use alternative materials. Halmatic (Scotland) Ltd set up a yard in Orkney to produce vessels with hulls made from glass reinforced plastic (GRP), while at Scrabster a firm began to build vessels from reinforced concrete.

The largest yard to be assisted by the Board was at Campbeltown. Here the English company, Thames Launch, developed the site at Trench Point to build steel hulled vessels. The company ran into severe difficulties when their first two vessels were built at a loss. Fortunately Lithgow Holdings took over the business and introduced a range of designs for seiner/trawlers up to 85 feet long. In the space of seven years, Campbeltown Shipyard built 34 vessels, one of them an 85 foot stern trawler for a crew in the Faroe Islands.

The boats built under the Board's scheme were modern in design and incorporated the latest equipment on deck and in the wheelhouse. The larger vessels were equipped to catch white fish or herring, while the smaller vessels concentrated on shellfish, contributing to the great rise in the catch of prawns and scallops in the 1960s and 1970s.

White fish, shellfish, freezing and processing. And the East Coast men go West.

The Board also set out to develop fish processing facilities, to cope with increased landings. Small shellfish processing units were started along the West Coast and in islands such as Westray, Stronsay and Islay, where they were of immense benefit to small communities for the jobs they provided. The HIDB also took over the freezing plant and cold store run by the Herring Industry Board at Stornoway and invested £100,000 in new machinery over three years. Under the name Gaelfish, it processed white fish, herring, prawns and scallops and was built up into a successful business, later acquired by a Norwegian businessman, Rolf Olsen.

It was in Shetland that the most spectacular developments in fish processing took place. Iceatlantic at Scalloway, having survived the lean years around 1960, received assistance from the Board and embarked on a period of rapid expansion. It was joined by other firms until, by 1971, there were 14 firms engaged in fish processing in several parts of the Mainland and in the islands of Yell, Whalsay, Out Skerries and Burra. The production consisted mainly of white fish fillets marketed as laminated block. Marketing within the UK remained a problem until the Scalloway firm, TTF (Fish Processing) Ltd, discovered an almost unlimited demand in the USA and arranged with a Danish shipping company for refrigerated cargo vessels to call at Scalloway, *en route* for America. In 1971 exports by this route amounted to 4500 tons. The building of a 1500 ton cold store at Scalloway confirmed the village's position as the fish processing capital of Shetland.

While local fleets expanded under the Board's scheme, it was men from the East Coast that made the biggest impact on West Coast fisheries in the 1960s and 1970s. Finding fish more plentiful than in the North Sea, they moved to the West Coast, using such ports as Lochinver and Kinlochbervie to land their catches and leaving their boats there while they travelled home each weekend.

At Kinlochbervie the pace of development was spectacular. Fish landings there in 1962 were worth £172,000, but ten years later they were worth £706,000, and the rush continued until Kinlochbervie became one of the top five ports in the UK, with a harbour and shore-based facilities to match.

The Board's first fisheries development scheme ended in 1971 when £3.5 million had been invested. As a result of the scheme the fishing fleet in the Highlands and Islands had increased from 167 vessels in 1966 to 411 in 1971. In the same period the number of vessels registered at East Coast ports had dropped from 819 to 789. The scheme had been so successful that the Board submitted a proposal to the Secretary of State for Scotland seeking an extension. Approval was given in 1973 for the provision of a further 40 vessels between 40 feet and 80 feet long, 110 second-hand boats and 100 new vessels for shellfishing and sea angling. When that scheme ended in 1979 it was calculated that the Board had invested over £20 million in the industry, 500 boats had been added to the fleet and at least 4300 jobs had been created or retained.

The invaders from Norway—and a ban on herring fishing

In the early 1960s the driftnet was still the most common method for catching herring in Scotland. A small quantity was taken by trawl and along the West Coast the ring net was highly effective in shallow sounds and firths, but the main summer fishery at Shetland and off the Buchan coast was in the hands of drifter-men, who used the traditional net introduced by the Dutch hundreds of years before. Their numbers had dropped considerably, but still around 40 vessels switched over from seine netting to herring fishing for three months each year. While curing was still the main outlet at Lerwick, an increasing proportion of herring was frozen for the home market.

Unknown to these fishermen, the long era of the driftnet was coming to an end because of developments in Norway, where the purse seine had been developed into the most effective mode of capture ever known. Innovations that made this possible were sonar to locate herring shoals, synthetic twine to allow larger nets to be handled, hydraulic winches to close the net and the Puretic power block to haul the net on board.

In 1965 over 150 Norwegian purse seiners fished in Shetland waters for the first time and the contrast between the two systems was soon apparent. In their huge nets, 280 fathoms long and 70 fathoms deep, the purse seiners often took 100 tonnes of herring from a single cast of the net, within sight of the small motor drifters for whom 30 crans, or 5 tonnes, was a good night's work. While the drifters could manage only one set of their nets per day and returned to port to land their catches fresh each morning, the purse seiners stayed on the grounds until they could carry no more and then set their course for Norway, where their catches were pumped ashore into fish meal factories. In 1965 the Norwegian fleet took 190,000 tonnes of herring from the Shetland area compared with about 10,000 tonnes by the British fleet—and that was only the start of the Norwegians' interest in the Shetland area.

The reaction of Scottish fishermen was predictable. Fears that the stocks would soon be wiped out led to indignant letters in the press and appeals to the Herring Industry Board, but no one took the slightest notice. Naturally there were fishermen who realised that the purse seine had come to stay and that they would have to adapt to a new situation or go out of business. The first British purse seiners were the converted white fish seiner, *Glenugie III* of Peterhead and the side trawler *Princess Anne* from Fleetwood, both of which fished in 1966. The following year the HIDB made its first investment in a purse seiner when it assisted a Shetland crew to buy a secondhand Norwegian vessel, which they renamed *Adalla*. Financially the scheme was a failure, but it showed the potential for this method of fishing.

In 1968 the first British vessels to be built specifically for purse seining began their careers. They were much smaller than the Norwegian vessels—generally 75 feet to 90 feet long and designed for trawling and seining for white fish during the winter and spring. By 1972 the British fleet included 12 purse seiners, four of which were based at Shetland.

Spurred on by its initial success, the Norwegian fleet had entered the second stage of its development with larger vessels—nearly 500 of them—equipped with more efficient gear. Other European countries followed Norway's example and the herring catch continued to rise. Prior to 1965 the normal catch by all nations from the North Sea was 600,000 to 700,000 tonnes, but in that year Norway alone took 615,000 tonnes and the North Sea catch doubled to 1,300,000 tonnes.

For some years the Scottish herring fishermen, with their purse seiners, raised their catch to a level unknown since between the wars. However the experience of the drifters gave a clear indication of the run-down of the stocks. The number of drifters dwindled steadily, until in 1970 they landed only 13% of the catch at Shetland. In 1972 only 17 drifters fished at Shetland and in 1975 the last of them put to sea. Her catches were so poor that she stopped fishing half-way through the season. In 1977 there was no herring fishery at Shetland, since the British Government had been forced to act unilaterally and impose a complete ban on fishing, to save the herring stocks from extinction.

Mackerel saves the day—until the herring ban is lifted

Attention then switched to the Minch, which until then had maintained its herring stocks. In 1965 pair trawling had been introduced for herring, to the great annoyance of the men who still fished with driftnets and ring nets. A few years later came the purse seiners and West Coast ports experienced an intensity of fishing they had never known before. Most of the activity centred on Mallaig, which became the main herring port in Britain. Most of the catch was transported by road to processing plants on the East Coast of Scotland, while Faroese, Norwegian and Dutch vessels arrived to cure herring on board or carry loads of fresh herring, iced in boxes, back to the Continent, just as the earlier 'klondykers' had done before and after the First World War. Sadly, the stocks in the Minch suffered the same fate as those of the North Sea and in 1978 a ban was imposed on the west coast herring fishery as well.

Fortunately for the purse seiners, which now constituted a large and expensive fleet, an alternative fishery was found in the mackerel, a species hitherto neglected by Scottish fishermen. Its movements around the north and west coasts of Scotland had never been properly investigated and there was, therefore, some surprise when large shoals of mackerel were discovered north of Cape Wrath in the late 1970s.

The success of the first participants in this fishery sparked off an undignified scramble on the part of the British fishing industry. New, larger purse seiners arrived each year and the English trawler owners had their large distant water trawlers converted to catch mackerel. In the absence of detailed scientific research, fisheries scientists set a total allowable catch which was clearly far too high. By 1979 the build-up of the mackerel fleet was described as a free-for-all and, incredibly, it seemed that the mistakes that had been made over the herring fisheries were to be repeated all over again in the case of the mackerel fishery.

The demand for mackerel in Britain was strictly limited and it was due to the entrepreneurial skills of a new group of merchants and fish salesmen that markets were found in East European countries, whose large factory trawlers (or klondykers) chose Ullapool as their base. This quiet West Highland village rapidly became the premier port in Britain for the weight of fish landed. Mallaig remained one of the 'top ten' ports, but its boom days were over—and it had a fine new harbour to remind it of the hectic years of the mid 1970s.

After the autumn mackerel season at Ullapool the purse seiners moved to Cornwall, where Falmouth became the klondyking port of the South-West. They were thus away from their home ports for nearly half the year, although their crews arranged a long weekend at home, usually once a month. Shetland fishermen found it more convenient to charter an aircraft to fly them from Cornwall to Sumburgh.

Surprisingly, the herring stocks recovered from their mauling. The ban on fishing in the Minch was removed on 1 August 1981 and the North Sea fishery was reopened two years later. Lessons had been learned, however, and a new regime had been introduced, under which a total allowable catch would be calculated for each fishery and quotas allocated to each vessel. A licensing scheme had also been introduced to freeze the number of purse seiners at the current UK strength of around 50 vessels.

The most unfortunate result of the ban was that UK processors had lost their markets for herring products and, as in the case of the mackerel, the East European klondykers emerged as the major outlet, now able to virtually dictate the price that fishermen would receive.

Because of the licensing scheme, the distribution of the purse seine fleet when it was introduced was to determine the future of the fishery. More than half the fleet carry the registration letters of Peterhead, Fraserburgh and Banff, the traditional herring ports of North East Scotland. Shetland found itself in the fortunate position of having ten licences and of these no fewer than eight were held by fishermen in the island of Whalsay. Orkney had two licences and Mallaig initially had four, although three of them were subsequently sold to other ports.

In the early days of purse seining the fleet used to box part of the catch for the home market, while the rest were carried in bulk for curing or for fish meal. It was soon discovered that the most suitable means of storage was in tanks containing chilled sea water. Older boats then had their hold space sub-divided by steel partitions and installed refrigerated systems, while each new vessel had these incorporated when being built.

Although the Government had managed to restrict the size of the fleet, it had reckoned without the ambition of Scottish fishermen to continue to invest in the industry. Each new vessel was bigger and more powerful than the one she replaced and many of the older vessels were lengthened to increase their capacity.

A good example of this can been seen in the case of a crew from Northmavine in Shetland, led by Skipper John Peter Duncan. In 1977 they had the small seiner/trawler *Altaire* built at Sandhaven. A year later she was replaced by a 120 feet long purse seiner of the same name. Finding her too small they had her lengthened by 34 feet in 1982. Even this was not enough and she was replaced in 1987 by the third *Altaire*, a 200 feet long vessel built in Norway at a cost of over £5 million. Only two years later she was back in Norway for a 'stretch' which involved cutting her in two and inserting a 60 feet long section amidships, making her by far the longest fishing vessel in the UK.

The Search for 'New' Species

One of the greatest sources of controversy in the past twenty-five years has been the role of industrial fishing, the catching of fish for reduction to meal and oil.

British fishermen had long been opposed to this practice, maintaining that fish should be caught for human consumption and that only fish offal, surplus fish or fish that had deteriorated on passage should be sold for fish meal. The fish meal factories at Bressay, Stornoway and Fraserburgh were indeed regarded as essential components of the industry since they prevented the dumping of unwanted fish.

These plants received a boost in the late 1960s with the advent of purse seining, when traditional markets were glutted and large quantities of prime herring were sold for reduction. The price was low, but the huge volume of fish made the practice worth while.

In the late 1960s, Danish industrial trawlers moved into the Shetland area to fish for Norway pout—a small fish unsuitable for human consumption, although important as a food for larger species. Because of its small size it can be caught only with small meshed nets and these posed a threat to other species. On the sea-bed, pout and young haddock are often mixed together and they attract larger fish, such as cod and whiting that feed on them. The catch of a pout trawler is thus a mixed bag of fish of different ages and different species.

To make this fishery legal, a concession had to be introduced which allowed pout fishers to take up to 10% by weight of protected species. In other words, a trawler carrying 100 tonnes of fish could legally land, for fish meal, 10 tonnes of finger-length haddock, which would have produced several hundred tonnes of large fish had they been allowed to grow to maturity. Because it was difficult to restrict themselves to a 10% by-catch, these vessels received particular attention from British protection vessels and Danish skippers appeared frequently in Lerwick Sheriff Court, charged with illegal fishing.

In 1975 some Shetland vessels took part in this fishery and they landed a total of 14,000 tonnes of pout at the Bressay fish meal factory. The following year they landed 11,000 tonnes. Shetland Fishermen's Association, however, took the view that this was a retrograde step and local participation declined thereafter. Eventually the EEC introduced measures to control this fishery because of the threat to white fish stocks. Fishing for pout was banned within an area east of Shetland, to protect the main spawning grounds for haddock and whiting. This area became known as the 'pout box'.

The 1960s also saw the rise of the Scottish sprat fishery, with landings exceeding 80,000 tonnes in 1966, most of the catch being sold for fish meal. Confined mainly to sheltered firths on the mainland, it also provided a small fishery at Shetland between 1970 and 1978. This fishery too caused considerable disquiet because it also contained, at times, a significant proportion of young herring.

Sand-eels for fish meal, while the birds starve

Another major development at Shetland in the 1970s was the rise of the sand-eel fishery, a species which had been taken in the North Sea by Danish and Norwegian vessels for several years. In Shetland sand-eels are found on the sandy bottom near the shore, especially around the islands of Noss, Mousa, Fair Isle and Foula. It was regarded as a clean fishery in that there was no admixture with other species. There was, therefore, less opposition to this fishery than had been the case when pout fishing was introduced. Nevertheless many seine net fishermen maintained that the sand-eels had attracted large quantities of haddock to inshore grounds in the 1960s, where these formed the basis of a lucrative summer fishery—until the sand-eel fishery started and the haddocks disappeared. Environmentalist groups also pointed out that the sand-eel was the main food for several species of seabirds.

The fishery started in 1974 with a modest catch of 8000 tonnes, sold for fish meal. The catch rose steadily to reach a peak of 52,000 tonnes in 1982, by which time HBP Ltd, the owners of the factory at Bressay, had decided to build new premises to handle the expected increase in the catch of sand-eels. Unfortunately the catch declined steadily thereafter to reach a figure of only 4,800 tonnes in 1988. By this time it was clear that something had gone badly wrong at the seabird colonies. First to suffer were the Arctic terns which, from 1983 onwards, failed to rear any young. Then in 1985 it was noticed that Shetland's kittiwakes were experiencing the same problem, with large numbers of abandoned nests which were found to contain dead or dying chicks. The situation got worse in the next few years—until, in 1988, only three young kittiwakes fledged on the island of Noss out of 10,000 pairs of birds that had nested there.

A seminar was held at Lerwick on 15 and 16 October 1988, when it was established that the main reason for these breeding failures was a scarcity of sand-eels, but fisheries scientists said that there was no proof that the crisis was caused by overfishing. It was suggested that a possible explanation might be found in the recovery of the herring stocks from their low point in the mid 1970s to the stage when the dense shoals of herring were eating enormous quantities of young sand-eels. Other possible causes, it was suggested, were anomalies in salinity and water temperature—due, perhaps, to an influx of Atlantic water, which might be preventing the sand-eels from rising to the upper layers, where they could be available to surface feeders. The seminar ended with agreement that more research was needed into all aspects of the life history of the sand-eel and of the fishery at Shetland, as well as into the breeding failure of seabirds.

In the early 1980s the HIDB carried out surveys into the potential for sand-eel fishing in the Minch. It is still an important source of raw material for the HBP fish meal factory at Stornoway, which took its first supplies in 1977. In 1984 it handled over 11,000 tonnes of sand-eels out of a total intake of more than 18,000 tonnes of industrial species.

Blue Whiting let the investors down

While some species are an essential part of the food chain of larger fish, there are still fish stocks at the upper end of the chain that are under-exploited. One such is the blue whiting, found in deep water to the west of the Hebrides at certain times of the year. The Board's interest in blue whiting started in 1976 when it purchased the trawler *Hebridean* and chartered the Peterhead vessel *Shemara* to carry out exploratory voyages. They landed their catches at Stornoway where the Industrial Development Unit of the White Fish Authority and Torry Research Station were carrying out trials on machinery to process blue whiting, which is palatable in spite of its rather dark flesh. Further experiments were carried out at Iceatlantic in Scalloway in 1982, by which time it had been established that stocks of blue whiting were within reach of Scottish vessels from March to May each year.

So far efforts to start a fishery for human consumption in this country have failed, although landings are made from time to time at the fish meal factory in Stornoway. The plant at Bressay had its first supplies in 1980, when the purser/trawler *Azalea* made several trips and landed 2600 tonnes.

In 1976 the HIDB started to investigate the merits of a revolutionary new system for drying fish artificially. The following year a factory and pier were built at Breasclete on East Loch Roag in Lewis to process such species as white and blue ling, tusk, dogfish and blue whiting, all of which were believed to be abundant west of the Hebrides. A company, named Lewis Stokfisk, was formed with Norwegian involvement, the Board holding a 75% share.

Unfortunately the supplies of these species were less than expected. Few local fishermen responded by investing in larger trawlers and there were problems in getting Norwegian line fishing boats to land at Breasclete. In 1982 Lewis Stokfisk went into receivership, the final blow being the closure of the Nigerian market, for which the company had a considerable stock on the premises.

Undeterred by the experience at Breasclete, the Board embarked on an ambitious project to establish a fish meal plant at Ardveenish in Barra, in conjunction with Hull Fishmeal & Oil Company Ltd. The move followed the establishment of a 200-mile economic zone around Britain when, it was believed, large reserves of fish such as blue whiting would be available for British fishermen. The Board invested more than £2 million in building a pier and factory at Ardveenish, which opened in May 1985. It opened at an unfortunate time, when the world price of fish meal experienced a sharp fall—and supplies of fish were less than expected.

Early in 1987 Hull Fishmeal & Oil Co Ltd was taken over by HBP Ltd and the move resulted in a considerable improvement both in supplies and in the running of the factory. But even HBP, with all their experience, could not make the operation a success and the factory closed in 1989 with the loss of 20 jobs.

One of the reasons given for the failure of the Ardveenish factory was its inability to handle a new generation of bigger industrial fishing vessels, which require a considerable depth of water alongside the quay. This was a problem faced by the HBP plant at Bressay until 1987, when a new quay and conveyor system were built with assistance from the HIDB and Shetland Islands Council. Since then the factory has obtained supplies of capelin from Icelandic purse seiners and catches of blue whiting from the largest vessels in the Irish fleet. Early in 1989 the local vessel *Altaire* made her first landing of argentines—another 'new' species which has considerable potential, both for fish meal and for human consumption.

Brussels, bureaucrats—and too many boats

The 1970s brought many problems for Scottish fishermen. The greatest worry was Britain's decision to join the Common Market and the probable effect on fish stocks if the 12-mile limit was abolished, thus allowing continental fleets to fish right up to the beaches. After much discussion a compromise was reached and incorporated in the Brussels Treaty of Accession of 1972, whereby the inner 6-mile belt would continue to be reserved for British fishermen until the end of 1982, when the situation would be reviewed.

These terms did not satisfy Scottish fishermen, most of whom were bitterly opposed to Britain's entry into the EEC. It is significant that two areas where fishing is important to the local economy—Shetland and the Western Isles—actually produced a majority against British membership in the referendum of 1975.

The Fishery Limits Act of 1976 established a 200-mile economic zone around Britain and gave the UK government power to regulate fishing within the area, while the allocation of the catch was left in the hands of the EEC. Disagreement between Britain and other member countries led to constant wrangling and postponed the signing of a Common Fisheries Policy.

By this time the herring stocks were nearing extinction and concern was being expressed over the future of the white fish stocks, because of the presence of large British trawlers displaced from their traditional distant water grounds in the North Atlantic. It is not surprising that Scottish fishermen demanded a 50-mile exclusive zone for British vessels.

When that campaign failed, fishermen in the Northern Isles introduced their own Orkney and Shetland Fishing Plan, the aim being to give local vessels preference in a wide area around the islands and with recommendations to limit the total catch to ensure conservation. The plan was not accepted, the only concession to local fishermen being the establishment of a 'box' around Orkney and Shetland within which the largest European trawlers would be limited by licences.

The Common Fisheries Policy was finally agreed in 1982, following a series of compromises which pleased no one. At least the years of uncertainty were over and there began a period of renewed expansion on the part of Scottish fishermen, resulting in a big increase in applications for assistance to buy new boats. The Board's Fisheries Development Scheme ended in 1979, but it was still prepared to assist in the purchase of vessels. In 1983 the Board approved six such applications, of which three came from Shetland, two from Caithness and one from Orkney. Several of those contracts were placed with Campbeltown Shipyard, which by now had established a high reputation for the quality of its vessels. In 1984 the Board approved eight applications and six of these were for Shetland. Again Campbeltown Shipyard obtained several valuable contracts.

Ironically, part of the reason for this spate of boat-building was the growing scarcity of fish on inshore grounds. The old 70-footers that had sparked off the developments of the 1960s were sold and were replaced by steel-hulled vessels 80 to 87 feet long, costing around £1 million each, their wheelhouses packed with the latest electronic aids to fishing and navigation. Whereas a typical seine-netter of the 1960s was powered by a 150 hp engine, the big boats built at Campbeltown often had engines up to 800 hp. It was only their greatly increased towing power that resulted in increased catches, masking the inevitable conclusion that the stocks of ground fish were being steadily depleted. Larger trawls were required to get a bigger share of the declining catches and the boats were forced to operate on hard bottom, where their predecessors had been unable to fish. Special trawls, known as rockhoppers, were developed. They were armed with heavy rubber discs along the ground rope, which could roll or jump over obstructions in their path—hence the name.

Fishing on hard bottom, as far out as 200 miles west of Shetland and as far away as Rockall, the catches now contained a high proportion of 'rough' fish, such as cod, ling, saithe and a once-despised species, the monkfish, an ugly brute with an enormous head and teeth to match, whose slender tail has a meat which is now a gourmet's delight in top restaurants all over the world. Before long a box of monks was fetching over £70 on local markets and the success of a week's fishing depended on the proportion of monks in the catch.

There were many reasons for the decline in the stocks of haddock and whiting on inshore grounds. The fishery for pout (mixed with young haddock) in the 1970s certainly played a part, as did the persistent use of nets with a mininum mesh size of 80mm which, although legal, was too small to allow all the immature fish to escape. The biggest single reason, however, was simply a fishing fleet that was too large and too powerful for the available stocks of fish. The British fleet alone is too large—and we have to share our waters with trawlers from all over Western Europe. When a resource is a 'common' one no one feels personally responsible for the protection of stocks.

Fisheries scientists have tried for years to set Total Allowable Catches based on scientific assessment of the available stocks and the amount of fish that is being taken. It has been discovered, however, that catches are mis-reported by many European fishermen who operate a two-sale system, disposing of their over-quota fish on the Black Market. Besides, scientists are often unable to calculate how many tonnes of undersized fish are being dumped at sea.

The minimum mesh size is being increased and quotas of species that are in danger are being reduced. It must be recognised, however, that ground fish are not separated according to species—they swim in mixed shoals of cod, haddock, whiting, etc. Fishermen are permitted to fish for cod and whiting when the haddock quota has been taken, but they have to ensure that all the haddock they catch are thrown back into the sea. Such fish are dead, of course, and the system does nothing for conservation.

Some ports go up—others go down

The decline in fish stocks has brought severe problems for fishing communities. Many fishermen have survived by switching to other forms of fishing—indeed most of the West Coast fleet is now heavily dependent on prawns and scallops. Worst affected are the fishermen who have invested heavily in a large white fish vessel, for which there is no alternative fishery. The Campbeltown Shipyard itself is facing a crisis, since the EEC has placed a ban on grants to British fishermen because, it argues, the existing fleet is far too large.

Because of the scarcity, fish of all species are now in great demand and higher prices have certainly enabled many fishermen to remain in business. White fish processors, who used to export to the USA, now face severe competition from the fresh fish retail sector. The huge industry of which Shetland was so proud has been reduced to a handful of factories.

Scalloway, the main centre of the industry in the 1960s, has been devastated, due in part to the activities of an English firm which, in December 1986, purchased Iceatlantic, the main employer in the village. Having no experience of working in Shetland and no commitment to the people of Scalloway, it closed down the fish meal and pelagic processing lines, leaving the factory totally dependent on white fish. When these became scarce, the white fish section, too, was closed and over 100 people lost their jobs. Scalloway, with a population of 1200, was totally dependent on fish processing and the knock-on effects have been severe. Now the large cold store is virtually empty and the harbour traffic is severely reduced.

The bright spot in Shetland at the moment is the new pelagic processing plant at Lerwick, which opened in July 1989. It was built at a cost of over £4 million with assistance from the HIDB and Shetland Islands Council. It carries out primary processing of herring and mackerel, thus lessening the fleet's dependance on the East European klondykers. To guarantee supplies of mackerel the Government had to reverse a previous decision that Ullapool should be the only transhipment port for this species. Lerwick is now a designated transhipment port for both herring and mackerel.

The recovery of the herring stocks and the continuing success of the mackerel fishery shows what can be achieved by strict management. It is mainly due to the pelagic fisheries that the balance has shifted from the east coasts of Scotland and England to the Highlands and Islands. In 1983, for the first time, landings by weight in the Board's area exceeded that for the rest of the UK. The following year the Board's area handled 60% of the Scottish catch—some 328,000 tonnes, worth £74.6 million. It is significant that six of the 'Top 12' UK ports are in the Highlands and Islands. They are Ullapool, Lerwick, Stornoway, Kinlochbervie, Mallaig and Wick.

The politics of fish farming

After so much despondency over the stocks of wild fish it is heartening to note the success of fish farming in the Highlands and Islands within the last fifteen years or so. In its first report the Board stated: 'We are keeping under review the potential in our area to sustain fish farming enterprises.' That potential was to surpass their wildest dreams. While keeping all their options open, the Board clearly expected that fresh water fish farms held most promise and members had

18   Lerwick fishmarket. [HIDB]

19   Fish farm, Crossbost, Lewis. Photograph by Sam Maynard/Eolas.

already paid a visit to Denmark 'to assess the potential for fish farming in the Highlands and Islands on the fresh water pattern, as practised in other countries.'

Experiments in marine fish farming were already under way at Ardtoe near Fort William where, in 1965, the White Fish Authority had set up a unit to rear young plaice. After modifications to the original tidal pool, the work diversified into the use of floating cages for rearing plaice to marketable size. In its third report the Board stated: 'A good deal remains to be done before commercial fish farming is a reality and we are giving the Authority (WFA) financial help to carry out further research.'

During 1969 work began on a large oyster hatchery at Loch Creran, near Oban, promoted by Scottish Sea Farms Ltd, with help from the HIDB. It was claimed that the new technique would enable mature oysters to be harvested only three or four years after planting. In 1973 the Board gave assistance to three commercial projects for rearing oysters and four years later the first attempts to cultivate mussels were also giving promising results.

The Board continued its efforts in the farming of rainbow trout and encouraged several local firms to get started in this sector. There was an early setback when one farm was badly affected by disease and it was realised that the main problem lay in the quality of the eggs being brought in from Denmark. In 1971 the Board decided to set up its own hatchery, at Moniack near Inverness. Pure water was essential and this was obtained from bore holes. In 1974, following events in the private sector, the Board decided to diversify the hatchery to include a small amount of salmon to be taken through to the smolting stage.

The history of salmon farming in the Board's area goes back to 1964 when the multinational company, Unilever, set up a wholly-owned subsidiary, Marine Harvest Ltd, with a modest budget, to examine the prospects for farming salmon and trout. A year later Unilever instructed its research division to assess the potential for marine fish farming. At that time salmon was considered the least likely to be reared in captivity because of its strong migratory habits. It was realised, however, that only a highly priced, quality fish was likely to justify the considerable expenditure required, and by 1968 Unilever had realised that salmon was the obvious choice for fish farming on a commercial scale.

The first salmon farm was set up at Lochailort, by Marine Harvest, where they and Unilever Research had carried out most of their development work. In 1973 this farm produced 50 tonnes of farmed salmon and grilse, which were marketed successfully. The implications were obvious and from that date the salmon farming industry made rapid strides.

It became apparent that the clear waters of the West Coast of Scotland, with its many sheltered sea lochs, were ideally suited for salmon farming. A constant flushing by the Atlantic Ocean ensures unpolluted water, while the influence of the Gulf Stream ensures warmth for rapid growth throughout the year. Moreover the people of the area have a long history of farming and fishing and this combination of skills was to become of considerable importance.

By this time the Board had retained a fish farming consultant to give advice on disease and other aspects of the industry and had assisted a private company to set up a consultancy service. In 1976, in conjunction with Inverness Technical College, Stirling University and the Scottish Marine Biological Association, the Board helped to institute the first training courses for the fish farmer.

The Board, however, was convinced that salmon farming was not suitable for crofter-fishermen. In its 13th report, covering 1978, it stated: 'Farming of salmon has been shown to be a highly skilled operation, demanding considerable capital investment and expertise. While we still hope to see salmon farming applied as a small scale operation and have encouraged small scale pilot schemes towards this end, it is at present an activity more suitable for companies who have substantial financial resources behind them.'

In 1979 a long-running issue between the Board and Unilever was finally settled. Unilever had applied for a patent to cover their system for transferring salmon smolts from fresh water to the sea. The application was originally refused, but was granted following an appeal to the Patent Appeal Court. The Board decided to oppose the patent on behalf of the salmon farming industry, its case being based on the view that the technique was a natural process. The situation was resolved when the Board accepted an offer from Unilever to assign to the HIDB the UK rights of the patent for a nominal sum of £1. The Board then withdrew its opposition to the granting of the patent, the rights of which it decided not to apply, and made it clear that it would allow the patent to lapse. This enabled the industry to develop unhindered by exclusive rights to the important technique involved.

A major deterrent to the growth of the industry was an inadequate supply of smolts, which was not rectified until the late 1970s, when output from hatcheries could meet the ever-rising demands from salmon farmers. The Board's 20th report, covering 1985, described the 'burgeoning interest in fish farming' when, at one stage in the summer of 1985, there were 150 applications or pending applications involving a total of £7.8 million, against a budget allocation of £2.8 million. After a policy review it was decided to reduce the level of assistance to schemes that were 'up and running' and able to fund their own development, while preserving the level of funding in priority cases such as smolt supply, locally initiated salmon farming developments and shellfish culture.

The greatest interest in salmon farming at this time came from Shetland. Visitors to Norway had been impressed by the success of salmon farmers there and realised that what had been achieved along the west coast of Norway could also be done in the sheltered voes of Shetland, in spite of the earlier predictions of fish farming experts that Shetland's sea water was too cold.

The first smolts to enter the sea at Shetland were put into cages at West Burrafirth in June 1982 by John White, then in partnership with two Norwegian salmon farmers, Messrs Holterman and Meland. After a few months the cages were transferred to Garderhouse Voe, following a change of partnership which gave rise to Shetland Salmon Producers Ltd under the management of Jim Scott.

Shetland has no large rivers and the scarcity of clean, fresh water held back smolt production for a long time. This was overcome with the introduction of well boats—ships fitted with seawater tanks—which could bring in cargoes of smolts with only minimal losses during transit. Shetland's purse seiners have proved that they, too, are suitable for this job.

Shetland Islands Council played a major role in encouraging salmon farming for the maximum good of the islands. Under the ZCC Act of 1974, which gave the council power to control oil-related developments in coastal areas, the SIC also has power to issue or refuse works licences and this provided a procedure for applications to start salmon farming as well as for objections to be raised. To prevent the growth of large farms, owned by foreigners or multinational companies, it was decided that at least 75% of the capital for any farm must be raised locally. As a result, a large proportion of Shetland's salmon farmers are also crofters. In 1988 there were 58 salmon farms in Shetland and they produced 4600 tonnes, with an estimated value of £18 million, accounting for over one quarter of Scotland's production of 18,000 tonnes.

In its report covering 1988, the Board stated that a total of 1335 full-time jobs and 418 part-time jobs had been created in salmon farming while 'downstream' employment throughout Scotland was estimated at 5000. Throughout the Highlands and Islands the industry has provided jobs in packing salmon for export, producing polystyrene boxes and making everything from nets and cages to salmon feed.

The success of salmon farming tends to detract from achievements in rearing other species. Native species, such as oysters, mussels, scallops and queen scallops, are now farmed successfully. It has been found that the Pacific oyster *Crassostrea gigas* produces better results than the native oyster *Ostrea edulis* and the former is now the main species for farming. Another exotic species that promises to do well in Scottish waters is the Manilla clam.

The research station at Ardtoe still plays a key role in the industry. It is now run by the SFIA which replaced the White Fish Authority in 1981. Having developed a system for farming turbot, now being practised commercially, it achieved a major breakthrough in 1987, when it successfully reared halibut from the egg stage through metamorphosis to the juvenile fish—a natural transition which they had until then been unable to repeat in captivity. The station has now assembled a broodstock of young halibut from Iceland so that farming on a commercial scale can begin. The halibut is now extremely scarce in British waters, due to the intensity of trawling. High prices, allied to scarcity, should ensure a good demand for farmed halibut.

In 1987 the produce of fish farms in the Highlands and Islands reached a first sale value of £60 million, compared with £63 million for white fish landed in the Board's area. Of this salmon accounted for £50 million. Clearly this is only the start of a major new industry which is perfectly suited for the Highlands and Islands. It is comforting to know that, as the wild stocks continue to decline, fish farming can fill the gap.

However it would be unwise to regard fishing as a dying industry. The natural stocks have a remarkable ability to recover from a low point and there is no reason why the industry should not recover and strengthen the already important position it holds in the Highlands and Islands.

20   Oyster farming, Loch Fyne, Cairndow. [HIDB]

21   Mussel farming provides alternative incomes to many crofters in rural areas.
This crofter holds a rope of mussels on his raft at Uig, Lewis.
Photograph by Sam Maynard/Eolas.

At the moment the nation is obsessed with the wealth that flows from under the North Sea; but in many ways fishing is far more important than oil. The reserves of oil are finite and must become exhausted some day. Fish stocks, on the other hand, are renewable—or at least they should be if exploited at a rate which ensures that enough young fish are left to grow to maturity and to spawn in their turn.

Dr James Robert Nicolson was born and brought up in Shetland and has lived there most of his life. He has had a varied career which included five years working as a geologist in Sierra Leone, West Africa, and five years working as a fisherman in Shetland. He is now a full-time writer with several books to his credit, including *Shetland* which has already sold out four editions. He is editor of the monthly publications *Shetland Life* and *Shetland Fishing News* and is local correspondent for the national weekly *Fishing News*. He and his wife Violet live in Scalloway. They have a family of two daughters and a son.

GLOSSARY

Creel:	A pot for catching shellfish. In many parts of Scotland the word refers to a large wicker basket.
Driftnet:	A long net, floating on the surface and drifting with the tide, to catch pelagic fish such as herring.
Economic fishing zone:	A fishing area up to 200 miles from the shoreline, reserved for the sole use of one country, eg Iceland, or a group of countries, eg the EEC.
Fifie:	A sailing vessel which originated in Fife. Hundreds of them had motors installed between the wars and they provided a cheap alternative to the steam drifters.
Klondyking:	A practice started at the end of last century whereby large quantities of fresh herring from Scotland were rushed to the Continent for processing. At that time the gold rush in the Klondyke area of Canada was the main talking point. The fishing industry has always been quick to take over a topical word—as in the case of the Zulu. The East European factory ships of today are also known in the trade as Klondykers, but their operation is different from that of their predecessors.
Pair Trawling:	Two vessels working together, their increased power enabling them to tow a much larger net.
Pelagic:	Referring to fish that swim in upper layers of the sea as opposed to demersal fish that keep to the sea-bed.
Purse seine:	A large net which can be drawn tight and closed after enclosing a shoal of pelagic fish.
Ring net:	A much smaller and earlier version of the purse seine.
Scaffie:	A sailing vessel once common in the Moray Firth.
Seine net:	A net for encircling fish. The special Scottish seine net, an adaptation of the Danish seine, is similar, in some respects, to a trawl.
Smolt:	Young salmon migrating to the sea for the first time.
Zulu:	A type of fishing vessel developed at Lossiemouth about 1880—the time of the Zulu War.

Chapter 7

Industry

ALF YOUNG

I have a memory, culled from some newspaper or magazine, of this African tribal leader building, at baffling expense, a great, unfinished cathedral somewhere on the southern reaches of the Sahara. A powerful man's grand religious gesture, so apparently at odds with the subsistence existence of his people.

That same image, metaphorically, has been used by Italian social scientists to describe attempts in that country to graft large industrial complexes onto the more marginal economies of peripheral regions like Calabria. Building cathedrals in the desert, they've labelled it. And there are those, surveying post-war attempts at industrialisation in the Highlands and Islands of Scotland, who can feel the strong resonances of that same image as they contemplate the stripped-out pot lines at the Invergordon aluminium smelter or the current run-down of the fast-breeder reactor programme at Dounreay.

Did it ever make sense to try to bring major industrial projects this far north? Are the closures at Corpach, Invergordon, Kishorn and Arnish not conclusive evidence that the dream was, indeed, flawed from the start? Would the Highlands and Islands not be more profitably employed exploiting tourism, small business and economic activity based on the natural resources of the area?

The HIDB has lived with that fundamental debate since Day One. In its first annual report, the Board's first chairman, Sir Robert Grieve, wrote that modern industrial enterprises were 'absolutely essential' to Highland regeneration. Under Grieve, a majority on the fledgling board identified three areas—Lochaber, the Caithness area around Dounreay, and, most significantly, the greater Moray Firth—as areas with significant industrial development potential.

They commissioned the Moray Firth Plan, against Scottish Office opposition; they even put up a proposal to commission a private power station in the area, ring-fenced from the tariffs being charged by the Hydro Board. The search for viable industrial projects convulsed the HIDB in its early years, notably during the infamous Frank Thomson affair. Then the closure of the Fort William pulp mill in 1980, followed by the shutting of the aluminium smelter on the Cromarty Firth a year later, seemed to shatter for ever the industrial growth point philosophy which Grieve and others had fostered in the first five years.

The debate has rumbled on throughout the remainder of the 1980s. But the conclusion was not, and is not, as starkly inevitable as those who would have us rubbish the aspirations of that anonymous African leader would like to believe.

Smelters come and go

Take aluminium. The process which converts bauxite ore to alumina and then reduces that oxide to aluminium metal ingots requires massive amounts of electrical power. Extensive supplies of low-cost hydro power, readily available in places like Canada and Norway, have ensured that these countries have long been major primary aluminium producers.

But the industry, it may surprise some to learn, is also nearing its centenary in the Scottish Highlands, where hydro capacity, on a more modest scale, is also available. Work began on the first British Aluminium smelter at Foyers, on the east side of Loch Ness, in 1895, with Lord Kelvin as scientific adviser. When production began in 1896 the plant could produce 200 tonnes of metal a year, a tenth of total world output. By 1909, British Aluminium had built a second hydro-scheme and aluminium reduction plant at Kinlochleven, capable of quadrupling the UK's then total output of aluminium. The capital required nearly brought the company to its knees, but one financial reconstruction and one world war later it embarked on a third, much bigger, smelter project, in the shadow of Ben Nevis.

That was an extraordinary civil engineering undertaking for its time, involving the carving of a 15-mile-long tunnel through the solid rock beneath the mountain, to take the waters from Lochs Treig and Laggan and the headwaters of the Spey to the power station and smelter by Fort William. By the time the Lochaber plant was producing metal, in December 1929, questions were already being asked about the economic viability of the whole exercise. Today, a refurbished Fort William, like Kinlochleven, is still in business and regarded by some industry professionals as the most efficient smelter in Western Europe.

So what went wrong at Invergordon, which had produced aluminium for little more than a decade before its closure was announced so suddenly on the 29 December 1981? The 100,000 tonnes-a-year plant was one of three developments triggered by Prime Minister Harold Wilson's Labour Party conference speech at Scarborough in 1967.

It was not forced to locate in Easter Ross, in the way Premier Macmillan had twisted Lord Rootes's arm to build his car plant at Linwood. Indeed, two of the firms competing to build the Wilson-inspired smelters, British Aluminium and the Canadian giant Alcan, wanted to go there. A third consortium, led by Rio Tinto Zinc, short-listed Invergordon, but finally chose Anglesey off the North Wales coast.

The Wilson case for encouraging smelter developments in the UK was three-fold. First, for a Government haunted by balance of payments problems, the imbalance in aluminium supply was particularly stark. Total UK consumption of primary aluminium in 1967 was 356,000 tonnes. Between them, Lochaber and

22   British Aluminium smelter, Lochaber. The pipes taking water through Ben Nevis can be seen leading down to the Fort William smelter. [HIDB]

Kinlochleven—the UK's only operational smelters—could meet just 39,000 tonnes of that demand. Second, as Wilson told the Scarborough delegates, a source of cheap power was to hand. 'As a result of great advances in nuclear generation', he said, 'where Britain now leads the world ... the new nuclear generating stations of the 1970s will be able to provide electricity for industrial use far cheaper than electricity costs today.' And third, with government grants of 40% available towards capital investment in development areas, a substantial carrot was being deployed to encourage aluminium producers to locate in the more depressed regions of Britain.

That Whitehall carrot, however, was just as juicy if swallowed in Anglesey or north-east England rather than Invergordon. But the sheltered deep-water facilities of the Cromarty Firth were attractive to an industry that depended on shipping vast quantities of raw material from the Caribbean, Latin America or Australia. And although there was no nuclear power station within 200 miles of Easter Ross, under the joint generating agreement introduced in the wake of the 1961 MacKenzie Committee Report, between Scotland's two electricity utilities—the South of Scotland Electricity Board and the North of Scotland Hydro-Electric Board—the costs and output of all future generating plant (including Scotland's planned first AGR nuclear station, Hunterston B on the Ayrshire coast) would be shared. So any Invergordon operator could tap this brave new form of electricity through the grid.

We can ask, with hindsight, why the Invergordon smelter, like Foyers, Kinlochleven and Lochaber before it, did not plump for a proven, dedicated supply of hydro-electricity from the start. In part, the Wilson government was determined to push the virtues of nuclear power, whose drawbacks were a lot less visible then than they are now. And in part the sheer scale of the Cromarty plant would have required the lion's share of all the Hydro Board's installed dam capacity. Before it closed, Invergordon was taking nearly a quarter of all electricity sold in the Hydro Board's area. According to the then Secretary of State for Scotland, George Younger, the plant would have required some 60% of the board's full hydro capacity to meet its power needs on a continuous basis.

Of the two contenders, Alcan wanted to build its own coal-fired power station on the firth and ship fuel supplies from the pits of Northumberland. British Aluminium was prepared to sign a contract which meant it was, in effect, paying (with the help of a government loan) for 21% of the construction of Hunterston B in return for a guaranteed tranche of its output until the year 2000. Despite some Scottish pressure to build its smelter next door to Hunterston B, BACo won the political battle to build its plant at Invergordon. Alcan opted instead for a site at Lynemouth, near Blyth in Northumberland, where its smelter, powered by its own coal-fired station fuelled from a local pit, operates to this day.

Work on the £37m BACo plant at Inverbreakie Farm on the edge of Invergordon village began at the end of 1968. For Grieve and the others who believed in the industrialising of Highland growth points, it must have seemed that a large slice of their dream was about to be realised. The first aluminium was poured in May 1971.

Two years later the directly-employed labour force had grown to 669, 74% of them under 40. More than 60% of the workforce lived in the Highlands when they applied for jobs at the smelter, two-thirds of that group within the East Ross area. Another quarter came from the rest of Scotland. By 1975 Invergordon was employing 850. When it closed at the end of 1981, 890 smelter workers were given two days' notice that their jobs were lost and, on the Scottish Office's own estimate, those indirectly affected took the total number of jobs at risk to 1400.

The main causes of the smelter's premature demise were a disastrous slump in the market for primary aluminium during the recession which followed the election of the first Thatcher Government, and that special nuclear power deal, which failed dismally, to stand the test of time.

The brave new nuclear age ushered in by Prime Minister Wilson in 1967 was soon in trouble. In the early years Hunterston B failed to reach its designed output. By 1976, BACo was given access to an extra 5% of the lower capacity the station was achieving, with the Government picking up the tab. By 1981, that tab amounted to £113m. Then, in 1977, an accidental inflow of sea water put one of the two reactors out of commission for 30 months. By the late 1970s provisions being made by the SSEB and the Hydro Board for the eventual reprocessing of spent nuclear fuel added their own impact to rising unit costs, already outstripping anything anyone had predicted in the heady days of 1968.

Indeed the adverse impact of escalating reprocessing costs has continued to the present day, with nuclear stations being withdrawn from the proposed privatisation of the electricity supply industry and projected AGR decommissioning costs still a matter of considerable dispute.

Back in the late 1970s these emerging uncertainties were being increasingly felt on the bottom line of BACo's operations at Invergordon. For several years the company had disputed with the Hydro Board the prices it was being asked to pay for power. The dispute, involving an unpaid £47m by 1981, was heading for the Court of Session. In 1980–81, the smelter paid 1.26p for each unit of power. In April 1982, the Hydro Board instituted court proceedings. By September it was telling BACo that the provisional charge for that year would be 1.67p a unit, well in excess of the power costs faced by either of the other two Wilson smelters.

With operational losses at the plant mounting to £500,000 a week, a showdown was inevitable. BACo confronted ministers with three stark options: renegotiate the power contract to make it competitive; allow the whole BACo business to go into liquidation, jeopardising its 2700 other Scottish workers; or terminate the power contract and allow Invergordon to close.

Conflicting accounts of what took place in the subsequent negotiations between BACo and the Scottish Office have never been fully reconciled. At one stage Scottish Office negotiators insisted that any continuing subsidy on the power price, put at £16m a year, must have a break clause after three years. The company rejected that proposal. But in a briefing note to MPs, BACo's chairman Ronnie Utiger said 'The package discussed on the last day of negotiations on 17 December 1981 did not include a break clause. On 18 December BACo was informed that the package had been rejected as too costly and that termination was the only possibility.'

In the Commons on 21 January 1982, Under-Secretary of State Alex Fletcher said 'The Government and the company disagreed, not so much on the price, but on the period over which that price would have to be directly subsidised by the taxpayer. The difference between three years and 18 years was, in the Government's view, too long to give a blank cheque to any company.'

These conflicting claims of what was offered and what rejected have never been satisfactorily resolved. But it is clear that while Scottish Office ministers baulked at a long-term power subsidy for Invergordon the Kaiser/RTZ smelter on Anglesey was enjoying an even larger subsidy from the Central Electricity Generating Board and Alcan at Lynemouth was getting coal from the National Coal Board well below the price other NCB customers were paying. 'It is no secret' said Mr Younger at the time 'that both contracts now involve the respective boards in heavy losses.' But he and his colleagues were not prepared to go down that same road at Invergordon—not for more than three years, at any rate.

The Hydro Board was equally adamant. In its 1981–82 annual report it said 'The Board has always maintained and continues to maintain that it would be inequitable for its half-million other customers to have to carry any burden in respect of cheap power to the Invergordon smelter by means of higher electricity tariffs'.

So Invergordon closed. BACo got £79.3m for its residual rights to its share of Hunterston B through to the year 2000. The Government waived repayment of £21.2m of the outstanding loan granted back in 1968 to allow the company to buy into the nuclear station. In return BACo coughed up the £47m disputed power charges and another £4.15m due to the Hydro Board in the normal course of business. The Government was repaid £12.3m of the 1968 loan. BACo walked away with a net £15.5m in cash, an injection which kept the rest of the company's operations afloat—it ran up a pre-tax loss of £19.9m in 1981—until, within the year, BACo was taken over by Alcan.

The HIDB was given extra funding of up to £10m spread over three years to help the Invergordon area adjust to its new circumstances. But it was clear even then that Board members were far from convinced that the situation had been well handled. In a letter to *The Times* the outgoing chairman, Rear Admiral David Dunbar-Nasmith, attacked the Hydro Board for its attitude to power pricing. Quoting the Hydro Board's founding charter, which charged it with exploiting the water power resources of the Highlands to help regenerate the local economy, he asked 'What has happened to the vision of those who set up the Hydro Board in 1943?'

In a private memo to George Younger on his retirement as Board Chairman, Dunbar-Nasmith warned that, psychologically, the smelter closure was 'extremely destructive to the strategy of the Highlands and Islands Development Board, which has been laboriously built up over 15 years'.

In a nine-point shopping list, he called firstly for the transfer of the smelter plant to a new company for a nominal price of no more than £5m. And Dunbar-Nasmith went on to argue for a guaranteed electricity supply at a realistic price of between 1p and 1.2p a unit. Reiterating what he had said in his *Times* letter, the outgoing chairman called for that power to be supplied by the north's Hydro resources. Invergordon, he accepted, would require 60% of all the available capacity. The remaining 40%, he continued, would allow a modernised pulp mill to re-open at Corpach, with enough left over to run several metal-producing industries, such as ferro-alloys.

'What would be the cost, as costs there must be?' he had asked in *The Times*. 'Those of us in the Highlands would have to pay the same rate for our domestic electricity as those throughout the United Kingdom, instead of a marginally cheaper rate. I suggest that the people of the Highlands would much rather have worthwhile long-term secure jobs contributing significantly to the country's balance of payments while paying the going rate for their domestic electricity.'

The Scottish Office failed to take the argument on board. A world-wide search was mounted to find a successor operator for Invergordon. But without a significant re-think on power prices, it was always a charade.

On 27 April 1982 the new HIDB chairman, Robert Cowan, warned publicly that the overwhelming case for re-opening the smelter was being lost by default. 'We are deeply concerned and disappointed by the government's inability to find a solution to the power problem from the detailed proposals submitted to them' he said. 'Meanwhile time is running out for Invergordon.'

By June, BACo revealed the terms under which it and rival aluminium companies had been negotiating with the Scottish Office about re-starting production in Easter Ross. In a statement it said 'During the discussions the Scottish Office did not make a firm offer of power terms, but indicated that the base price would be higher than the company had previously been paying at Invergordon, and close to bulk tariff plus escalation. The base price would be subject to government subsidy—to be negotiated—but any subsidy would probably be on a reducing scale and would in any case be for a maximum period of five years.'

Needless to say BACo broke off the talks and every other operator decided that the terms were unrealistic. The smelter was dismantled. There were those only too ready to conclude that this, the grandest of all the great industrial cathedrals of the north, had been lured to the wrong place. But Bob Cowan was emphatic in rejecting that view. In his foreword to the HIDB's 1981 annual report (published in May 1982) he wrote 'It is perhaps worth making the point that our area is not ... suffering from a peculiarly Highland failure. The closure of the Invergordon smelter and Corpach pulp mill had nothing to do with their geographic location.'

There is no doubt that recession, fast-changing technology (in the case of Corpach) and, above all in Invergordon's case, uncompetitive power prices—not location—conspired to force closure. Ironically, British Alcan is now hinting, nearly a decade on, that the smelter may one day resume production. And the Hydro Board, moving towards privatisation, is now keen to do special deals with big industrial customers as far away as the north of England. Large quantities of sour gas from a growing number of North Sea fields, including the output of the Miller field (which is already contracted to the Hydro Board for burning at its Peterhead station from 1992) holds out the prospect of a variety of new, lower-cost power deals for industry.

From the Trees, Value to be Added

If location was not a major factor in the smelter's demise, location has worked against the Highland interest, since the Corpach pulp mill closure, and prevented the region from exploiting to the full its forest resources. Plans to build pulp and paper-making plants at a site outside Fort William pre-dated the creation of the HIDB. When the plans first surfaced in 1959 there were worries about the environmental impact. *A pulp mill will smell like cooking cabbage, warned one press report.*

But the supplies of maturing conifers in the West Highlands opened up a processing opportunity and originally four companies—Bowater, Reed, Thames Board Mills and Wiggins Teape—formed a consortium company to create the £15m complex. Bowater and Reed quickly withdrew and in 1962 Thames Board also lost interest. But Wiggins Teape, a subsidiary of British American Tobacco, decided to go ahead with the project on its own. Indeed, such was the optimism at the time that a second phase development was mooted, taking the capital cost to £20m and the projected workforce to 1200.

When Reggie Maudling announced the go-ahead, with the help of a £10m government loan, early in 1963, the then Scottish Secretary Michael Noble was forecasting work for 3200, including security for 700 existing forestry jobs. The government also pledged £2.5m to upgrade roads and create the community infrastructure that would be needed to cope with the influx of new families into Lochaber.

When production at the pulp mill started in March 1966 the project immediately hit problems. The plant lost £1.6m that year and £1.7m in 1967. Market conditions were tough and the innovative sulphite process for making the chemical pulp was not proving the world-beater that had been predicted. Wiggins Teape made vain efforts to get cuts in the price of its timber supplies and blamed the high transport costs of getting timber from the forests to Corpach for some of its losses. The advent, in the early 1970s, of a chipboard factory near Stirling, targeting 100,000 tonnes a year of precisely the same Sitka Spruce plantations as the pulp mill, added to Corpach's problems. 1973 brought severe shortages of suitable local timber.

Although the paper-making side was doing well, the pulp mill limped through the 1970s. In 1978 Wiggins Teape commissioned the Finnish consultants Jaakko Poyry to examine the pulp mill's future viability. The nine-month study made bleak reading. The sulphite process, the consultants concluded, was out of date. Even if it were upgraded—at a projected cost of £10m—the mill would still not be viable against bigger and more technologically advanced Scandinavian and American competition.

In April 1979 Wiggins Teape told the 450 pulp mill workers that their plant—which had lost £3m in each of the three previous years—would close in nine months' time. 'This is the gravest news in the Highlands for a decade', said HIDB chairman Sir Kenneth Alexander.

Jaako Poyry, with an eye to the vast quantities of standing timber which would

23   Highland Forest Products Ltd, near Dalcross, Inverness. The largest advance factory built to date by the HIDB at over 120,000 sq ft. [HIDB]

be maturing all up the west coast of Scotland in the 1990s, did suggest the possibility of building an integrated newsprint mill in Lochaber, with a price tag of £100m. Wiggins Teape, a fine and special papermaker, had no track record in that technology. So the first people to look at the idea's viability were a Reed/Bowater consortium, the very companies who had dropped out of the Corpach project 20 years before. They quickly lost interest a second time and Wiggins Teape then turned to the Montreal-based Consolidated Bathhurst and for a time in early 1980 a deal looked possible. But by the end of April the deal was off and the Corpach pulp mill finally closed in November.

The two companies blamed the high cost of future timber supplies and the then weakness of the dollar, the currency in which newsprint is traded. The current state of the dollar hardly seems a basis on which to judge the economic viability of a plant that might expect to go on producing newsprint for decades. In fact the principal reason why Consolidated Bathhurst walked away appears to have been the refusal of the Scottish Office and the Forestry Commission to underwrite the project with a £30m capital injection and a timber subsidy amounting to £1.75m a year.

There were two attempts, led by the Duke of Argyll and Highland Region vice-convenor John Robertson, to put together plans to re-start the pulp mill, but to no avail. However that maturing natural resource, so much of it planted throughout the West Highlands and set to triple in available volume by the 1990s, was not going to go away. In the immediate aftermath of the Corpach closure, Scotland exported a lot of its surplus timber to Scandinavia for processing. Undeterred, a group of interested parties, including the HIDB, the SDA, the Forestry Commission and the Scottish Office, formed the Scottish Forest Products Development Group to promote downstream processing projects. That strategy has paid handsome dividends during the rest of the 1980s. But sadly for the Highlands, where most of the trees are growing, only one of the crop of new processing plants which have come into existence has put down its roots in the HIDB area. That was Highland Forest Products, now owned by Noranda of Canada, which started production in 1985 at a site at Dalcross near Inverness, using Scots Pine to make oriented strand board, an innovative substitute for plywood.

But the biggest projects either settled in the industrial heartland of Scotland or located themselves even further south. Of the new integrated pulp and paper mills, at the start of the decade Thames Board sited its £83m complex at Workington in Cumbria; the Finnish-owned Shotton Paper, making newsprint, went to Deeside in North Wales; and the latest arrival, Caledonian Paper, also Finnish-owned, took its £240m coated paper line to Irvine on the Ayrshire coast. Closeness to markets for its finished product weighed more heavily on Caledonian Paper's decision on where to locate than the need to shorten the transport link with the plantations. The former car factory site at Linwood, not Corpach, was the disappointed underbidder in that case.

Demand for coniferous small round wood for all three modern integrated mills, as their expansion plans mature, and the continued growth of the now German-owned Caberboard particle board plant near Stirling (which, incidentally, also chose Irvine for a spin-off plant in the interim) will again put a heavy strain on existing timber supplies through the mid 1990s. So the pressure to continue planting large tracts of the West Highlands will remain. But the real economic spin-off, sadly, will be felt elsewhere.

Sunshine and storm with oil

If location has largely worked against the Highland interest in timber processing, the discovery of North Sea oil has left its indelible imprint on many Highland and Island communities since that first significant oil strike on the Arbroath field in December 1969, followed by BP's Forties discovery 11 months later.

From the start the Highland Board was an enthusiastic supporter of oil-related developments in its area. Given where the oil was being discovered, there was a clear economic and strategic case for many of the platform fabrication yards and landfall terminals to be built on sites around the Highlands and Islands coastline. But the real prize would have been a major downstream petrochemical plant. In his 1982 memo to George Younger, Rear Admiral Dunbar-Nasmith argued that government support for a gas-gathering pipeline into the Cromarty Firth, where there had long been a dream of processing the gases and natural gas liquids associated with the oil, was 'imperative'.

At earlier stages in the story of North Sea oil the HIDB had made itself unpopular in some parts of the Highlands by support for planning applications for new fabrication facilities in environmentally sensitive areas. One inquiry rejected the American company Chicago Bridge's plans to build platforms at Dunnet Bay in Caithness. But the real *cause celebre* which attracted the most intense media interest was the Drumbuie inquiry which opened in late 1973.

Two UK companies, John Mowlem and Taylor Woodrow, wanted to build concrete platforms at Port Cam, Drumbuie, at the mouth of Loch Carron. They were supported by both the HIDB and the Department of Trade and Industry (which, at the time, included responsibility for energy policy). Pitted against them were a small community of 23 people, the National Trust for Scotland—which owned the land—and an outraged environmental lobby. The green case prevailed.

Hindsight indicates that the enthusiasm of the government and many of the contractors in the early days for the Norwegian-inspired concrete platform designs was grossly inflated. One excavated site, at Portavadie on Loch Fyne, never received a single order and became infamous for obscure property dealings on remote tax havens.

Even where productive construction yards were created—the Highlands Fabricators facility at Nigg Bay, McDermott's at Ardersier, Howard Doris on Loch Kishorn and the Olsen- (later Hereema-) owned facility at Arnish Point outside Stornoway—the inherently boom-or-bust nature of the industry placed heavy strains on those who had the task of providing housing, education and other services for the influx of workers. HiFab, for example, which specialised in steel structures and won important orders for the Forties field as soon as it opened in

1972, was employing 3300 people within 30 months. At peak recruitment the recently-opened smelter along the road was hit hard by the high wage rates traditionally associated with the oil sector. It lost as much as 35% of its workforce annually to Nigg in those early years.

The limited social amenities of an Easter Ross faced with thousands of high-spending single or unattached males exacerbated the difficulties. HiFab resorted to mooring two cruise liners in the Cromarty Firth to accommodate some of the temporary workers at peak times.

When the first steel jacket was floated out, 1600 of the HiFab workers were laid off within a two-month period, bringing home what was to become an enduring feature of the offshore fabrication scene. A yard employing up to 5000 at peak production knew how to enjoy the boom times when the oil majors were spending up to £1300m a year on platforms and associated equipment. They say that when the biggest steel jacket of all, for the Magnus development, was floated out from Nigg in 1982, the celebrations—now committed to legend as 'the feeding of the ten thousand'—were such that innocent tourists were diverted off the A9 to join in the hoolie. But the same yard could be orderless and in mothballs a few months later.

Despite periods of famine, particularly after the 1986 oil price slump, yards like HiFab and the American-owned Ardersier facility have survived and are, at the time of writing, prospering again. Others have been less fortunate.

Early on, the swing from concrete to steel technology became unstoppable. The Anglo-French Howard Doris yard at Kishorn, across the loch from Drumbuie, managed for a time to make the transition, but succumbed to the receivers in 1986. In Lewis, the Arnish yard which had provided work for up to 1000 men in a particular unemployment blackspot finally closed for good in December 1988.

The arrival of oil also brought major landfall terminal developments at Sullom Voe on Shetland, Flotta in Orkney and at Nigg Bay, to handle the output of Britoil's inshore Beatrice field in the Moray Firth. Together they represented a capital investment of more than £1700m. But although Sullom Voe in particular has had a dramatic impact on life in Shetland, all three are essentially tranportation points in the onward journey of the crude oil to final processing.

A dream that died

The HIDB's long standing dream of a major petrochemical development being located in the Moray Firth remains unrealised. 'The opportunity created by the existence of feedstock to initiate a new petrochemical industry' Dunbar-Nasmith told Secretary of State Younger in his 1982 memo 'is unique'. He went on: 'The case studies commissioned by the Board in 1977–78 demonstrated the economics of processing associated gases and natural gas liquids at a location near to pipeline landfalls and safe port facilities. Ethylene produced from ethane in the Cromarty Firth would be competitive in Europe in five to six years' time'.

Such a project, involving a gas-gathering pipeline, was, he added, 'the key to the future of the Highland Board's industrial strategy.' But it was not to be. The main reprocessing spin-off from the North Sea oil boom went, instead, to Mossmorran in Fife—and, ironically, the cost to the Exchequer of supporting that capital-intensive project, and Sullom Voe before it, was the main motive force in reshaping (and reducing in cash terms) the Thatcher government's commitment to regional policy.

The nuclear North-East

If terminals like Sullom Voe are cathedrals which function with few direct worshippers and the fabrication yards have congregations with a highly volatile attendance record, the last great Highland cathedral, created in the post-war period—this time paying homage to the nuclear age—now looks set, like the Invergordon smelter and the Corpach pulp mill before it, to go out of business. In July 1988 the government announced that the prototype fast-breeder reactor at Dounreay in Caithness would finally close in 1993–94 and the associated reprocessing plant by 1997. The Dounreay workforce, 2100 strong at the time, would drop to 1600 by the mid 1990s and to 500 when the reprocessing plant finally closes its doors.

The economic blow to the Thurso area is hard to overstate. If the government's present plans are carried out the whole economic mainstay of that part of Caithness will go. A facility which directly employs 20% of the local working population (30% when sub-contractors are taken into account) and contributes £1.4m a month in wages to the local economy is, if the truth is faced, virtually irreplaceable.

The Dounreay plant first arrived in the 1950s. The first experimental reactor gave way to a prototype station and the infant Highland Board had to lobby hard, with others, to ensure that the stage two development went to Caithness. But now, with the prototype station in maturity, feeding power into the Hydro Board grid, and the fast-breeder development programme having cost an accumulated £3500m over more than three decades, the government has concluded that the fruits of the research will not be needed commercially for another 30 or 40 years.

Hopes that the PFR would be succeeded by a full-scale demonstration fast-breeder have been sunk by low growth in elecricity demand, substantial existing generating over-capacity, the government's commitment to the building of a new generation of pressurised water nuclear stations now abandoned and a new-found caution about the virtues of nuclear technology. Dounreay's fate is not entirely sealed: its owners, the UK Atomic Energy Authority (in its new guise as AEA Technology) is determined to build up the plant's growing expertise in related contract areas; and the nuclear waste disposal executive, Nirex, has shortlisted Dounreay (against the opposition of Highland Regional Council and other groups) as the possible site for a national nuclear waste repository—a project which could cost up to £4000m, creating between 350 and 700 jobs.

If closure does go ahead the consequences for the HIDB, as the principal agency charged with picking up the pieces, are substantial. Put bluntly, the options are to

12 Aonach Mor Ski Development. Photograph by Peter Davenport.

13 Ski-ing in the Cairngorms. (HIDB)

14   Wind surfing, Lewis. Photograph by Sam Maynard/Eloas.

15   The farmhouse of Achnambeithach, Glencoe. Photograph by Peter Davenport.

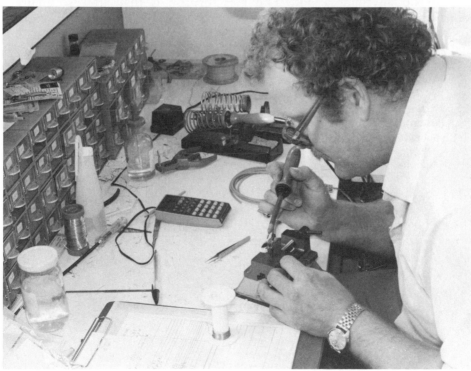

24a and b Gaeltec, Skye. [HIDB]

find substitute inward investment for the area; sponsor emigration from an area where the population has quadrupled since the 1950s; or face up to the social consequences of escalating unemployment in the area.

There can be little doubt that the Board will concentrate all its efforts on option one. And there are successful precedents. When the Invergordon smelter closed much of the extra funding the HIDB received from the Scottish Office was channelled into the new Enterprise Zone created at Invergordon and Alness.

Despite initial scepticism, that zone has had considerable success, attracting small to medium-sized firms, working in a whole range of industrial sectors, to locate there. The companies—from a BP offshoot making food products for the fish-farming industry to a German-owned recording tape manufacturer escaping the skills famine in south-east England—now employ as many people as lost jobs when the smelter closed.

There is already a similarly diversified industrial base in Caithness, from glass-making to electronics, to the wife-and-husband Grant team at Norfrost, the celebrated domestic freezer manufacturers. It will not be easy, but at least there is something to build on.

The post-war history of the industrial cathedrals of the Highlands and Islands does not make particularly happy reading. The failures have been dramatic. The reasons were often outwith the power of the region or its people or its development agency to do anything about. The real surprise is that after so many dis-appointments the resilience of all concerned has continued to shine through.

ALF YOUNG is Economics editor of the *Glasgow Herald*. After earlier careers in education and politics, where he was research officer of the Labour Party in Scotland during the devolution years of the late 1970s, he made a late career switch, at the age of 35, to journalism. He has worked for Radio Clyde, the late-lamented *Sunday Standard*, BBC, *The Scotsman* and the *Glasgow Herald*, where he specialises in the Scottish economy.

Chapter 8

Leisure—The Fourth Wave

JOHN FOSTER

In 1965 Michael Dower (son of Arthur Dower, architect of the National Park system of England and Wales) published the results of a survey he had carried out for the Civic Trust. This was entitled *The Fourth Wave*. He described the first three waves that had broken over Britain since 1800 as the growth of large industrial towns, the outward thrust of railways and the spread of car-borne suburbs. This fourth wave, he thought, would be more powerful than all the others, although contained in one modest word—leisure. A quarter of a century on, there can be no doubt that Dower's assessment of the impact of leisure was right—and this applies as much in the Highlands and Islands of Scotland as elsewhere in Britain.

But in 1965 the Highlands and Islands were not ready for this fourth wave. Visitors were already coming in considerable numbers, driving, by today's standards, rather unreliable cars and encountering rough, single-track roads. There were too few hotels and B & Bs, and an equivalent dearth of information about places of interest and local traditions. Muirhead's *Scotland* and the books of H V Morton were among the popular sources of reference at the time.

Nevertheless more and more people came north as outdoor activities—walking, climbing, ski-ing, fishing, camping—became ever more popular. Some first-time visitors were disappointed by the lack of creature-comforts, but many were not dismayed and returned again and again, penetrating farther and farther into what was, to them, the unknown. They particularly appreciated the relative freedom of access to the mountains and glens and were impressed by the vast tracts of country open to them through the landholdings of the National Trust for Scotland—from Goatfell on Arran and Ben Lawers in Central Perthshire to Glen Coe, Kintail and (by 1967) Torridon in the west and north.

Into this scene of tourist potential came the Highlands and Islands Development Board in 1965. Its first chairman, Robert Grieve, recognised this potential at the outset and described it as 'the second great prop of the regional economy'. (The others were forestry, manufacturing industry and fishing.) He also saw that tourism had to be selective and must be developed without spoiling what the First Annual Report of the Board called '... one of the last great unspoilt beautiful landscapes in Europe'.

116 HIGHLANDS AND ISLANDS

Some local authorities, voluntary bodies and private individuals realised the opportunities to be grasped, but many landowners, crofters and local residents viewed the matter differently and were opposed—or at best indifferent—to the establishment of the Board (for a variety of personal reasons). As to tourism, they feared adverse consequences from the influx of too many outsiders.

The Years Between.

In 1965 a poorly funded voluntary organisation—the Scottish Tourist Board—was responsible for tourism in Scotland. It did not achieve statutory status and reasonable resources until the Development of Tourism Act was passed four years later. The need to encourage tourism, however, was urgent and the challenge was quickly taken up by the HIDB.

The Spey Valley was an immediate focus and the Board helped to bring into being the Aviemore Centre, opened in 1966, and to get the very new Cairngorm Sports Development Company onto a more secure financial footing. In the West Highlands and in the Islands, it recognised the need for new hotels and planned a £1 million development scheme to be implemented over a period of years. In the meantime it put money into improving guest houses, providing caravan sites and helping to establish several new types of sport, including sand yachting on the magnificent beach at Dunnet Bay in Caithness.

The Countryside Commission for Scotland came into being in 1968, with an all-Scotland remit to help to provide informal recreational facilities in the countryside and to protect the quality of the scenic environment. The two agencies quickly made common cause on a number of ideas. In the same year the Board launched its first campaign specifically designed to attract visitors to the Highlands and Islands, with the particular aim of extending the tourist season at both ends. This proved successful both within the UK market and internationally. Its success in turn put greater pressure on the limited accommodation and public transport facilities then existing, but this was very much within the Board's philosophy of increasing demand on the assumption that supply would expand to meet it. In its second year the fledgling agency directed £500,000 to tourism development, nearly one-third of its total finance for grants and loans—a modest sum by today's standards, but a welcome commitment.

At that time the small information centres scattered throughout the region were poorly funded, unco-ordinated and run by a variety of associations and public-spirited individuals. The Board helped with cash and as an interim measure tried to bring them into an overall network with an assured source of income—a task which was to prove more daunting than at first thought.

Meanwhile, out on the ground during the late 1960s, two things were happening—one encouraging, the other worrying to the Board. First, Michael Dower's Fourth Wave, helped by the Board's own efforts, had well and truly broken over the mainland Highlands and was lapping tentatively on the shores of the Islands. Local employment in tourism increased. The £500,000 invested in 1967 was estimated to have produced 400 new jobs, with more to come as cash flowed into the industry from the Board and other sources.

The worrying aspect was the continuing reaction of many local people to the Board generally. The Highlander's suspicion of bureaucracy and of organisations and people imported from the south surfaced in a number of ways, not least in tourism. Many crofters and others saw it as purely seasonal in character and second-rate on that account. Robert Grieve, sensitive as always to the local pulse, had recognised the possibility of this attitude at the outset and sought to overcome the prevailing view, as he observed it, that '... any manufacturing industry, no matter how useless or dubious its product ... is somehow more honourable than an industry which is designed to give a visitor a warm welcome, a comfortable bed and good food'.

Some local people considered tourists to be a threat to their distinctive cultural heritage, while others felt that they were put at a disadvantage in getting jobs by the annual influx of hotel workers from the south and from overseas. Inevitably, too, as more people came into the area and bought and improved cottages for retirement or as holiday homes, it became more difficult for young local people to buy their own first homes.

These problems of disapproval in some quarters were to remain for a long time. The Board took them very seriously and continually made efforts to bridge the gap of misunderstanding by demonstrating through example the positive advantages to local interests of tourism of the right kind. One such example occurred at Carrbridge in the Spey Valley in 1970. This was European Conservation Year (ECY) and efforts were being made throughout Britain to raise public consciousness about the environment. David Hayes, then living in the Highlands, inspired by his experiences of travelling in the US National Parks, built a major visitor centre to interpret local history and the natural environment. *Landmark*, as it was called, was opened by the Duke of Edinburgh in the summer of 1970. This was local enterprise, employing local people, and was substantially aided by the HIDB. Its success (with its multi-screen audio-visual programmes and one of the best ranges of Scottish books on sale anywhere in the country) helped to improve local understanding and appreciation of the Board's policies. *Landmark* still thrives today, 20 years on and despite the new trunk road A9 having bypassed the village some years ago.

Putting the Highlands and Islands on the tourist map was one thing, but meeting the consequent demands of visitors was quite another. The Board (along with local authorities, voluntary bodies and private interests) had many problems to overcome in record time. It had tackled accommodation at an early stage and this continued. A holiday cottage scheme, initiated in 1972 to help the growing self-catering market, met early problems, mainly because many of the applicants did not have the necessary land ownership and/or planning permission. After a few cottages had been built, mainly by crofters, the scheme was quietly abandoned.

Tourist pressures also brought problems in getting about. The single track roads were a joy to the 'getting away from it all' travellers of the 1950s and early 1960s. But by 1970 (accelerated by the growing popularity of trailer caravans and by accident statistics) road widening and improvement became a priority. The delightful old winding route along Loch Maree, among others, was replaced by a wider, straighter road. Deplored by many as a frightful scar beside the loch, time has dealt kindly with this road and today it sits in the landscape of the lochside as a restrained piece of highway engineering.

Among other improvements were sections of the roads between Gairloch and Ullapool, Garve and Balmacara and along the far north coast between Thurso and Durness, to list but three. The slow ferries at Ballachulish and Kylesku were replaced by efficient bridges (the more recent, the curving high-level bridge at Kylesku in Sutherland, designed with grace and character). Major improvements to the road north from Inverness—more to provide fast access to the Cromarty Firth oil-related developments than to speed tourists on their way—came with the Cromarty and Kessock bridges. Together with improvements to the A9, journey times from Edinburgh to Wick and Thurso were dramatically reduced.

The fact that the Fourth Wave was still little more than lapping on the shores of the Western and Northern Isles by the early 1970s had much to do with the lack of car ferries. The first major car ferry in Scotland—the *Arran*, operating between Gourock and Dunoon—had begun in 1954, followed by a regular service to Brodick with the *Glen Sannox* three years later. Farther north, the *Columba* sailed out of Oban from 1964 and in the same year the *Hebrides* was commissioned on the run between Uig, Tarbert and Lochmaddy. These were drive-on, drive-off ferries, with vehicular lifts on board. The ultimate convenience of roll-on, roll-off did not arrive until 1970, when the *Caledonia* began sailing (literally) from A to B—Ardrossan to Brodick! Through the 1970s roll-on, roll-off increasingly became the norm on many of the Western Isles routes and in 1973 the service to the Outer Isles was significantly increased by the establishment of the Ulla-pool/Stornoway run.

In the north the *St Ola* began the roll-on, roll-off service between Scrabster and Stromness in 1975. Two years later the long-established passenger steamer service to Shetland was converted to ro-ro with the introduction of the *St Clair*. More recently, in 1987, roll-on, roll-off convenience to the Northern Isles has been increased by the *St Sunniva*, operating on the Aberdeen-Stromness-Lerwick run. While the various improvements to services to the Western and Northern Isles have undoubtedly increased the flow of car-borne visitors over the years, compared with the mainland the movement is nevertheless still light.

As the freedom of movement was improved and accommodation increased in quantity and quality (although the latter not entirely to everyone's satisfaction) the flood of visitors needed guidance about what to see, what to do, and where and when to see or do it. Very important too were bad-weather facilities—the Board has never succeeded in achieving control over rain or midges. What to see on any one visit to the Highlands and Islands was a problem of the first order. Should it be the gardens at Crarae or Inverewe? Or a visit to the Northern Isles to see Skara Brae or Jarlshof? Again, what about castles—perhaps Dunvegan— or battlefields, Culloden maybe? The list could be extremely long, always provided that visitors knew of the existence of the places.

Board help to the voluntary information centres developed fast and by 1970 some fourteen local tourist associations were in business, each with an elected council and a paid tourist officer in charge. The day of the professional in tourist promotion had arrived. At first the centres were mostly asked to help visitors find accommodation, to produce and distribute literature and to organise local entertainment. With the establishment of the Regions following the reorganisation of local goverment in 1975, Area Tourist Boards were set up throughout Scotland, with 17 in the HIDB area. By 1980 they were employing 150 full and part-time staff. By then the Board itself was firmly in the marketing saddle, in concert with the area boards and through its membership of the Scottish Tourism Consultative Council. Among its own widely distributed promotional publications, *Escape to the the Highlands* (1978) was a classic of high quality presentation and content and must have attracted many new visitors.

The area boards were pioneers in developing the Book-a-Bed-Ahead scheme, and introduced the Travel Pass Ticket (providing inclusive-priced journeys) and the Highland Holiday Card (making discounts available for accommodation, shopping, entrance fees and the like during the 'shoulder' months).

There was initial reluctance—partly due to typical Highland canniness—on the part of local trade to pitch in and support the Area Tourist Boards. By the time local enthusiasm had been generated, a new crisis was looming. The tourist flood of the Fourth Wave of the 1960s and early 1970s had landed up on the rocky shore of inflation, increasing unemployment, and the huge increase in petrol costs after the fourth Arab-Israeli war in 1973. Accommodation and transport costs rose fast and the Highlands and Islands gradually became a long and costly way off for the holidaymaker from the south. At the height of the recession the Board joined with the Scottish Tourist Board in major advertising campaigns to attract visitors to Scotland, with assurances that petrol was not as scarce as it was at that time in parts of England.

The crisis passed slowly and by the mid 1980s visitor traffic was flowing at a steady rate—though not at the flood level of the earlier decade. Cheap package holidays had attracted many potential visitors to the Mediterranean sun. There was another difference too. The Board had always sought to reassure its critics that it respected the need to balance development with conservation, particularly in relation to tourist provision. Those involved with protecting the environment were not entirely sure that it always got this balance right in its formative years. Now, however, greater environmental awareness in the 1980s began to be reflected in the Board's attitude towards development and in its support for a new range of sporting provisions for the enjoyment of visitors.

In 1970 David Hayes's *Landmark* had been a pioneer in a very new field. 'Interpretation' was now the name of the game. It had been promoted by the Countryside Commission for Scotland from its establishment and had found favour in the 1970s as a technique for helping people to enjoy and understand their experience of the wider countryside and of places of specific interest. Visitor Centres, like those of the National Trust for Scotland at Glen Coe, Culloden and Glenfinnan, were interpreting the natural, social and political history of their localities to thousands of appreciative tourists every year. In the Spey Valley the private estate of Rothiemurchus opened an interpretive centre, with guided walks organised by its ranger service to inform visitors in a friendly way of the main features of the local enviromnment and the management of the estate. Many other enterprises of a like kind were established: centres such as the Clan Donald Centre on Skye, the Sea Life Centre near Oban, the Hydro-electric Board's Ben Cruachan Centre on Loch Awe and the Highland Wildlife Park at Kincraig. A Monster Exhibition Centre at Drumnadrochit on Loch Ness may seem a slightly bizarre attraction, but Nessie's very elusiveness had made her an intriguing tourist 'draw'.

Activity holidays, rather than passive sightseeing trips, brought more people north with definite purposes in mind for their visits. The Board reacted to this demand. It expanded yacht cruising facilities in small communities, installing moorings on Gigha, Mull, Jura and Coll. 'Put and take' salmon fishing was launched jointly with the National Trust for Scotland and a number of hoteliers. The Board also supported the expansion of winter ski-ing in the Spey Valley and

25   Ben Nevis hill race: the Fort William smelter can be seen below the runners. [HIDB]

the development of a new ski centre at Aonach Mor, near Fort William. Less physically demanding are the interests of visitors, mostly from overseas, who come in search of 'roots'—genealogy is a thriving business and most of those who come seeking ancestors from the Highland diaspora return home satisfied with the results of their enquiries.

Today, 1990.

In 1965, before detailed figures were recorded, it is estimated that probably around a million domestic and overseas tourists visited the Highlands and Islands. By 1989 this figure had risen to well over three and a half million. However statistics alone cannot do justice to the changes that have taken place in tourism in the region over the past quarter of a century. What has happened on the ground tells the story much more effectively.

The range of attractions and activities available or provided for visitors today is far beyond that which could possibly have been envisaged by the HIDB, or anyone else, in the 1960s, when the Fourth Wave began to flood across the Highland mainland. A number of factors, as we have seen, have played an important part in the changes which have occurred. Some of these have been triggered by the Board, some initiated by others. The improvement in the roads, largely for economic and community reasons, have increased tourist opportunities dramatically. Most of these engineering works have been achieved with minimal damage to their surroundings, the new A9 from Perth northwards being a good example of careful choice of route and sensitive landscaping following construction.

New bridges and ferries have also improved mainland communication, and inter-island ferry services are much better than they were 25 years ago. The principal remaining bridge still in the offing is that to link Skye with the mainland. No doubt this will be in place well before the end of the century and will be welcomed by islanders and tourists alike, all too familiar with the long ferry delays at Kyle and Kyleakin during the summer. Sadly, though, 'over the sea to Skye' will lose its long-standing romantic association, for first-time travellers at least! (Though the Prince was, of course, speeding across from the west—from South Uist—not from the mainland.)

Despite threats of closure from time to time, the three far-flung railways to Thurso, Kyle and Mallaig have remained open, with the new 'super sprinter' trains in service and, in summer, steam trains to Mallaig. Long may good sense prevail. Not only do they relieve roads that are all too narrow for their present traffic, but they are also tourist attractions in their own right. Nowhere else in Britain can so much dramatic scenery be enjoyed through the window of a railway compartment. This is a tourist resource which could be exploited far more than it is and which, unlike some other visitor provisions, does not put environmental quality at risk.

The prosperity which has come with a variety of new industries since 1965, tourism one of them, has helped to reduce the extent of dereliction and rusty

26　　Culloden Moor and Visitor Centre, near Inverness. [HIDB]

corrugated iron long associated with many Highland communities. Crofters' cottages are increasingly being improved and painted up and new dwellings are appearing in once declining communities. Torridon is a good example of this.

In 1972 a study of the Torridon area undertaken by the then Ross and Cromarty County Council and the Countryside Commission for Scotland, assisted by the HIDB and other public and voluntary bodies, indicated a group of communities in serious decline. A follow-up study in 1987, 15 years on, showed 38 new houses built in the area, more pupils in the school, a lower community age structure and more permanent jobs available locally. The improvement had been generated by the well paid employment opportunities, shortlived though they were, at the Kishorn oil platfrom construction yard. This had put money into local pockets which was prudently used to build new homes, buy boats and set up small fish farming enterprises. The result is that today Torridon is a visually more attractive area and on that account draws more visitors.

The general worry about incomers buying up local cottages for renovation still exists and, while the new owners have undoubtedly added to the outward attraction of places, the effect on prices has often worked against the interests of local people. The 'white settler' syndrome is unfortunately all too real in some parts and not always in the best interests of community life. Time share development, with HIDB assistance, might help to reduce this problem, always provided it is not located in remote places or in large concentrations in small communities.

The HIDB, with the Area Tourist Boards and the local authorities, has exploited the scenic and wildlife qualities, the historic associations and the opportunities provided for active outdoor pursuits in magnificent surroundings. Visitors seldom arrive with expectations of bright lights or candy floss—except, possibly, at Aviemore. This marketing principle has helped to ensure that new tourist development has been of a character appropriate to the area and—with a few exceptions—of a standard worthy of its surroundings.

The use of interpretation as a positive tool for increasing the awareness of visitors has added a new dimension to their experience and has helped to make people a little more sensitive to the environment around them and the need to protect it. (There is still a long way to go, as the empty beer cans along some remote roads testify, but a start has been made.)

Today access to mountain and moorland for walking, climbing and cross-country ski-ing is still generally easy, although not backed by all the legal rights that many associate with moving around the open spaces of Scotland. Two long distance walking routes exist in the Highland area now—the West Highland Way and the Speyside Way—and a third, a Great Glen Way, is in prospect. Some local authorities have established and signposted short distance footpaths convenient to tourist areas and picnic sites. Laybys and viewpoints are now commonplace along tourist routes. In addition to walking and cycling tracks in some of its forests, the Forestry Commission has provided a motor trail in the Queen Elizabeth Forest Park in the Trossachs.

Downhill ski-ing has long been recognised as an important economic opportunity in the Highlands and the uplift facilities at Cairngorm and the White Corries in Glen Coe are of long standing. Recognising the overcrowding at Cairngorm, the Board is supporting an extension of ski-ing opportunities into the nearby Lurchers Gully, a controversial location being fiercely resisted by nature conservationists and climbers. It has also looked at smaller-scale developments farther up the Spey Valley and at Drumochter Pass. Aonach Mor, near Fort William, has been on the cards for many years as an area known to hold snow well. Through the enterprise of the Board and a number of private interests, Ski Lochaber has come into existence, with the first ever gondola system in Scotland. These facilities should be able to absorb 3000 of the 15,000 skiers who queue for uplift at the other Scottish ski slopes on a good winter weekend. This particular enterprise, firmly based as it is on the area's natural resources, will also add significantly to the attraction of Fort William as a summer resort.

The tartan image of the Highlands has two faces, one acceptable and the other not. The acceptable face includes the traditional highland games which take place in many communities and are appreciated by thousands of visitors every summer. It also includes real tartan, such as is still handwoven to order by Peter Macdonald at the Highland Tryst in Crieff, and the work of those many craftsmen who

27   Tom Shearer, Weaver, Orkney. [HIDB]

fashion wood, bone and clay with skill and sensitivity. What it does not include are the myriad of plastic, overdressed tartan-clad figures and other geegaws, usually manufactured far from Scotland, which fill the windows of all too many souvenir shops today. Among major enterprises of the highest quality, Caithness Glass and Highland Stoneware at Lochinver stand out.

While wide-ranging tourist facilities now exist on the Highland mainland, this is not yet so on some of the islands. Skye has long been a tourist destination, Mull (with Iona) too, and Islay has the special attraction of its seven famous distilleries. But others among the Inner Hebrides are less well known. Jura has but one road and little accommodation. Coll and Tiree have their afficionados and perhaps it is well that they should not be developed much further lest they lose their particular magic.

The Outer Hebrides are another world. It would be all to easy to lose their remote, strangely beautiful quality with development of the wrong kind. The Board has a difficult balance to maintain here in dealing with applications for tourist development assistance—a balance shared with Comhairle nan Eilean (the Western Isles Islands Council) as the planning authority.

The Northern Isles are more robust in character and already have considerable experience in providing for visitors. The short sea passage from Thurso to Stromness has increased the popularity of Orkney and this may increase still further if the John o' Groats—South Ronaldsay ferry becomes operational. Shetland, on the other hand, is still a long way off to many people and even from Lerwick it is a long island-hopping ride to Unst in the extreme north. Shetland, like the Outer Western Isles, has a very special quality of bare uncluttered landscape, in this case inhabited by a people who look to Norway rather than Scotland for their history and traditions. Like Orkney, it is a place rich in wildlife and archaeological interest. Here again a balance between the preservation of individuality and the creation of thriving tourism is paramount.

The same need for balance applies on the Highland mainland. Here the pressures

28   Day trip on a ferry boat in the Sound of Harris. Photograph by Sam Maynard/Eolas.

are heavier and the risks for the environment commensurately greater. The HIDB currently spends around a quarter of its budget on tourism and leisure and has therefore a significant power for good or ill in relation to the environmental future of its bailliewick. Its current three-fold strategy for tourism provides some reassurance. The first element concerns the major centres—Inverness, Aviemore, Fort William and Oban—which the Board sees as having an important role in attracting and keeping visitors in the region. These are the places considered to be able to sustain larger-scale facilities. The second element calls for smaller centres, such as Tobermory, Portree, Thurso and Lerwick, to be developed on a realistic scale, with remoter areas only moderately enhanced through assistance to small-scale projects and with encouragement in them for visitors to move out and explore more widely. The third aspect is the acknowledged need for local area development strategies, combining local and Board thinking.

The scale and nature of tourism have changed vastly since the HIDB came into being in 1965. A viable industry now exists and, although there are still some rough edges, local people are now happier about it—they have come to recognise the economic opportunities that catering for tourism and leisure interests offer and are prepared to grasp those opportunities which fit their community needs. Most important of all, the Highlands and Islands have survived the Fourth Wave in good environmental heart and without the loss of character which the pressures of tourism have wrought on so many parts of Britain, to say nothing of parts of the rest of the world.

Postscript—Tomorrow

Who knows what tomorrow may bring? We do know, however, that in the UK generally a trend is developing for ever greater concentrations of tourist accommodation and leisure facilities in specially designed and very expensive centres, usually located where the catchment area will provide a high enough revenue for profitability. Although this trend has less future in the Highlands and certainly none in the Islands, it is one which nevertheless needs to be watched carefully. Aviemore was a useful creature of its time, but hardly one to be repeated in the Scottish Highlands.

The key to a successful future for tourism in the Highlands and Islands must lie in maintaining their distinctive character, providing for leisure in a manner befitting that character, always to a high standard and always leaving the remote places strictly for enjoyment by those who value that quality.

By doing this, discerning visitors—of whom there are plenty today—are more likely to beat a path time and again north of the Highland Line, not only from elsewhere in the UK, but also from continental Europe, from across the Atlantic and from farther afield still. Providing for the type of visitor who is sympathetic to the Highland environment and way of life makes economic sense and is much less likely to conflict with the traditions and aspirations of local people than the mass tourism common to so many other holiday destinations.

Over the past 25 years the record of the HIDB and others concerned with tourist provision in the Highlands and Islands has, in the main, been one of commendable restraint. The Board's strategy, as presently declared, is designed to maintain that policy of restraint. If this strategy is applied, with adequate resources from central government, the future of tourism in the Highlands and Islands has good prospects well into the next century.

JOHN FOSTER Born and educated in Glasgow. Qualified as surveyor, architect and planner. Wartime service with Air Ministry. Early post-war experience in local government planning in Kirkcudbright and Lincolnshire. 1954–68 Director of Peak District National Park Planning Board. 1968–85 first Director of Countryside Commission for Scotland. Retired 1985. CBE 1985. Now part-time consultant in countryside conservation, recreation and interpretation. Interests: photography, hill walking, travel, reading, writing.

Chapter 9

The Natural Environment

J MORTON BOYD

> With inexpressible delight you wade out into the grassy sun-lake, feeling yourself contained in one of Nature's most sacred chambers, withdrawn from the sterner influences of the mountains, secure from all intrusion, secure from yourself, free in the universal beauty ... go where you may, you everywhere find the lawn divinely beautiful, as if Nature had fingered and adjusted every plant this very day.

So wrote John Muir in *The Mountains of California* of his joy at walking upon the glacier meadows of the Sierra Nevada, which he describes as 'smooth, level, silky lawns embedded in the upper forest'. His words bring alive comparable high moments in our own lives, coming face to face with the beauty of Muir's native land—the greenery of spring in the old oakwoods of Loch Lomond, the flowery machair of the Hebrides in June, the wine-red Moor of Rannoch in August, the gold of Glen Affric's birches in autumn, the white-quilted pinewoods of Rothiemurchus and Mar in winter. We all have our favourite places and seasons which we would wish added at their brilliant best to the broad tapestry of the year's round in Scotland. These scenes are among our most personal and sacred experiences, always to be tenderly remembered, unquenched by the beauty of foreign climes. The collective memory of Scotland by Scots throughout the world is charged with the beauty of Nature in our wild country, kept alive in song and poem.

John Muir (1838–1914) hardly knew the Highlands and Islands when he left Dunbar as a child with his family to settle in Wisconsin. Yet when he reached his *ultima thule* in the High Sierra of California he met on a colossal scale the re-run of a great deal of the history of the Scottish Highlands of about a century previous. The wholesale destruction of the glorious redwood and pine forests, the development of intensive sheep farming, the annual burning of hill pastures to rid them of dead foggage and give an early spring bite to sheep, and the harnessing of great rivers for water supplies and power. Muir opposed the piece-meal development of the Sierra and was one of the great conservationists of all time. Yosemite is testament to his endeavours, but he also left behind him the concept of *wilderness*—not a place of savagery to be tamed, nor of waste to be transformed for profit, nor a curse to be shunned and feared, but a sacred place of natural renewal and adjustment and a civilising influence upon all mankind.

16   Adult Sea Eagle, Isle of Rum. Photograph by John Love.

17   Rum from west side of Eigg. Photograph by John Foster.

18   Muckle Flugga. (HIDB)

19   Esha Ness Cliffs, north of Lighthouse. Photograph by John Foster.

In his old age Frank Fraser Darling (1903–1978) retired to the Laigh of Moray and pondered a lifetime's endeavour in the footsteps of John Muir. In Scotland he is remembered for one thing above all others—his description of the Highlands as a wet desert which, in its devastation, possessed an inexorable wild beauty deeply touching to the human spirit. He chimed with Gerard Manley Hopkins in the poet's impression of the Highlands:

> What would the world be, once bereft
> Of wet and of wildness? Let them be left,
> O let them be left, wildness and wet;
> Long live the weeds and the wilderness yet.

Fraser Darling and John Muir have different places in history, but they both had a heroic sense of beauty and subtlety in Nature, and a rare insight into natural processes. They trod the ground between philosophy and science, often between reality and mysticism. Their utterances were instinctive rather than researched and carried a ring of truth which was at once arresting and admonitory. Their names have become a shibboleth for environmental concern. Fraser Darling's name is still used more with nostalgia than in precise context, as a slipway when the debate on Highland landuse fails. His *West Highland Survey—An Essay in Human Ecology* (1955) is full of quotes of timeless worth to the people who prevail upon the resources of Nature.

Fired by the success of integrated policy-making, planning and action on a large scale by the Tennessee Valley Authority (TVA), and the contemporary work on the Clyde Valley Regional Plan by Robert Grieve, much influenced by the planner-biologist Patrick Geddes, Fraser Darling sought a much higher level of integration of effort in the Highlands and Islands than had ever existed. His 'ecological' approach was wholesome—the vision of a TVA-like authority embracing all the natural resources north of the Highland Line was at the heart of the *West Highland Survey* and was shared by the then Secretary of State for Scotland, Tom Johnston. The creation of the North of Scotland Hydro-Electric Board in 1943 added an indigenous power base to a gathering group of Highland industries in agriculture, forestry, fisheries, minerals, tourism, recreation and now fish farming. In hindsight, there was a golden opportunity to create an integrated department of Highland Affairs. Instead, the hydro-power was fed as a contribution to the Great Britain grid and the industries remained distributed in a group of different deparments of the Scottish Office and the Forestry Commission.

The creation of the Highlands and Islands Development Board in 1965 served to stimulate thought and action towards integrated social and industrial development. However, it fell short of providing *inter alia* the integrated planning of agriculture and forestry which could have greatly influenced, for the greater good, the nature and condition of the Highland environment for centuries to come. It is a measure of the historical significance of these days of opportunity that Fraser Darling and Robert Grieve, the two great visionaries in human ecology and planning, became leaders in their respective spheres of action and were both knighted.

Into this multiloculate system came the Nature Conservancy in the 1950s and the Countryside Commission for Scotland in the late 1960s, new agencies with duties which impinged upon the activities of industrialists, farmers, crofters, estates and local authorities. The 'environmental' movement which had its rooting in John Muir's America with such early adherents as James Audubon, Theodore Roosevelt and Ralph Emerson, was initiated in Britain by Patrick Geddes, Charles Rothschild and more recently continued by Arthur Tansley, Julian Huxley, Fraser Darling, Peter Scott, Max Nicholson and HRH The Duke of Edinburgh. The movement was poorly understood, reluctantly recognised and grudgingly accepted and there were difficulties ahead.

The creation by Royal Charter of the Nature Conservancy, whose sole purpose was the conservation of the flora, fauna and geological and physiological features of Great Britain, raised few eyebrows, even though it was accountable to the Privy Council and not to a departmental Minister. From the beginning there was a presumption that the voice of conservation in government should be independent of trade and industry, agriculture and fisheries, forestry, defence and later development and energy. A corollary of this was the freedom of the Conservancy to establish a science base, formulate standards of scientific expertise, and conduct research in support of both. Had the new body been of greater size and influence its inception would have attracted more notice, but its founding fathers did not know the extent to which it would grow and the influence which it would have following its transformation into the Nature Conservancy Council in 1973 and its greatly increased funding following the Wildlife and Countryside Act in 1981. It was only a matter of time until a 'David and Goliath' confrontation would develop and this was between the Conservancy and the Central Electricity Generating Board over the nuclear power station at Dungeness in 1958. The CEGB won the day, but the tiny Conservancy escaped unhurt and displayed a fearlessness of industrial giants which has endured ever since.

The confrontation which exists between conservation and development throughout the world is especially strong in Britain. In most countries on either side of what was the Iron Curtain, nature conservation has grown out of departments of government: lands, forestry, national parks, game, fisheries and wildlife and occasionally tourism and information. From its inception in these countries, conservation had a strong affinity to current regimes of land use and to some extent may have been compromised by them. In Britain, nature conservation had different beginnings in the animal and plant protection movement (including prevention of cruelty) and in academia, as a form of applied ecology. It was purposely vested in the Privy Council which gave it the necessary independent voice, though later it became an agency within the Department of Education and Science and ultimately within the Department of the Environment, all London-based.

The fifty years following Darwin's *Origin of Species* (1859) had seen the dawn of ecological science. The core concept of 'conservation' of nature evolved from simple 'preservation'. However it soon became obvious that to perpetuate a wild creature it was essential to perpetuate the habitat of which it was an integral part. The 'nature reserve' as the open-air laboratory became an ideal in experimental ecology in which nature was protected, but perhaps more important, where the processes of nature could be revealed unaffected by human disturbance. The National Nature Reserves at Beinn Eighe and Rum with their well-equipped field stations represented the attainment of the ideal. From the beginning, therefore, conservation in the Highlands and Islands with all their great potential in wildlife and geology assumed a grand scale. If the functions of the Nature Conservancy in Scotland had been vested, say, in the Forestry Commission or the Department of Agriculture and Fisheries for Scotland, it would be very different today in organisation and achievements.

When the Nature Conservancy bought Rum in 1957 and decided not to renew the grazing lease there was a hostile outcry from agricultural interests; yet Rum, largely because it possessed no sheep, was to become part of Unesco's Man and Biosphere Programme and is today a world-class nature reserve, while sheep farming is in serious decline. In the same year work began in the construction of the Guided Weapons Range in the Outer Hebrides, with much concern expressed about the future of St Kilda and the environment and Gaelic cultures of the Uists; yet today the National Trust for Scotland (NTS), Nature Conservancy Council (NCC), the Army and the crofters of Stilligarry, Drimsdale and Howmore in South Uist all have a world-class endeavour in conservation and development. St Kilda is the first natural area in the United Kingdom to be designated under the World Heritage Convention and the three crofting townships are part of a Reserve designated under the International (Ramsar) Convention on Wetlands. The issues raised by these early cases had portents for much greater ones to come, but the few cases which in the past ten years became a *cause celebre* should not obscure the achievement in conservation and development north of the Highland Line, which has resulted in the quiet and amicable designation of about 100 nature reserves ranging in size from Cairngorms (25,949 ha) to Corrieshalloch Gorge (5 ha). These reserves are mainly those of the NCC, Royal Society for the Protection of Birds (RSPB) and the Scottish Wildlife Trust (SWT).

Sites of Special Scientific Interest (SSSIs) was the name given in the National Parks and Access to the Countryside Act (1949) to sites which did not merit the status of a nature reserve, but which nevertheless deserved some conservation. A duty was laid upon the Nature Conservancy to notify SSSIs to the planning authority and the owner. This process took many years to have full effect, since, as it transpired, there were over a thousand such sites in Scotland, representing coasts, woodlands, grasslands, heaths, wetlands, peatlands and uplands. It was not until the Wildlife and Countryside Act (1981) that the SSSI system was placed on a firm administrative and financial footing, which required the re-survey and re-notification of all SSSIs, the assessment of potentially damaging operations (PDOs) and, where necessary, the making of management agreements between the NCC and the landowner. This is now a base-line for habitat and geological conservation, but it came after the advent of North Sea oil and gas.

The speed with which the oil and gas fields in the North and Norwegian Seas were explored and put into production took everyone by surprise. The late 1960s and early 1970s saw the Nature Conservancy as a component body of the Natural

Environment Research Council (NERC), underfunded and undermanned for the job of keeping pace with developments in Scotland. To start with, many areas lying in the line of development were proposed SSSIs, which had not yet been notified. That fact, coupled with a lack of consultative apparatus in the early stages of proposed development, left the Conservancy very exposed to public ridicule as a latecomer to the planning scene, often with what appeared as trivial objections. Regional Council chambers resounded with the heated 'ducks versus jobs' argument. The struggle to deal with each development as it arose in quick succession from others was immense. It was punctuated by Public Inquiries, of which a proposed oil port in the Cromarty Firth and the proposed platform construction yard on the inalienable NTS property at Drumbuie, Balmacara, were perhaps the most celebrated. In both cases the outcome favoured the objectors, but in the former, the Secretary of State for Scotland overturned the Reporter's recommendation. Both demonstrated the power with which the conservation case could be delivered and its high level of acceptance in the community.

Looking back, these were years of great excitement and endeavour in the Highlands and Islands, with some outstanding environmental initiatives. In Shetland, the concordat between the Islands Council, the industry and the conservation bodies resulted in the Shetland Oil Terminal Environmental Advisory Group (SOTEAG) which still operates and has the oversight of the planning and management of the great oil port. Similarly in Orkney the Flotta terminal was created with immense care for the environment of Scapa Flow; and the aerial monitoring of tankers at sea round the Northern Isles has contributed greatly to the security of the seabird assemblies for which the islands are famous.

In 1982 there came the Integrated Development Programme (IDP) for the Western Isles by which European Community funds gave an opportunity to revitalise agriculture in the Outer Hebrides. As initially arranged, no funds were made available for the care of the environment. Public opinion was polarised. On the conservation side there were those who, having seen the demise of wildlife through agricultural development on the mainland, feared the same in the Hebrides; on the other there were the crofters and their advisers, whose concern was for livelihood and prosperity. The corncrake, which has disappeared from most of the mainland in the face of modern agriculture, but still flourishes in the Uists and Tiree, became the symbol of the conservation *cause celebre*. After seven years, the worst fears of the conservation bodies have not been confirmed, but from the IDP many lessons were learnt on both sides which have been applied in the Agricultural Development Programme (ADP) which followed in the Inner Hebrides, Orkney and Shetland. For example, funds for the care of the environment were available in the ADP from the beginning.

The Scottish Highlands and Islands are rich in wildlife and geological phenomena, especially when compared with most parts of Europe of similar size. The remnants of the native pine forest represent the most western survivors of the great Eurasian pine forest which has been substantially destroyed by man. The efforts of the Forestry Commission, the NCC, RSPB, and private estates to conserve these woods, some of which are standing on ground which has been tree-

29   Village Glen, St Kilda in the summer of 1957. The RAF construction squadron is encamped between the ruins of the village and the sea. Photograph J Morton Boyd.

30   A dominant grey seal bull in his breeding territory on Shillay, Sound of Harris in September. Photograph J Donaldson. Copyright J Morton Boyd.

covered for thousands of years, have been a success story. The regeneration of the native pinewoods across the Highlands from the Loch Maree islands to Glentanar in Deeside bear testimony to this, with such names as Beinn Eighe, Affric, Stathfarrar, Abernethy, Rothiemurchus, Ballochbuie and Rannoch writ large. Nor have the native broadleaved woods been overlooked. The blast furnaces of the seventeenth and eighteenth centuries consumed the native oak/ashwoods/birch/alder, but the coppiced successors of these, together with their native communities of plants and animals are cared for within the series of SSSIs and reserves, of which Letterewe, Rassal, Ariundle, Carnoch, Taynish, Inchcailloch, Craigellachie, Morrone and Dinnet are a few among many.

In the 1980s attention became focused on peatlands. The landuse history of Britain tells of how the primeval blanket of peat has been systematically removed by advancing agriculture and, in more recent times, drained for afforestation. Like the native pine forest, only a few remnants of undisturbed deep peat remain, the most extensive lying north of the Great Glen. These are part of a short world series of such peatlands, as far apart as Newfoundland, Alaska, Tierra del Fuego, New Zealand and Kamchatka, generated and maintained in climates of at least 1000mm of annual rainfall within a range of annual mean temeratures for the warmest month of 9–15 degrees Celsius. The actions to safeguard the 'flows' of Caithness and Sutherland from afforestation, and Duich Moss in Islay from peat extraction for distilling of whisky left a deep and enduring impression in the public mind of the political scale and depth of ill feeling to which these cases were taken on both sides. Perhaps there are redeeming features in the lessons which such hard fought cases give to those who, in the next decade, decide the form which the 'green alliance' will take in Scotland.

The golden eagle soaring over the high summits has become an emblem of Highland life. Rightly so! It is at the top of the food chain in its spacious, mountainous world. It is a most serene creature of great beauty when seen on the wing or when perched on its eyrie. It is an object lesson in wildlife conservation, for, despite persecution with traps and poisons, damage from pesticides in the 1950s and 1960s, and the depredations of collectors on eggs and young, it continues to flourish in the Highlands and Islands.

Between 1975 and 1985, the NCC, RSPB and five other bodies have reintroduced the sea-eagle to the Hebrides. Eighty-two nestlings were transferred from Norway, reared on Rum and released. They are now grown, paired and settled to breed among the islands. So far, thirteen young Scottish-born eagles have fledged and the oldest of these will soon be mature and ready to breed. This is a great achievement which will go down for all time in the natural history of the Highlands and Islands. It will mark a time of prosperity for our array of raptorial birds—think of the return of the osprey to the Highlands in the past thirty years— which is possibly the finest in Europe. Last century such an array would have made the Highlands a 'verminous land'; today it is a glorious heritage, cared for and appreciated.

In 1960 the first report of the newly constituted Red Deer Commission began with these words: 'Whatever success may attend the efforts of this new permanent

31   Red deer 'royal' stag (twelve points on the antlers) in Glen Feshie. Note the fine
body condition and mane. Photograph David Gowans, Nature Conservancy Council.

Commission, its setting up, as a matter of history, marks the first comprehensive attempt to deal with a controversial problem which has vexed the Highlands for the best part of two centuries ...'. At that time Fraser Darling, following his survey of red deer in the Highlands, concluded that there were 155,000—including calves of the previous year. That number he considered much too high for the general good of Highland land and for the deer themselves. The deer are in direct competition with sheep, and combined they exert excessive grazing pressures on hill and coastal pastures, often accompanied by muirburn. This results in increasing frequency of unpalatable, fire-resistant herbage and a spread of bracken and purple moor-grass. It also prevents any chance of regeneration of the native forest and causes damage to commercial crops of trees, roots and cereals. And it increases winter mortality of deer.

Today the Red Deer Commission estimates about 300,000 deer, including those in woodland. Louis Stewart, the Commission's Chief Field Officer and one of Fraser Darling's surveyors of the 1950s, has been witness to this great increase over thirty years during which much deer land has been enclosed for forestry and agriculture. It is not surprising therefore that the Commission's reports for many years have been urging a reduction in the numbers, particularly of hinds.

Stags are the trophy animals, the sporting challenge and the unit by which the value of the deer forest is assessed; the hind has none of these attributes and is left to the stalker to cull in the dead of winter. Stags tend to range more widely than hinds and are therefore more susceptible to being shot in forestry plantation or farm. Both sexes provide good venison. The general result—stags are culled to the limit and beyond, and hinds are underculled.

There is a tradition in red deer management which is not borne out by research, that a large stock of hinds is required to maintain high numbers of shootable stags. This is sometimes offered as the reason for not culling hinds when, in reality, the hinds are geographically inaccessible (except at great cost) and straddle estate boundaries (which necessitates a co-ordinated effort between estates, possibly in snow). When hinds become too numerous they extend their grounds on to those of the stags and so displace the stags, which take to wandering and are sometimes lost to the the deer forest. To add to the problem of overpopulation, the market for wild deer is being blunted by the production of farmed deer and to some extent by the hand feeding of stags in winter.

The reasonable way to reduce the size of the population is to reduce the number of wild brood hinds. The alternative could be natural destruction of large numbers of deer by starvation in which, again, the hinds will survive much better than stags. Meantime the devastation of the deer forest will continue with the gradual build up of numbers to the next 'crash'. Fortunately, a gigantic 'crash' throughout the Highlands as a whole is unlikely, since different forests are in a different part of the population cycle. However, it could happen, with tens of thousands of deer dying between January and March. Perhaps then the government will bring in the necessary legislation to cure this malaise in Highland landuse.

Most of the world population of grey seals breed in the Scottish islands—about 80,000 of them producing 20,000 pups annually. An increase in numbers can be traced back to the middle of last century, when hunting ceased and, later, through protection following the Grey Seals Protection Act of 1914 and subsequent measures until the Conservation of Seals Act of 1970. Fishermen claimed that the grey seal reduced the catchable stocks of fish, acted as an intermediate host of the codworm parasite, and damaged fishing gear. However the situation was confused by fish stocks having been heavily exploited by man for over a century with increasing efficiency in fishings. Fishery biologists estimated that 65,000 tonnes of fish, valued at about £17.5 million, were 'lost to seals' annually in UK waters and about 85% was attributed to the grey seal and the remainder to the common seal.

In 1977–78 culls of adult grey seals were mounted in the Outer Hebrides and Orkney, in an attempt to placate the fishing industry and in numbers which would not put at risk the future of the grey seal. This was to be done according to a control plan provided by the Natural Environment Research Council (NERC) to reduce numbers to levels of the 1960s over six years. A Norwegian sealer was contracted to do the work, but the entire plan was frustrated and abandoned due to bad weather which prevented operations in the Hebrides, and because of a campaign of resistance in Orkney, including the Greenpeace vessel *Rainbow Warrior*. Though the fishermen and fish-farmers still complain of seal damage, especially at coastal salmon stations, the grey seal issue has never reared its head since the Orkney action of 1978. This is due partly to the diet of the seals as described by the fishery biologists being superceded by that described by biologists from NERC, and partly by the fact that salmon and sea trout fishermen and fish farmers can, under licence, shoot seals with a rifle in the vicinity of their nets, cages or river runs. The case for the mass slaughter of seals as a means of improving catchable stocks of fish on the continental shelf has never been proven and is unlikely to be raised again in the near future.

This is but part of the tapestry of the natural environment of the Highlands and Islands as it has been woven in the past 25 years. It contains a vivid, serene portraiture of flora, fauna and landforms, but it also contains people—with the joys of being together with nature, and the agonies of being in conflict with nature and with each other. There are the panoplies of wild creatures, each fitting the beauty of their own place—as with the otter in still, deep waters. There are men and women working in and for a better countryside; as with the crofter who leaves uncut the thistle which gives shelter to the lark's nest. The vignettes of wild and human life are too many to count. Seen together they are the fabric of heritage. They have an epic quality, as if part of a continuing saga!

Dr J Morton Boyd—educated Darvel School, Kilmarnock Academy and Glasgow University. War Service RAF (Flt. Lt.) Nature Conservancy Council Regional Officer 1957–68; Nuffield Travel Fellow in Africa 1965; Assistant Director NCC 1969–70; Director (Scotland) 1971-85.

Leader, British Jordan Expedition 1966. Conservation adviser in Mid-East, USSR and Oceania 1967–85. Since 1985 consultant to Forestry Commission, North of Scotland Hydro-Electric Board, National Trust for Scotland and others. Many publications, including *Fraser Darling's Islands* and *The Hebrides—a Natural History*.

Chapter 10

The North and Western Isles

10a   Oil and the Shetland Spirit

JOHN J GRAHAM

Today in Shetland past and present sit side by side, often in stark contrast—the modern house with *en suite* bathroom, central heating, etc., alongside the derelict crofthouse, with rusting black stove, no electricity, no running water; the crofter fishing for piltocks from his small open boat as the 200 foot purser sets off for the distant grounds; people working peats in the hill while against the sky burns the great Sullom Voe Terminal flare. All vivid testimony to the hectic pace of change which has swept Shetland life along in recent years. And all reminders that while much has changed much remains.

In many ways the past twenty-five years have been the most turbulent in Shetland's history. The discovery in 1971 of oil a mere 150 miles off our shores threw us virtually overnight into the front line of a multi-million pound operation to get the oil ashore. Had this happened ten years earlier, when the island economy was at a low ebb, the oil industry would have been welcomed with open arms. But community confidence and sense of local identity had grown during the 1960s and we could afford to regard the coming of oil with a healthy scepticism.

In 1962 a County Council delegation had returned from Faroe with the message that the prime reason for the Faroese success story was their 'right and power ... to manage their own affairs, and the application of special measures to special problems.' This prompted the Council to suggest, soon afterwards, to the Secretary of State for Scotland that Shetland be granted a degree of autonomy. But the political tide was running the other way at the time, with the Labour administration bent on a policy of more and more centralisation. Shetland's Police and Fire services were amalgamated with mainland authorities. An attempt to centralise all secondary education in Lerwick was vigorously opposed and the local alternative of seven junior high schools at strategic points reluctantly accepted by the Scottish Education Department.

This centralising process reached its climax in 1969 with the publication of the Wheatley Report recommending the amalgamation of Shetland's local authority in the Highland Region. Vehement local protest focused attention as never before

on the importance of retaining our existing local government, and the announcement in 1971 that Shetland, along with the other two island authorities, was to
receive most-purpose status, was seen locally as an important victory.

A further boost to local confidence was the fact that from the mid 1960s Shetland
had been coasting along on the back of an economic mini-boom, partly the result
of local initiative and planning, partly access to capital funding from the newly-
formed HIDB. Fishing and fish processing were flourishing, fourteen factories
having opened in the preceding decade, knitwear was selling well on the European
markets, and there was virtually full employment.

Shetland did not need oil and could afford to give the oil industry's advances a
cool appraisal. The County Council was keenly aware of the destructive forces
klondykes can unleash on vulnerable communities and they took steps to protect
Shetland and its economy. They acted swiftly to control the developments, and
in 1972 promoted a special parliamentary bill giving it more wide-ranging powers
than any other local authority in the UK—powers of compulsory purchase to
acquire the land to be used for oil developments and to establish itself as harbour
authority over Sullom Voe and its approaches; also powers of conservancy and
development inside a three mile limit of the entire coastal area, and the ability to
invest in oil-related ventures. Finally, the Council could use the income from its
Sullom Voe harbour operation to establish a Reserve Fund.

The bill which passed through parliament in 1974 as the Zetland County
Council Act was an extraordinary, even bizarre achievement. A County Council
with few radical pretensions had obtained a substantial degree of control over a
major industrial development; had demonstrated to both Labour and Conservative
Governments how to handle the oil industry; and had secured the right to take
shares in ventures associated with that industry. And the impetus had sprung not
from dogma but from a dogged desire to survive as a community.

Shortly after the passing of the Act and before construction of the Terminal
was allowed to start, the Council concluded a series of hard negotiations with the
oil industry, resulting in payments in compensation for the disturbance created in
the community because of oil developments. These payments, together with
the Reserve Fund, were to be used in the long-term interests of Shetland. The
Disturbance monies have been regularly placed in a charitable trust which, by
1989, stood at over £90 million.

The construction phase lasted from 1975 to 1982, with over 7000 workers
engaged at the peak period in 1980. The industry's initial forecast of 1200 was so
wildly inaccurate that one can only assume they were trying to play down the
scale of the 'disturbance' to the Council.

It was a classic boom situation. With high wages and plenty of overtime, the
fat pay-packet from Sullom Voe was a lure to many. At the peak, over 1000 of
the construction workers were local, representing about 10% of the local labour
force, with obvious distortion of the indigenous economy. Fish processing and
knitwear suffered in particular, while both private and public sector service industries struggled to retain workers. Fishermen displayed their traditional commitment to their occupation. I asked a veteran skipper if he felt that fishing-boats

might accept contracts as oil-rig guard boats and received the contemptuous response: 'Nae right fisherman would ever wirk for an oil company.'

While the oil industry undertook the task of building the terminal, Shetland Islands Council, as local authority, faced up to its responsibility to develop infrastructure to support the new developments—water, sewerage, roads, housing and schools.

During the 1970s the population grew by a remarkable 35%, from 17,327 to 23,386. To accommodate the new families 455 new houses were built between 1975 and 1981 at a rate unprecedented in Shetland. Like all crash programmes it was executed at the expense of quality and now Shetland Islands Council, a decade on, is having to undertake a massive repairs programme.

An increase of almost one-third in the number of schoolchildren meant newer and bigger schools. In a decade which saw drastic government cutbacks in school building, Shetland's role as host to North Sea oil enabled it to obtain government support for a remarkable programme of educational building. Between 1975 and 1987 thirteen new schools and major extensions were built, at a cost of over £20 million. Only three of those were in the parish of Delting, where Sullom Voe is situated, but the Council had successfully advanced the argument to government that it could not set about the creation of two standards of provision—one for the oil-related, another for the rest.

Planning in the wake of a boom can be a precarious operation. Sumburgh airport became a key staging-post in flying workers off to oil-rigs, with a fleet of helicopters operating the final leg from Sumburgh offshore. In the late 1970s, with about 1700 employed at the airport, local schools were overflowing. A new secondary school at Sandwick was planned, but by the time it was completed in 1983 the industry had decided to fly its workers direct from Aberdeen on long-range helicopters, avoiding Sumburgh. Airport staff fell to 250 and the school opened with a roll much below expectations. The children planned for had gone, but the Council's capital debt remained.

The influx in the 1970s consisted mainly of young families. During this period the number of people in their twenties increased by almost 60% and in their thirties by 85%—an injection of vitality into the Shetland population which has transformed community life. Young men and women in these age groups are not only the customers for leisure facilities, but the potential leaders and organisers of sporting and social activities. Immediate pressure was placed on Shetland's very modest leisure facilities—consisting almost entirely, in rural areas, of fairly spartan village halls. Lerwick was better provided, but even there social provision for young people was limited. In 1965 its one youth club had one half-size billiard table, one table tennis table, and a small sitting-room. It had about 100 members, mainly under 16, but an indication of its inadequacy was that 200 young Lerwegians between 15 and 20 had no connection with it—nor, in fact, with any organisation.

The Council's Leisure and Recreation Department met the challenge and launched a community development programme focused on village halls. The emphasis was placed on local initiative, with Council money used to prime the fund-raising pump. In this way 44 hall projects were undertaken, involving new-build, extension or renovation, at a total cost of over £4 million. Of that, a remarkable £449,000 was raised by voluntary effort, the balance being contributed by SIC, HIDB and government. From the new generation of village halls came a heightening of social life, with a growth of new clubs, sporting activities, and resurgence of voluntary effort.

Village halls could not cater fully for the leisure aspirations of an increasingly sophisticated population, and the Council planned to create a network of Leisure Centres incorporating games hall, swimming pool and outdoor pitch. Three have already been completed (winter 1989–90) and a fourth is in progress. The Centres have proved phenomenally successful, with more people using them than had ever been predicted. I was told in Unst that the Leisure Centre and the ro-ro ferry were the best things to come to the island in recent memory.

The sheer scale and pace of oil developments generated many doubts and fears about Shetland's future. Drastic social changes were predicted, radically altering the way of life. To expect a small island community to absorb the impact of this major intrusion without becoming changed in the process was to ask the impossible. We could only hope that the changes remained superficial, without affecting the character of the community—its general friendliness and caring outlook, where people counted for more than money, where the individual felt he mattered, and where family life was central.

It is difficult to sift out and quantify the various elements of social change, but it can be said that, despite all the gloomy predictions, the fabric of local society has borne the brunt of the onslaught surprisingly well. And that in itself is a tribute to the robustness of the social structures. The large numbers of incomers have been accepted without friction, whether in workplace, school playground or leisure situations. They have integrated remarkably smoothly and many now regard themselves as confirmed Shetlanders. The local population have had to adapt to their new neighbours and in doing so have widened the range of their social landscape. All in all, Shetland society has emerged more adaptable, more enterprising, more dynamic, and in many ways better equipped to face a testing future.

It is a truism that people fully appreciate something only when they think they are about to lose it. Certainly the threat of the oil invasion made Shetlanders more aware than ever of their local culture and its value. There was increased interest in Shetland dialect and folklore, together with a growth of local history groups and small local museums. The advent of the BBC local radio station—Radio Shetland—in 1977 was a fortuitous and entirely fortunate development. It helped to reinforce a Shetland sense of identity. The nightly programme presented important local news alongside local weather, local announcements. There was a fine sense of proportion about a thirty minute programme which included the latest state of negotiations between BP and SIC together with details of a missing kitten. In interviews it encouraged people to use their natural tongue and in so doing enhanced the status of the dialect.

Oil brought new people to Shetland, but it also brought new jobs and better wages. At the peak of the construction period the average income per head was higher than in the UK as a whole. This in turn brought a higher standard of living—reflected, for example, in the vastly improved standard of housing. In 1966 a mere 58% of local houses had hot water, bath and inside toilet, whereas in 1981 almost 92% had these amenities. A further index is that between 1971 and 1981 the number of private cars had almost doubled.

Higher incomes provide people with what they would previously have regarded as luxuries, especially in homes and private possessions. But they also provide the luxury of planning ahead, not possible when living near subsistence level. New houses have been built, money invested in business projects, holidays taken abroad on a scale never before encountered. The confidence which enabled Shetland to look oil's gift horse in the mouth in the early 1970s has been enhanced by the new prosperity which followed.

Modern schools and houses, better roads, more jobs, greater affluence are all pluses in any community. Affluence can liberate, but it can also fetter. While many used the extra resources to good purposes, there were those who abused them. Some blew their wages improvidently, some in excessive drinking. For many years there has been a pattern of hard and habitual drinking in Shetland, but it is only in comparatively recent times that it has surfaced as a serious social problem. It is estimated that 10% of all adult males have an alcohol-related problem. Family life is threatened, with children particularly vulnerable. The number of children in care has increased dramatically during the past twenty years, with 22 in public care in the autumn of 1989. Of these, half are from homes where there is alcohol abuse. The Council's Social Work Department has established an Alcohol Resource Centre, funded by the Charitable Trust, which provides counselling and support for people with alcohol-related problems. Tackling the situation in the long-term involves more than individual counselling. Social attitudes to drinking embedded deeply in local culture have to change and that involves a long, slow process of community education.

A great deal of the stability in Shetland society of the past stemmed from the family unit, with three generations living together not uncommon. Pressure on the traditional family has accelerated in Shetland in recent times: there has been a dramatic increase in broken families, divorces, single parent families. The Scottish statistic of one in three marriages ending in divorce is gloomy enough, but in Shetland it is in the region of one in every two—a sad commentary on the role of the family in the community. Although this is a trend which cannot but undermine social stability, it is too soon to detect any significant social changes. The number of child offenders has increased steadily during the period, but it would be wrong to ascribe that to any one factor.

From the outset the Council was keenly aware of the need to take positive steps to safeguard the community as much as possible. A key role here was performed by the Social Work Department. Its staff had to encounter not only the casualties of modern living heightened by the stresses of rapid industrial development, but also the elderly and the disabled who could not participate in the benefits of oil, yet who were penalised by its side effects—such as increased cost of living and decline in general services. The Council gave Social Work spending high priority and with generous grants from the Charitable Trust launched a number of initiatives. These included a generous heating subsidy for pensioners in sheltered housing, a £200 Christmas bonus to all pensioners, sturdy vehicles for the physically disabled who would otherwise be housebound, free bus services for the elderly in remote areas, and a variety of social assistance grants to those in need. Also, from 1979, almost five hundred homes have been modernised at a cost of about £3 million. This is all part of a policy to make life for the elderly as secure and comfortable as possible within their own communities. This policy has been extended into the concept of the Respite Care Units. One such care centre has already been completed in Yell, one of our North Isles, and another four are planned throughout rural Shetland. When completed these—in conjunction with Home Helps, Meals on Wheels and Home Improvements—will provide a network of care for the elderly.

A prime concern throughout the boom days of oil was that the traditional industries of fishing, crofting and knitwear, together with tourism, should survive and continue into the post-oil period as the backbone of our economy. The 1970s saw a steady drift of workers away from fish processing and knitwear to Sullom Voe. Tourism suffered as hotel accommodation was absorbed by oil personnel. By the early 1980s, with the construction period drawing to a close, the Council took positive steps to assist the limping local industries. Plans were prepared whereby grants, loans and equity imvestment were made available to finance development.

A 10-Year Agricultural Plan was launched, designed not only to promote agricultural production, but to rejuvenate rural communities. Low-interest loans, financed by the Charitable Trust, were made available and, by 1989, 237 had been granted, involving expenditure of £3.3 million on projects of land improvement, new buildings, acquisition of livestock and new machinery. These loans have activated further finance in the form of grants from the HIDB and DAFS, as well as the crofters' own money. All in all, the Plan has directed an investment of over £7m into local agriculture.

Knitwear and tourism catered for specialist markets and these had to be reached through the pervasive clamour of mass marketing. The only way was to enter the world market-place with modern advertising and presentation. Council support was given alongside HIDB finance to make this possible. Today the name 'Shetland' is well-known at world-wide trade fairs.

As Shetland looks to the future, there is no question but that the key component of our post-oil economy is fishing. Since the Second World War local fishermen, aided by grants and loans from HIDB and SIC, have displayed great enterprise and initiative in meeting the challenges of new technology in their industry. Today, with one-quarter of the total Scottish purse-seiners—all well over 100 feet—we have perhaps the finest fishing fleet of any community in the UK. Young crews, despite limited training facilities, have adapted astonishingly well to modern techniques. The floppy disc in the fisherman's back pocket is no uncommon sight these days. But for all their enterprise and industry they are

32   Lerwick Harbour. [HIDB]

20 St Magnus Cathedral, Orkney. Photograph A Hetherington.

21 Broch of Gurness, Orkney. Photograph A Hetherington.

22   Castlebay, Barra. Photograph by Sam Maynard/Eolas.

23   Hebridean Perfume, Isle of Barra.

caught up in the vicious circle that plagues all fishermen today. Modern boats mean increased costs, which involve bigger loans, which in turn demand bigger catches to enable them to be paid off. This inevitably leads to greater pressure on stocks—and therefore to the imposition of quotas.

To escape from this predicament Orkney and Shetland Islands Councils have prepared a regional Fisheries Management Scheme whereby all fisheries in the Orkney and Shetland area should be controlled by licence, with preference for local boats. This scheme would recognise the vital importance of fishing to the future of the Northern Isles, while at the same time allowing controlled entry to our grounds by boats of countries who have traditionally fished these waters. But the scheme failed to find favour with the British government and Shetland's main industry faces the future in shackles.

It is a rare event for a major new industry to surface in Shetland. Even now it is difficult to credit that local salmon farming, which accounts today for 26% of UK and 5% of world production, began in Scotland a mere eight years ago. For us it emerged naturally from our local situation—the sheltered voes, the clean environment, stable water temperatures, long hours of summer daylight—all providing ideal growing conditions. A further factor in the successful development of the industry was that the Council used its special powers under the ZCC Act to control allocation of licences within the 3-mile limit in the best interests of local people and the local economy, whereas in Scotland licences were issued by the Crown Estate Commissioners with no priority given to local people as against large outside commercial interests.

The positive manner in which local people responded to salmon farming is, in many respects, a reflection of today's Shetland. Oil sent a surge of energy through the community and the reverberations have shaken the foundations of local society, with a new industry, new people, new aspirations all making their different impacts. A new, bustling Shetland has emerged, superficially changed in many ways, but still with a firm hold on its heritage.

JOHN J GRAHAM was born in Shetland; served in the RAF as a pilot during World War II; took English at Edinburgh University post-war; taught English at Anderson Institute; Headmaster in Lerwick from 1966–82; 0n Shetland Islands Council since retiring in 1982. Publications: *The Shetland Dictionary*; *Shadowed Valley* (novel). Joint Editor of *The New Shetlander*.

10b   Orkney—A Better Life

LAURA GRIMOND

These twenty-five years have been eventful for Orkney, bringing increased prosperity without as yet any sacrifice of an enviable way of life. Material change has been visible, but the greatest changes have probably been social, making this quarter-century a time when Orkney people became conscious of their own advantages and learnt how to fight for them.

While not to be compared with the local and international dramas of the first quarter-century, when Orkney was a major theatre of the war at sea, this past period has witnessed the coming of oil and the development of transport, particularly of air travel, which has brought the whole world within affordable reach of a community, many of whose members, notwithstanding their seafaring traditions and international connections, had never left their own islands, even to visit Kirkwall. (There are 17 inhabited islands in the Orkney group, and there were more in the past.)

Several times during these years there has also been the challenge of major political decisions—on local government reform, on the Scottish Assembly and on entry into Europe, not to mention a proposal to mine uranium, which raised much local passion. Perhaps predictably in a farming community, Orkney returned an emphatic 'yes' to Europe, and surprisingly, given their constant support for the Liberal Party, they voted 'no' to the Assembly, an inconsistency which probably arose from a gut fear of being ruled from Clydeside. Had the package included proportional representation things might have been different.

Orkney was directly affected by the reorganisation of local government in 1974. After a hard-fought campaign against being yoked to a North of Scotland Water Board—which couldn't possibly share its water resources with people living on the other side of the Pentland Firth but could share its costs, and during which the late Lord Ross of Marnock was cast as one of the wicked Stewart Earls—the islands early resisted becoming part of Highland Region. This time the message was soon understood. Orkney, like Shetland and the Western Isles, was designated an 'All-purpose Authority', a decision never regretted, bringing greater efficiency and a better deal for the remoter islands.

Island problems had always centred round freight charges, and a glance at the complex pattern of the archipelago explains why: goods, supplies and farm produce have to go by sea. It had been easier in the days of oar and sail. Post-war nationalisation had done away with the inter-island air service pioneered by the late Captain Fresson, but this was restored in 1967 in the shape of the Loganair Islander, permitting a journey from the remotest island to Kirkwall in 14 minutes instead of a possible eight hours. The latest *St Ola* plying the Pentland Firth now carries as many as 400 passengers and 98 cars (or seven lorries and 50 cars), its service being augmented in summer by regular passenger crossings from John o' Groats to Burwick in S Ronaldsay, where the Firth is only some eight miles wide.

To return to 1975, when the OIC (Orkney Islands Council) took up its reins of office, one of its first tasks was to extend water schemes and improve council housing to all parts of the county—the old county council having left the ever self-sufficient rural population to fend for themselves. It was as well the council changed course, though some of the housing schemes, albeit of good standard, did nothing for the townscapes of Orkney mainland. Oil came hot on the heels of the new council, and housing was one of its most clamant needs. One benefit was that improvement grants allowed some of Orkney's delightful older houses to survive.

Today the familiar but-and-ben, often just four stone walls divided by two back-to back box beds in the centre, is quite a rarity; and where it survives it often turns out to conceal a modern interior. Compared to these, some of the modern homes look more like Dallas both inside and out, but they are warm, dry and convenient, which is more than many of their predecessors could claim.

The island's landscape as well as its way of life could have been threatened by the arrival in the early 1970s of North Sea oil, just as the new council was cutting its teeth. But good fortune decreed that the invasion was less massive than in the sister islands of Shetland; good management and geography allowed the pipeline linking Orkney with the Piper and Claymore fields to make its landfall on the island of Flotta, in the historic waters of Scapa Flow, so that the most visible evidence of the oil industry seen from shore is the gas flare, locally described as 'lightsome'. Orkney was lucky in having only one oil company to deal with rather than 16 like Shetland, the company being Dr Armand Hammer's Occidental, experienced both in the problems of bringing oil ashore and in getting on with local people. Formidable tasks faced the small Orkney authority in negotiating with a large international company over matters of a highly technical character; they were well served by their astute chief executive, Graeme Lapsley, who was able to profit from the experience of Shetland, and in some respects to improve on its measures.

Like Shetland, they promoted parliamentary legislation to deter land speculation by interests seeking to cash in on oil-related development. Orkney also established a Harbour Area stretching from the northern side of the Pentland Firth to Shapinsay, wherein shipping could be controlled and earnings charged on oil and gas coming in and going out. Moreover these earnings could be paid into a Harbour Reserve Fund free from the constraints which normally restrict local government expenditure to rate-supported projects only. Thus much of Orkney's earnings from oil can be used to help local enterprise as well as charity—a valuable source for development. Orkney benefited greatly from the oil revenue, even though only about 100 jobs have been directly created by oil. Together with the 'multiplier' effect on the island economy and the OIC's increased revenue, Orkney gained and became less closely dependant on agriculture.

Today agriculture still employs more people than any other industry, though fewer than formerly. Until the late 1960s, looking out from our home in Firth, an almost daily sight was of one or other of Orkney's numerous travelling shops making its stately progress over the skyline of Wideford Hill, packed with merchandise of every kind. Soon it would pause and be joined by customers from neighbouring homes and farms, many of them carrying baskets already laden. The goods they brought were of course eggs, which they sold to the merchant, often using eggs as currency. Not only farms but rural houses all over the county were then surrounded by flocks of poultry whose produce often paid the whole week's groceries.

Alas, today both eggs and travelling shops have dwindled away. The day when the entire egg ration of Glasgow sailed from Kirkwall in a single weekly shipment ended with the advent of factory farming—a big business against which the Orkney housewife could not compete. Like the kelp-burning of the eighteenth century and the herring fishing of the nineteenth, eggs have vanished and nothing quite like them has succeeded in lining the pockets of Orkney country folk.

In many ways the post-war period had been a golden age for farmers in the islands, who, with 'ploughing out' subsidies and grants for fertilisers, at a rate of many acres annually, were reclaiming hill land—the green acres rising like a flowing tide up the brown hillsides. Lately this has been halted, understandably in a European Community dogged by surpluses. In other ways, too, what a different scene meets the eye, particularly at harvest. Today a field of stooks is a rarity: the combine is king, oats have been ousted by barley unless for silage, the 'green revolution' having bred a strain called Golden Promise, short in stalk and able to ripen in our brief northern summer. Before that revolution we knew only the bere or Arctic barley, mainly grown for bannocks and home brewing. Everywhere now the green fields bear witness to the convenience of silage—which has almost banished the familiar agony of an October hay harvest or of hay lying black on the ground in November.

Cattle remain a highly profitable part of Orkney's farming, with stores still the biggest export, but barley has encouraged the finishing of cattle in the islands. The new slaughterhouse, built to European standards, has been able to increase the headage slaughtered from less than 2000 to over 5000 annually, bringing closer the aim of sending away more meat in carcass rather than expensively on the hoof. Large continental breeds have crept in at the expense of the traditional Aberdeen Angus, being preferred for leaner meat and live weight gain, but to my taste lacking the delicious flavour of the black cattle. However there are signs of a return to older traditions. An Aberdeen Angus bull was the 1989 supreme champion at the County Show, still Orkney's great event of the year.

The waning of the egg industry coincided with a low point for Orkney. Between the censuses of 1951 and 1961 the population loss reached 2500, a decline of 250 people annually, the greatest exodus coming from the North Isles. Although the lowest total of 17,000 was reached in 1971, the rate of loss had by then slackened and the trend has been upward since.

To attack the causes of this loss my husband, Jo Grimond, from the time of his first election in 1950, had put forward the need for a development agency in the north of Scotland. He had been inspired by the example of the Tennessee Valley Authority set up by President Roosevelt as part of the New Deal legislation. To tackle depopulation of small remote communities only an agency with a wide brief could be effective. Later, as leader of the Liberal Party, this personal prescription became the message of a political party, leading to the publication in 1964 of a pamphlet by Russell (later Sir Russell) Johnston, called 'Highland Development'. This made an impression in Highland constituencies, the only political publication in my experience to have achieved electoral results. In 1964,

33   Highland Park Distillery. [HIDB]

Caithness and Sutherland, Ross and Cromarty and Inverness all fell to Liberal candidates, while Orkney and Shetland was held with an increased majority.

The new Labour Government under Harold Wilson lost no time in setting up the Highlands and Islands Development Board under the chairmanship of Professor Robert Grieve. The new body undoubtedly raised spirits in the north. In Orkney its first fruits were the grants for developing the fishing industry. Since the decline of the herring fishing between the two wars, this had been confined in the main to the export of lobsters; crab or 'partans' were usually cast back into the sea. Few fishermen had the means to buy a modern boat (amazingly, pre-war, half of Orkney's fishing boats were without engines). Neither of the two grant-giving agencies, the Herring Industry Board and the White Fish Authority, were competent to grant-aid shell fishing. Into this vacuum stepped the HIDB with a grant-and-loan scheme, an opportunity eagerly grasped by Orkney men. According to Orkney Islands Council development officer Alan Coghill (himself a Shetlander) they took to fishing as ducks to water, making use not only of the grants but also of the training schemes wisely provided by the Board. The 1969 HIDB Annual Report notes that its first boat allocated under the new scheme went to Stronsay in Orkney and with two other boats was 'doing extremely well', one Orkney skipper being amongst the top earners in the Scottish inshore fleet.

The Board designed a special 'Pentland Firth' scheme for Orkney and Caithness based on boats up to 40 feet overall, primarily for lobster fishing but with emphasis now on partans and latterly on other smaller crabs, 'green' and 'velvet', previously discarded. There has also been a profitable diversion to clam fishing, partly by dredging and partly by diving: even razor-fish are now caught by diving. Partans, however, have the most important spin-off, for whereas lobsters are exported live, partans have to be processed immediately after landing, giving shore employment to many in the processing plants in Westray, Kirkwall and Stromness. Live shellfish of all kinds go weekly to Spain from Stromness by lorry.

Westray has developed a fleet of larger boats engaged mainly in the white fishing and Stromness has two purse seiners—one the largest fishing vessel in Scotland—but these do not land locally, working as they do from the Norwegian Sea to the English Channel.

The last decade has seen an explosion of salmon-farming and this, together with oyster and mussel rearing, is now quite big business.

The next objective of the Board was help for tourism, an industry then viewed with ambivalence both by the council and the public in Orkney, but now reckoned to be probably the second biggest industry of the islands. The Board had no hesitations and decided to contribute the salary of a full-time tourist officer, as well as acquiring the former County Buildings as the main Tourist Office in Kirkwall.

The short Orkney summer has always curtailed the season, inevitably restricting the number of hotel beds available when demand is high. Youth Hostels had already been established in the smaller islands as well as in Kirkwall and Stromness; now the Board came in with grants for hoteliers and for householders willing to provide bed and breakfast, a service which has won golden opinions among visitors. B & B, now a familiar sign throughout the county, has also been a top-up for many small incomes, the nearest approach to the role of the old poultry industry. It is to be hoped that the poll tax will not clobber another source of extra beds for holidaymakerss, cottages and caravans.

Because the attractions which bring visitors to Orkney are birds, flowers and wild life, as well as the growing interest in archaeology—and, above all, the unspoilt beauty of its varied landscape—there has been little temptation to let in developers. The Council has recognised the need to safeguard cliff and shore, the only exception being the rather over-lavish provision of public toilets in certain places of outstanding natural beauty. Not the least benefit conferred by Occidental has been a major contribution towards the salary of Orkney's Field Archaeologist, whose help has encouraged a popular activity ideally suited to stretching the season for visitors. To this must be added mention of Orkney's midsummer music festival, pioneered by Sir Peter Maxwell Davies, and its companion folk festival. Tourism has also boosted several existing industries such as knitwear and provided a market for crafts, as well as marine activities such as scuba diving in Scapa Flow.

Inevitably the growth of visitors introduced more people to the islands, bringing in their wake the first wave of settlers since the coming of the Scots Earls at the end of the Norse era. These have been mainly, but not exclusively, attracted to the depopulated north isles, in some cases by the low price of farms, others simply seeking peace and quiet. Given the alarming rate of emigration from the remoter isles, such inward migration must be welcomed. Without it Egilsay, with only one native-born inhabitant left, could hardly have survived; and Rousay, with only half its original people, would not have justified the new roll-on ferry. It was, however, inevitable that such close-knit communities, having for time out of mind preserved their own customs, language and unwritten laws, should have found the 'white settlers' hard to digest at first. It was not so much those whose hobby was drinking (a pastime not unknown in the islands) but the feckless, the tactless, the romantics who believed that you could live in a hard climate on five or six acres. Orcadians are good neighbours and will lend a hand with lambing ewes and mending fences, but broken dykes and straying animals can become tedious and a couple who arrived with a hundred dogs and cats were a testing experience for one community.

While farming novices could be trying, the proficient were not much more popular when they lacked a proper reticence about their own achievements. One of these had earned a headline in the local paper: 'Island stirks earn top prices' the day before I called on the neighbouring farm. 'Those stirks you read about in the paper, Laura', the proprietor exclaimed indignantly, 'Just a rickle o' banes!'

Now, more than a decade after the incomers started to arrive, the culture clash has lost its sharpness. There have been marriages between old and new residents, children have grown up in island schools and speak like local people. Many settlers have enriched the community with new industries and new skills, while others, particularly the elderly, are welcome for themselves.

I mentioned at the beginning of this chapter that the big changes of recent years have been social. Holidays abroad and at least across the Pentland Firth are now usual for everyone. Through school visits abroad, and still more through membership of Young Farmers' Clubs, youth has had its chance early in life to measure itself against its counterparts elsewhere and has gained in self-confidence by the experience. Everyone has witnessed the annual influx of around 100,000 visitors, who marvel at what they find and return to admire and enjoy. Contact with people from all over the world (many of Orkney's tourists come from overseas) has not diminished the old sense of community, given expression in a lively local paper and, since 1977, in the ever-popular Radio Orkney. Nor has television stifled sociability.

Fifteen years ago over one hundred organisations were affiliated to Kirkwall Community Centre. The other day I discovered a register in the County Library naming around five hundred active in Orkney— by no means an exhaustive list, but an indication of the richness of life in these islands, which combine so successfully unearthly natural beauty with stimulating human society.

LADY GRIMOND was a member of Orkney Islands Council from 1974–81 (Chairman of the Housing Committee 1974–76 and of Services Committee 1978–80). She was the first Chairman of Orkney Heritage Society and Chairman of the Management Committee of Hoy Trust from 1970–74. She has lived in Orkney since her husband, Lord Grimond, became MP for Orkney and Shetland in 1950. She is a former Honorary Sheriff of Kirkwall and is a member of the Ancient Monuments Board for Scotland.

10c   The Western Isles—A Cloud of Gloom Dispersed

Martin Macdonald

'The feeling of depression in Barra in 1959 was tangible; it was a very introverted society.'

The man who told me that has spent a lifetime in community development and knows his islands well. With minor local variations, his assessment was equally applicable at that time to any of the chain of islands that stretches 130 miles from the Butt of Lewis to Barra Head. A harsh climate and terrain, poor communications and a fractured, marginal economy were some of the factors underlying that depression. Lewis, the largest of the islands, was heavily dependent on a Harris Tweed industry prone to cyclical troughs; fishing retained a tenuous hold in small islands like Scalpay and Eriskay where no other activity was possible; the British merchant fleet and the South Georgia whaling stations fed families, but only at the expense of separating men from home and community for long periods. Few families drew a satisfactory livelihood from crofting, though for many others it provided an important economic boost and the social fabric of the islands was largely woven around the crofting townships.

And the less easily identified undercurrents of depression? Many observers— those for whom clearance and depopulation were unavoidable economic realities as well as those who take a more emotional view of such questions—would agree that history has left its mark. Some would also cite a dourly Calvinistic outlook as part of the depressive mixture, though that hardly explains why Catholic Barra should plumb the depths. And what of cultural despondency? A peripheral minority, whose language and heritage have been disparaged for years by much of the larger world outside, inevitably begins to accept such a valuation, with disastrous results for its self-image and its confidence. With such a combination of economic, social and cultural factors feeding off each other, perhaps we should not be too surprised that Hebridean depression should have been so pervasive.

Now, this quarter-century-and-more later? My development friend suggests that the smothering cloud of gloom has all but dispersed, or, if a few wisps do still linger in certain areas, they are at least that much lighter. And yet, despite 25

34   Callanish Standing Stones, Isle of Lewis. [HIDB]

years of active development by a number of agencies, the islands' economic base seems as precarious as it ever was. Tweed production has again hit a trough; the fishermen cast anxious eyes on dwindling stocks and wait, none too hopefully, for what succour they can glean from Brussels-made policies; the sons of the men who sailed the world's oceans do their stint on the North Sea platforms; across Stornoway Harbour the oil-related construction yard at Arnish lies idle, and the men who returned home from the mainland to work there are back on the dole. In January 1989, unemployment in the Western Isles ran at 22.2%, just over twice the Scottish rate, and not significantly lower than it was a quarter of a century ago, though frequent changes in unemployment areas and definitions make exact comparisons impossible. But at least the debilitating disease of despondency has been curbed if not cured, and, while no-one is foolishly optimistic about the future, the challenges it presents will probably be tackled with a degree of local determination that was hard to find 25 years ago.

The reasons for that circumstance are difficult to define with minute precision, but commonsense suggests that they stem largely from the creation of two agencies—the Highlands and Islands Development Board and Comhairle nan Eilean, the all-purpose islands local authority—and the initiatives they took. And almost certainly these reasons have as much to do with social initiatives which were taken as they have with direct economic stimulus. Most of the initiatives post-date the creation of Comhairle nan Eilean during the re-organisation of Scottish local government in 1975 and seem to derive from the interaction, whether in rivalry or co-operation, between the two organisations. It was a fertile period for exploring new directions; it saw the Board adapt the Irish experience with community co-operatives, the Co-chomuinn, to the Hebridean environment, while the Comhairle pioneered some interesting projects involving various concepts of community education. Some sceptics were scornful, since these activities did not promote mass employment, even on the diminutive island scale, but in the long run they may prove more important than many labour-intensive projects (again on the island scale) which have long since gone by the board. They had, and those that survive still have, the virtue of involving local people in communal activity, and that seems as good an antidote as any to apathy and depression.

When the Highland Board first visited the islands after its creation in 1965 it met with a deal of suspicion and, indeed, occasional open hostility. From the perspective of a crofter's home in Lewis, or a fisherman's in Eriskay, its intense preoccupation with the 'growth centres' and the semi-industrialised Eastern Highlands seemed to sit ill with its chairman's declaration that it 'will be judged by its ability to hold population in the true crofting areas'. What remains in my memory from a BBC Scotland film of the time is the wariness in the Scalpay fishermen's faces as that same chairman, Professor (now Sir) Robert Grieve, expounded the Board's new-found fishing policy.

As it happens they were wrong to be quite so chary. The Board's decision to build on the foundations already laid by the combined efforts of the White Fish Authority and the Highland Fund in small island communities like Scalpay, which had, by their own efforts, kept a tenuous hold on their fishing tradition in the lean post-war years, and where the only choice was between the sea and starvation, was a wise one. Eriskay, and the port of Stornoway, also benefited from an injection of cash to buy new and second-hand boats though, with hindsight, a greater concentration on training facilities might also have been invaluable.

In Barra one can still find a residual sense of grievance that it took so long for the Board to realise that islanders with such a long tradition of world-wide seafaring were quite capable of fishing their home waters, and would much prefer to do so. But even if opportunities were lost in Barra in the early days, by 1971 over 50 boats of various kinds had been added to the Western Isles fleet. Again with hindsight, the concentration on dual-purpose boats of around 50 feet, rather than on smaller boats with smaller crews working from home each day, and on larger deep-water boats capable of longer voyages, may have been mistaken. From that same BBC Scotland film a memory lingers of a magnificent shot of the Scalpay men night-fishing in Loch Seaforth and taking an equally magnificent catch of gleaming herring. As with other west coast sea lochs, there are no herring now to be found in Loch Seaforth. But, even with hindsight, the Board can hardly be blamed for that. It merely serves to show how little control the islanders, in their peripheral situation, have of their own resources.

The Board's fisheries initiative brought it some degree of credibility among the islanders, and by the time it published its fourth Annual Report it had decided that 'the general strategy for most of the islands must depend on exploiting natural resources and indigenous skills to the utmost'.

However, its most prominent projects seemed rather exotic in an island setting. Two small factories in Barra—one manufacturing thermostats and the other spectacle frames and both of them branch factories of mainland businesses— flourished briefly and then collapsed. A prolonged experiment in trying to set up a

35   Stornoway. [Aerofilms Ltd]

36   New road to Rhenigidale. Photograph by Sam Maynard/Eolas.

mini Dutch bulb industry in North Uist failed to flourish at all, despite the best
expertise that Holland could provide. Otherwise the Board began its continuing
concern with the precarious business of promoting local fish processing units that
offered some promise of permanence, and of channelling resources into provision
and promotion for the Western Isles' relatively low-key tourist industry.

It also became engaged with the islanders' centuries-long preoccupation with
transport and communications. The present Stornoway-Ullapool ferry crossing
was promoted by a Board investigation (the triangular Uig-Tarbert-Lochmaddy
route was established in 1964), but no government has yet seen fit to buy the
Board's early conversion to Road Equivalent Tariff, the concept that sea crossings
'should be seen as extensions of mainland roads and charged accordingly'. Thus,
while the extending network of fast, modern ro-ro ferries makes the islands' links
with the mainland ever speedier, it makes them no cheaper.

When it was established in 1975, Comhairle nan Eilean (otherwise the Western
Isles Islands' Council) also faced major communications problems. Perhaps the
least of them, though still no small matter, was to provide physical links between
the Lewis and Harris land mass, and the neighbouring Uists, and then on to Barra;

and en route link up to the smaller outliers like Scalpay, Eriskay and Vatersay. A rudimentary ferry system did exist, but the need to get councillors and officials quickly and frequently from the Southern Isles and the Benbecula office to the new council chamber in Stornoway demanded something more. Loganair's Islander aircraft, wave-hopping along the islands' spine from Barra to Benbecula and Stornoway, supplied the basic need, though the inter-island service has never been developed—as Orkney's has—to give a short-hop capability linking all the islands.

The other main communicative challenges were to weld the disjointed crocodile of islands into a coherent local government unit, and to persuade the mandarins in St Andrew's House that such a unit had inherited problems which demanded special financial consideration. The former task was blessed with initial success; the latter, which demanded only initial success, received none. The local challenge lay in the fact that the crocodile's lower quarters distrusted the shoulders and head—Lewis and the town of Stornoway, respectively. From Harris southwards the islands had previously been part of Inverness-shire, and been very much the poor, outlying relations of that sprawling county. Lewis, on the other hand, and the burgh of Stornoway, had enjoyed a degree of administrative independence within Ross-shire which had left it the richest member of the new family, though by no means a millionaire. Moreover, Lewis alone contained more than two-thirds of the new unit's population of 29,615, and the Southern Isles, suspicious as all minorities are of majorities, looked northwards with some misgivings. For the largely Catholic population of South Uist and Barra, these misgivings intensified whenever hardline Calvinist theology thundered from a Lewis pulpit. But when the South Uist Catholics'elected a Church of Scotland minister as one of their first councillors, it was obvious that a common Gaelic heritage was proof against such theological differences.

The Scottish Office, however, refused to be persuaded that the low level of infrastructural provision the new authority inherited, particularly in the former Inverness-shire isles, required special measures. No amount of talk of decrepit schools, inadequate roads, scattered population and a low rateable base was of avail. The new authority was being invited to sink or swim, and there was much press speculation about whether it would cope. But cope it did, with the Lewis councillors making a conscious effort to prove the suspicions of the other islanders groundless. The new council embarked on a series of adventurous and innovative community education projects, linked to the formal education system, with the broad aim of fostering local self-reliance. The approach followed the concept, outlined in the 1975 Dag Hammarskjold Report prepared for the United Nations General Assembly, that 'Development is a whole; it is an integral, value-loaded cultural process; it encompasses the natural environment, social relations, education, production, consumption and well-being.' A variety of vehicles carried this out. They included the Community Education Project, designed to use both Gaelic and English as teaching media in the schools and eventually destined to be absorbed within the formal educational system; and a number of more specific projects such as Cinema Sgire, a community communications initative, Fir Chlis, a Gaelic theatre group, and Acair Ltd, a Gaelic publishing company.

These various projects attracted funding from a variety of sources, including the Scottish Education Department and such internationally active organisations as the Van Leer Foundation and the Gulbenkian Trust. The Highland Board was involved with most of them in various capacities, ranging from the provision of grant aid to active partnership, as in the case of the publishing company. Meanwhile, the Board embarked on a programme of establishing Co-chomuinn in various island communities. These too were aimed at communal self-help by encouraging people to come together in co-operatives to provide a range of services and commercial ventures identified by themselves as necessary for their localities. If much of this activity seemed rather esoteric to people used to more mundane development initiatives, such as receiving grants for providing tourist facilities or for fishing boats, an imaginative use of the government's Jobs Creation Scheme by Comhairle nan Eilean provided a down-to-earth basis that was more readily understood. But this ferment of activity provided many interactive linkages, and if the older people were rather puzzled by it all, the youngsters enthusiastically embraced them.

The buzz was quickly around that something new and possibly very exciting was afoot in the Western Isles. The council's decision to declare itself officially bilingual had already attracted the attention of the Scottish press, for most of whom Gaelic was a moribund language in which romantic songs were sung once a year at the National Mod. The council's seemingly quixotic decision to recognise it as the workaday language of 80% of its constituents intrigued them. More importantly, it brought an immediate reaction from Skye, still largely Gaelic-speaking, which began to press Highland Region for similar recognition, particularly in the educational field. In fact, the council's espousal of Gaelic was a catalyst for much of the Gaelic promotional activity that has gone on in recent years, including the Highland Board's belated acceptance of the language and its culture as a development tool.

But the various attempts at communal and cultural regeneration in the islands had also begun to attract international attention. Very quickly a traffic built up between the islanders and world-wide network of cultures and economic groups with similar problems and aspirations. From being a marginal, peripheral fringe of Britain, the Western Isles had suddenly become the centre of interest among a widening circle of people interested in cultural and social development.

But in purely economic terms the islands remained distressingly peripheral. The fishing industry that was being built up began to come under pressure from EEC policy decisions and from a degree of over-fishing for which the island fishermen were in no wise responsible, though this was to some extent offset by the development of new markets for lobsters, crabs and shellfish, and also by the burgeoning of various types of fish-farming. The Highland Board's attempt to underpin the fishing industry by building major fish-processing factories collapsed in a flurry of recriminations about the island fishermen's reluctance to desert profitable, short-term markets to support a long-term future—or, on the other hand, about the Board's foolhardiness. The three alginate factories, which gave useful employment on both the factory floor and to those engaged in the traditional business of combing the shores for seaweed to service them, have been withdrawn in the face of international competition.

The only major industrial development was the establishment of an oil construction yard at Arnish, near Stornoway, in 1975. By 1980 employment there had peaked at nearly 2000, many of the jobs being held by local men who had returned from similar work in Easter Ross or who had taken the opportunity to return home from secure jobs in cities like Glasgow. Apart from the economic impact on the island, the return of an active and energetic sector of the community seemed to add to the spirit of confidence being fostered by the various new departures in communal development. Sadly, the Arnish construction yard is now moribund, and only the foolhardy would expect it to achieve its previous scale of activity.

From 1983 onward some £24 million was channelled into the islands under the EEC's Integrated Development Programme. Unfortunately, the project proved to be less 'integrated' than at first supposed, and much of this financial inject was spent on bolstering the agricultural infrastructure, with fish farming and fish processing and marketing being the other main recipients. Nor did all the cash come from European sources; the various schemes carried out under the programme depended on considerable matching subventions being available from bodies like the Highland Board and the Department of Agriculture and Fisheries at the Scottish Office. Clearly, such a massive financial contribution to an economy of the scale of the Western Isles must be immensely beneficial, though whether its long-term effects will be as successful as they might have been is a question raised by a number of critics. They feel that, because of its narrow concentration on certain sectors of activity, an opportunity of linking up with concepts of community development pioneered in the late 1970s may have been lost.

Much of the experimental fervour that characterised that period now seems to have been dissipated. Under the impact of financial stringency, imposed on its low starting base, Comhairle nan Eilean seems to have lost some of the sense of purpose and direction it showed in the early days. In recent years it has shown itself to be alarmingly accident-prone, and a degree of petty bickering and internal dissension seems to have taken the place of solid debate. A decision to close a number of local schools—allegedly in the name of educational progress, though most of the evidence suggests that financial considerations were uppermost—was badly mishandled and left the Southern Isles bearing the brunt of the closures. The ancient misgivings about Lewis's predominant weight in council matters were fanned into flame again. And a brief foray of evangelical Calvinism, which threated to intrude elements of Lewis Sabbatarianism into the easier tradition of the Catholic community, brought some rumblings of discontent, though it is difficult to believe that, at the grass roots, the old Gaelic tolerance will not continue to hold sway.

And what remains of the pioneering efforts to integrate social, communal and cultural development as an underpinning for the economic framework? Most of the Co-chomuinn are still there; Acair expands its output of Gaelic literature, concentrating particularly on the expanding children's market; the Bilingual Education Project has been subsumed under the council's formal education provision;

37   Barra Feis fiddle lessons, Barra. Photograph by Sam Maynard/Eolas.

and while the Fir Chlis theatre has disappeared, those who learned their craft with it are now active in a variety of Gaelic artistic fields. And perhaps therein lies the real value of that creative period. The young people who were involved in its experimental exertions are now approaching early middle age. If there is a confidence and determination in the Western Isles that was absent 25 years ago, they are the generation who were largely responsible for creating it, and who will hope to pass it on to a younger generation. It may prove a valuable bulwark against an extremely uncertain economic future.

MARTIN MACDONALD is an Inverness-based freelance journalist who contributes to both the press and the broadcast media. He became a journalist after graduating from Edinburgh University and has held a number of editorial posts with the BBC. Originally from Skye, he works in both Gaelic and English and is currently involved in developing Gaelic television programmes.

Chapter 11

Athbheothachadh na Gaidhlig [Gaelic's Recovery]

Domhnall Iain MacLeoid [donald john macleod]

Twenty-five years ago, there was considerable optimism regarding the future of Gaelic. Donald John MacLeod compares the situation now and concludes that, while the number of young Gaelic-speakers has declined, the current optimism may, paradoxically, be a better grounded one.

Bho chionn coig bliadhna fichead, bha mi a' tighinn gu crioch cursa ann an Gaidhlig ann an Oilthaigh Obar Dheadhainn. Bha gnothaichean a' coimhead gle dhochasach a thaobh na Gaidhlig aig an am sin. Bha Fionnlagh MacLeoid, a bha na oileanach comhla ruinn, trang a' sgriobhadh nan dealbhchluichean ainmeil aige; bha sgioba sunndach aig a' BhBC, fo stiuireadh Fred; bha dusgadh ann an foghlam sgoile Gaidhlig ann an siorrachd Inbhir Nis, bha sinn a' cluinntinn. Bha sinne, a bha air starsach saoghal a' chosnaidh, a' faireachdainn, le misneach—agus 's docha aineolas—na h-oige, gun robh an t-abachadh anns a' bhun agus nach b'fhada gus am bitheadh am fochann, agus as deidh sin am barr boidheach, a' tighinn gu ire.

A' sealltainn air ais a-nise, as deidh nan coig bliadhna fichead sin, de seorsa fogharadh a tha air a bhith againn? A bheil e comasach do dhuine reusanta a bhith cho misneachail mu staid na Gaidhlig an-diugh is a bha e an uair ud?

Gun teagamh, chan eil cus dochais no toil-inntinn ri fhaighinn as na cunntasan sluaigh, tha sin cinnteach. Mura bheil aireamh luchd-bruidhne na Gaidhlig air a bhith a' crionadh buileach cho luath is a bha, chan eil moran piseach air a bhith a' tighinn oirre nas mo, ma tha thu a' dol a reir nam figeirean lom. Tha seo gu h-araidh fior ma tha d'aire gu sonraichte air an oigridh.

Agus, ma tha an cothrom agad a dhol timcheall nam bailtean anns na h-eileanan, gu ire a bhith a' dol do na dachaighean—cothrom a bha agamsa nuair a bha mi ag obair aig CNAG—'s ann a tha an suidheachadh nas eudochasaiche buileach. Ann am bailtean far an robh a' Ghaidhlig laidir nuair a bha sinn a' dol timcheall nar n-oileanaich coig bliadhna fichead—agus fiu's coig deug bliadhna—air ais, tha e air tighinn uaireannan an-diugh gu bhith na annas gu bheil Gaidhlig aig leanabh.

Agus, tha moran air an dochas a chall. 'Fuirich gus an teid e don sgoil, cha bhit i fada aige': sin an duan a bha aig gu leor ann an Uibhist, Na Hearadh agus Leodhas nuair a chluinneadh iad an gille beag agam a' bruidhinn Gaidhlig fhads a bha sinn anns na h-Eileanan as t-samhradh seo chaidh.

Ach, an deidh sin is na dheidh, 's ann a chanainn gur ann a tha am barrachd adhbhair ann airson a bhith dochasach a-nise na bha an uair ud.

Tha iomadh riochd air an dochas sin. Iomadh iomhaigh.

Balach beag, can, no nighean bheag, ann an sgoil ann an Inbhir Nis no Glaschu, nach cluinn facal Gaidhlig san dachaigh, ach a tha nise siubhlach innte air sgath a bhith ann an sgoil Ghaidhlig.

Tha a' streap ri fichead de na bunsgoiltean beaga sin ann agus tha an tuilleadh a' tighinn am barr gach bliadhna. Tha sgoiltean-araich air a bhith a' nochdadh cuideachd, a' toirt taic dhaibh aig aon cheann, agus chan fhada gus am bi an doigh-teagaisg seo a' sgaoileadh gun ard-sgoil aig a' cheann eile.

Comharra eile, na tha de mhathraichean air feadh Albann a' saorachadh gus croileagain Ghaidhlig a ruith dhan cuid chloinne. Agus na parantan, ris am bheil mo ghnothach fhein cho tric, a tha a' faighinn misneachd as an obair sin gus a dhol am bad nan ughdarrasan ionadail airson gum faigh an cuid chloinne an rud a chaidh a dhiultadh dhaibh fein, foghlam sgoile anns a' Ghaidhlig.

Tha iomadh comharra eile ann cuideachd air feadhas na cuise. Tha barrachd leabhraichean Gaidhlig ann an-diugh na bha riamh, taing don Chomann Leabhraichean agus do fhoillsichearan mar Acair agus Ruaraidh MacThomais. Tha Brag air an teili agus Caithris na h-Oidhche air reidio, maille ri gu leor eile. Agus Run-Rig, caite 'n do dh'fhag sinn iadsan?

Tha an Riaghaltas taiceil. Agus na Roinnean. Tha barrachd airgead poblach— agus priobhaideach—a' dol chun na Gaidhlig an-diugh na bha riamh roimhe. Agus chan e a-mhain airgead ach suim agus deagh run cuideachd.

Tha poileasaidhean, saoghal-brath de phoileasaidhean 's docha gun can cuid, ann airson na Gaidhlig.

Tha craobhsgaoileadh agus foghlam Gaidhlig, agus na cothroman cosnaidh a tha nan cois, air leudachadh gu mor.

Agus tha barrachd a' faicinn a' cheangail eadar, air an aon laimh, neart canain agus uaill ann an cultar agus, air an laimh eile, leasachadh caithe-beatha. 'S e seo as bunait do Cholaisde Gniomhachais Sabhal Mor Ostaig agus a tha ga fagail cho soirbheachail. Os cionn nan uile, ghabh am Bord Leasachaidh trath ris a' cheangal seo, taing do dhiulnaich mar Bob Storey, agus tha sin air a bhith an da chuid gu math na Gaidhlig agus caithe-beatha na Gaidhealtachd.

Agus de mu na miltean de inbhich a tha ag ionnsachadh na Gaidhlig. Tha feill agus meas air a' Ghaidhlig an-diugh. Chaidh a radh rium le te Ghallda as aithne dhomh, bho chionn greise—le beagan farmad, shaoil mi—nach eil thu anns an fhasan an-diugh, mura bheil thu ag ionnsachadh na Gaidhlig agus a' cur do chuid chloinne do sgoil Ghaidhlig!

Nach ann air an t-saoghal a thainig an da latha bho bha Gaidheil air Ghalltachd a' cleith gun robh Gaidhlig aca.

Nise, bha cuid de na gluasadan sin, a tha mi a' cleachdadh mar chomharran air adhartas, a thoisich bho chionn greis mhath—cuid aca aig an am ud coig bliadhna fichead air ais mun do bhruidhinn mi aig toiseach gnothaich.

Ach tha aon rud ur ann an turas seo, a tha a' fagail an athbheothachaidh ur, saoilidh mi, nas fhallainne na am fear a bha ann an uair ud.

'S e sin gur ann *bhon t-sluagh* a tha moran den adhartas ag eirigh a-nise. Sluagh na Galltachd agus sluagh na Gaidhealtachd. 'S docha sinne a rinn uimhir de ghairdeachas ris an athbheothachadh a bha ann aig an am ud, o chionn coig bliadhna fichead air ais, nach do thuig sinn ceart rud a tha gu math cudromach. 'S e sin, gu feum siol talamh laidir mus tig piseach air fochann no barr.

DR RUGADH DOMHNALL IAIN MACLEOID anns Na Hearadh ann an 1943. Bha e na oileanach ann an Obar Dheadhainn agus Glaschu agus tha e air a bhith ag obair ann an oilthaigh, ann am foghlam coimhearsneachd, anns an sguil sgoil, aig Comunn na Gaidhlig agus, bho chionn ghoirid, na neach-comhairleachaidh Gaidhlig aig Roinn na Gaidhealtachd.

Chapter 12

Governors and the Governed

JOHN KERR

There used to be a convention in Highland politics as applied to local government that party labels were taboo. The rather attractive theory was that all candidates should stand as Independents, on their merits as individuals, committed to the common good of this or that burgh or county. Of course it did not require much discernment to make a political choice at the polls between, say, a laird with extensive land holdings and a local trade unionist with a sizeable programme of public spending on schools, housing and secondary roads at the top of his list of pledges and priorities. It was really the coming of the new surge of nationalism in the late 1960s and early 1970s and the prospect of local government reform that put paid to that amiable little understanding between the parties. Surprisingly, perhaps, it was the Conservative party—at least its leadership in Edinburgh—which first decided to stand up and be counted under true blue colours, although this concept is still far from generally accepted in Highlands and Islands councils.

Coyness among politicians towards spreading the party gospel did not, of course, obtain in the national arena, where all the traditional social and economic divisions were reflected in votes cast left, right or centre for aspiring members of parliament.

With the exception, perhaps, of the Outer Isles, where since the war Malcolm MacMillan had commanded unswerving support for Labour, the basic Highland and Island instinct was Liberal. There are still crofters in Skye who will say that they and their families have always been Liberal since the 1884 Crofters' Act, under Gladstone's administration, provided them with security of tenure. That Act may not necessarily have been an unqualified economic success, but it worked wonders for crofters' morale.

So perhaps, in a way, the Liberals were reclaiming something they might regard as home ground when they won the three mainland Highland seats of Inverness, Ross and Cromarty, and Caithness and Sutherland at the General Election of 1964. They already held Orkney and Shetland—a northern insular fastness for the party leader Jo Grimond since 1950—and this at the time enabled the victor in Caithness and Sutherland, George Mackie—now Lord Mackie of Benshie—to claim that the Liberal writ in Scotland ran from Ballachulish to Muckle Flugga. This was

165

38   'Highland Development' pamphlet being studied by Russell Johnston, Jo Grimond
and George Mackie, now Sir Russell Johnston, Lord Jo Grimond and Lord George Mackie
of Benshie.

originally one of Mr Mackie's jolly quips intended to catch a headline for his party
in an hour of triumph. But there was more to it than perhaps even he imagined.
That Liberal Highland victory, taking three Conservative seats, was in the overall
context of an election which left Harold Wilson with a majority of 4 to sustain
his Labour Government in the House of Commons.

Sir Russell Johnston, who won the Inverness seat in that turn-up for the Tory
book, suggests that it was no mere chance that Mr Wilson with his slender majority
was prepared to adopt the centrepiece of the Liberals' domestic policy for Scotland
during the election campaign—the creation of a Highland development authority.
Had there been no sign of unrest among the natives, as it were, the concept of
special measures to stimulate Highland development might have been left to
slumber in peace.

As it happened, Russell Johnston was a prime mover on this policy issue. Two
years before the 1964 election he proposed a resolution on the subject at the party's

annual conference in Aberdeen. This was expanded into one of the Liberals' familiar yellow pamphlets which had an appendix recording previous party proposals on the same theme. In 1928, under the heading 'An undeveloped colony' the Liberals were proposing the creation of a Highland Development Commission 'to prepare and carry into effect a comprehensive scheme for developing the full resources of the Highlands'. The detailed tasks specified in 1928 for the achievement of this objective bear an uncanny resemblance to the declared aims of the Highlands and Islands Development Board as constituted in 1965.

Sir Russell Johnston can now look back at that time more than 25 years ago with a smile and say, with perhaps justifiable satisfaction, 'We began to think something was going to happen when the Scottish Office at St Andrews House ordered 40 copies of that pamphlet.'

Fickle as political allegiance may be, and usually is, the beneficiaries of the setting up of the Highlands and Islands Development Board, the great voting public, did not remain entirely true to the Liberal cause in the years that followed. Sir Russell survived in Inverness, with a comfortable cushion of support apart from one moment of deflation in 1974, when his majority was drastically reduced during the second wave of the Scottish National Party's great push for power. In Ross and Cromarty in 1964 Alasdair Mackenzie, a lifelong advocate of land settlement to encourage crofters, won the seat; he held it in 1966 but was toppled by Hamish Gray (now Lord Gray of Contin) for the Conservatives in 1970. In Caithness and Sutherland George Mackie got shorter shrift, losing out in 1966 to Robert Maclennan, then Labour, but later a Liberal Democrat. The tradition of Liberalism held totally unshaken in the Northern Isles of Orkney and Shetland, where Jo Grimond, like ol' man river, just kept rolling along until he retired in 1983, to be honoured with a peerage and so have another platform for his powerful performance as orator and debater.

The specialised mould of party politics in the Western Isles took longer to crack. It was not until 1970, at the first time of asking, that Donald Stewart, one of the outstanding figures in modern nationalism, unseated Labour's long-established member, Malcolm MacMillan, and unfurled the SNP's banner to fly over the Hebrides for 16 years. While SNP fortunes fluctuated with some rapidity in other parts of the country, and sundry factions came and went within the inner councils of the party, Donald Stewart maintained an even keel and provided for his constituents probably the most effective parliamentary service they ever had.

The new authorities

One of the most dramatic changes in public life for which Donald Stewart, as MP, did much to smooth the way in the Western Isles, was the reform of local government following the 1969 report of the Wheatley Commission. In addition to running controversy over the size and extent of Strathclyde Region and such other issues as the division of Fife or its retention as 'The Kingdom'—a region in its own right—there was much debate about the status of the island communities.

For Orkney and Shetland the answer at the end of the day was relatively simple. Under the old system both these island groups had operated their own County Councils. The Outer Isles, however, had been administered partly by Ross and Cromarty County Council and partly by Inverness County Council.

While it seemed natural to give Orkney and Shetland separate all-purpose Island Council status, which conferred most of the powers exercised by the mainland Regions—though with some collaboration over police and fire services and aspects of education and social work—that formula was not immediately agreed for the Western Isles. The case, however, had been argued in a 'note of reservation' to the Wheatley Report, written by Russell Johnston and Betty Harvie Anderson, the Conservative MP for Renfrew East. This rationalisation of the Western Isles, already a Parliamentary constituency, into a local government unit had an obvious appeal for the islanders' Nationalist MP, and Donald Stewart brought all his campaigning and lobbying skills to bear in that cause. And so, when the new authorities were instituted in May 1975, the Outer Isles, from the Butt of Lewis in the north to Barra Head in the south, were united—after more than 70 years of division—under Comhaire Nan Eilean, or the Western Isles Islands Council.

This change was enormously significant for the Western Isles. In Orkney and Shetland, with the existing County Council framework to develop, virtually all that was required was to do away with the old town councils. After that it was more or less business as usual with a nice new letter-head, and possibly even a tidy increase or two in officials' salaries.

But west of the Minch the councillors of Lewis, Harris, Uist and Barra found themselves in a position to make decisions in a way that had never happened before. Under the old regime Lewis was relatively well off, with 15 members out of a total of 50 on Ross and Cromarty County Council, and carrying a certain amount of clout with Stornoway as the largest town in the county. As a result, Lewis did quite well in terms of local authority attention and expenditure, and benefited also from a generally progressive outlook which prevailed in council deliberations in Ross and Cromarty.

By way of contrast, Harris, the Uists and Barra had only ten members out of 60 on Inverness County Council; there was no large centre of population to wield influence, and these islands were, in effect, three separate communities. As a result, and dealing with a more reactionary county council in Inverness, the southerly parts of the Long Island suffered by comparison with Lewis. Barra, for instance, most island-watchers would agree, was ill-served in several respects by the former Inverness County Council. One official recalls that on Vatersay, Barra's small neighbour, school meals were cooked by the head teacher, who had to keep provisions in a worn out fridge—a cast-off from another school—which did not always work.

More general grievances about education under rule from Inverness still rankle in all three of the more southerly islands. It is very much a clash of class in which island crofters see themselves in conflict with mainland landlords. The island view would be that the laird-dominated county council operated on the principle that children of the professional classes were well able to go to the school of their choice; and for the rest Inverness Royal Academy or Portree on Skye were available: all of which did not constitute a particularly compassionate view of education for children in the remoter island areas. But with the coming of Comhairle nan Eilean there also came a marked improvement in services of all kinds for the more deprived parts of the islands.

It had been feared in some quarters that there might be some sort of north-south divide derived from weight of population and religious persuasion. For the most part this fear was unfounded and what happened in practice was that virtually all spare resources were ploughed into the three southerly island groups. Perhaps the major achievement was the opening in 1988 of a 6-year secondary school at Liniclete to give the children of Uist a chance to stay at home during the latter years of their education. There was also a new school, taking pupils up to 4th year, built at Castlebay in Barra.

There were improvements, too, in health and welfare care. It seems hard to believe that in those southerly islands of the far west—Harris, Uist and Barra—there was virtually no provision at all for social work prior to the reform of local government: this in spite of the fact that the islands must have registered degrees of deprivation much more acute than many an inner city area, well staffed with social workers and endowed with funds to relieve the effects of hardship. As with schools, the social services have been brought more into line with national standards since 1975, and at least part of the credit for that must go to the Islands Council.

On the Highland mainland the 1975 reorganisation brought into existence one Regional Council and eight District Councils. After fifteen years, many people are still confused as to the division of powers between Regional and District Councils. There is talk in some quarters of amalgamating them: Liberals and Nationalists in particular have always considered that a single tier of local government is enough, particularly if a Scottish Assembly is contemplated. Under present arrangements an Assembly would add a fifth tier of government—Westminster, Assembly, Region, District, Community Council—making Scotland the most over-governed territory in Europe. District Councils, closer to local communities than Inverness (centre of the Regional Council) deal with matters such as housing policy and allocation, leisure and recreation, cleansing and environmental health—leaving education, roads water and sewers, sociaL work, regional planning to the 52 Regional Councillors.

The call for devolution to a Scottish Assembly has always been strongest in the Central Belt of Scotland. The 1975 reorganisation had, in any case, already brought administrative devolution and considerable local autonomy to the Regions. The Highlands and Islands have been ambivalent about the idea of government from Edinburgh, where there was some anxiety that such an option would leave most of the political clout—and finance—in the hands of Lothian and Strathclyde Regions: the needs of the deprived industrial West of Scotland, would, some feared, overwhelm the available budget. During the referendum on devolution held in March 1979, Highland Region voted narrowly in favour (51% yes, 49% no; only 45% voted). The Western Isles, with its SNP tradition, was more positive, with 55.8% of those voting in favour, 49% against. But Orkney and Shetland (whose inhabitants, with their Norse heredity, do not share the 'Scottish identity') were overwhelmingly against. Almost 73% of those voting disapproved of devolution to Edinburgh. (45% of Orcadians abstained, as did 50% of Shetlanders.)

It is perhaps worth observing that the anxieties which caused the Highlanders' doubts in 1979 may no longer be valid: Glasgow and Clydeside, with imaginative local management and substantial injections of Government and EEC money, have become 'Miles Better' since the time of the Referendum.

The coming of 'Scotland's Oil'

The run-up to local government reform in the early 1970s coincided with another revolution, this time an industrial revolution, with profound effects on the life and politics of the Highlands and Islands: the discovery and the exploitation of massive oil reserves in the North Sea. Probably the first real intimation of this great wealth waiting to be extracted from below the sea-bed came at an industrial forum in Aviemore organised by the Scottish Council Development and Industry. That was in 1970, and when the respective chairmen of Shell and BP outlined to an audience of Scottish businessmen the great bonanza that was about to cascade about their ears it all seemed something of a fantasy. But in no time at all the reality was there for all to see. By October 1970 BP had discovered the huge Forties Field 110 miles north-east of Aberdeen. By the end of the following year the race was on to get that oil ashore.

It was at this point that the economics of oil emerged as one of the main issues dividing the political parties. Edward Heath's Conservative Government of that time seemed largely content to give the oil companies their head. Harold Wilson's Labour Party wanted as great an element as possible of public ownership. The Liberals argued for an arrangement that would bring a share of the Government oil revenues to Scotland, in particular to the areas of the Highlands and Islands directly involved in oil production. And, with much less inhibition, the SNP adopted the campaign cry in pursuit of independence—'It's Scotland's Oil'.

A lot of skirmishing was conducted on Highland and Island territory: the Drumbuie Inquiry, for example, into a planning application to build concrete oil production platforms on a site between Kyle of Lochalsh and Plockton in Wester Ross. This was the culmination of a controversy that raged for some time over the now familiar conflict between developers and conservationists. On the one hand heavy industry coming to a West Highland backwater would bring with it untold benefits in terms of jobs and a massive boost for the local economy. On the other, a delightfully scenic part of the country would be despoiled and there could be all sorts of social problems arising from a largely imported work force. And, inevitably, there was the national interest. It was on this last point that the government, through the Department of Industry, leaned heavily when short of any other argument. And it was on this point that they were badly exposed at the Inquiry as being far from in control of what the oil companies were up to in the early days of oil-related development.

One Whitehall mandarin, sent north to tidy up what must have seemed in London a needlessly time-consuming charade, produced the national interest in evidence for the aspiring developer. It was, he said, imperative in the national interest that planning permission be granted for a concrete platform yard at Drumbuie if the demand for production platforms was to be met by British construction firms in time to satisfy the needs of the off-shore industry. *Could he say how many platforms were required?*—the question came from counsel for the National Trust for Scotland, who, as fate would have it, owned the disputed site and opposed the planning proposals. *Well, that depended very much on the time scale,* said the man from Whitehall. There was a gypsy's warning in the learned counsel's follow-through. *Could, perhaps, the leading authority in such matters in the appropriate government department hazard an estimate as to the anticipated order book for such platforms over the next twelve months? ... Ah, it was quite pointless to pursue this line of inquiry, you see: the level of orders in fact changes from day to day. ... Perhaps then that resolves our difficulty: would you be so kind as to tell us what the level of orders was yesterday?* Collapse, as the cartoon captions in *Punch* used to say, of stout party. There was no answer.

That exchange from the Drumbuie inquiry took place in the last weeks of 1973. It illustrates one of two options—either the Department of Energy was attempting to mislead the public inquiry in the interests of its own oil policy, or it just did not know what was happening in the North Sea. Charity, and a clear recollection of early oil politics, would come down in favour of the less sinister conclusion.

The muddle that oil-related development generated in Shetland at about the same time as the Drumbuie controversy was just another example of lack of government grip on an issue not only of real national interest but of far-reaching international significance. There was a people's uprising in the local elections of 1973 in Shetland, as a result of which seven county councillors, including the convenor and vice-convenor, were defeated. The leader of this revolt was the Rev Clement Robb, the minister at Brae in the Sullom Voe area, where 5000 acres of land had been earmarked for development. He was a founder of the Shetland Democratic Group, which campaigned on the issue of secrecy within the council on oil plans. Mr Robb and his supporters were opposed to a private bill being promoted by the council, seeking extensive powers, including compulsory purchase, to control oil development. They also expressed concern at what they described as the close liaison established by the county clerk, Ian Clark, and leading councillors with four oil companies.

At the time there were all sorts of allegations of hanky-panky and malpractice flying around. Shetland became a focus of world news. The heavyweight press flew into Sumburgh from all directions—most of the visiting firemen, though, conceding defeat in the face of the complications of island relationships: the Deputy Editor of the *Guardian* found Shetland politics too Byzantine for analysis, and the *Wall Street Journal* took to bed with a headache.

Although the Shetland Democratic Group operated as a non-party organisation, its driving force, Mr Robb, was also chairman of the Shetland Conservative Association and briefly commanded the attention of Mr Heath's office in Downing

Street. From Mr Robb, through the Scottish Office to the Prime Minister and the Cabinet, the feeling and stated belief of the Conservatives was that all matters relating to oil development were nicely under control. The only concession that Mr Heath made to all the rumpus over planning issues in Scotland was the appointment of Lord Polwarth as a so-called 'trouble-shooter' and the creation of an advisory 'Oil Development Council' appointed by the Secretary of State for Scotland. It was one of those amateurish arrangements beloved of senior civil servants and government ministers, giving semblance of action and concern but, if the chips were down, not really capable of getting in the way of decisions from on high. And, as history was soon to relate, it all ended in tears.

The downfall of Mr Heath's government in 1974 is usually attributed to his misjudgment of public feeling for the miners' cause. In Scotland that was certainly a major factor, but the oil issue and the Englishness of the government's attitude to oil development also had a very direct bearing on the Scottish vote.

As compared with the Conservative line that all was well and the oil industry was in good hands, the Scottish National Party's battle cry 'It's Scotland's Oil' was bound to have wider appeal, if only to the baser instincts of self-interest. And indeed in that first election of 1974—hot on the heels of the Drumbuie inquiry, another inquiry into a proposed rig yard on Dunnet Sands in Caithness, and all the Shetland fuss—the SNP won seven seats, their 'Magnificent Seven', as they called them. In the second election of 1974 they increased this to eleven—their '1st XI'—most of which were to be lost again in 1979. Probably the most significant of these victories was that of Mrs Winnie Ewing over the Conservative Secretary of State for Scotland, Gordon Campbell, in Moray and Nairn. That seemed to be the ultimate slap in the face for the outgoing government in the Highlands. The other Highland seat won in February 1974 was Argyll, which had been held for 16 years by the former Scottish Secretary, Michael Noble; it fell to Iain MacCormick, son of John MacCormick, one of the founders of the original National Party of Scotland. There was also, of course, Donnie Stewart in the Outer Isles, but he had been MP there since 1970 and was a forerunner of the 1974 Nationalist push.

Winnie Ewing, an even earlier forerunner when she won the Hamilton by-election 1967, went on from her dramatic success in Moray and Nairn. In June 1979 she became the first elected member of the European Parliament for the Highlands and Islands and has twice successfully defended that seat. One of the great election campaigners in Scottish politics, Mrs Ewing quickly acquired in Europe the courtesy title of 'Madame Ecosse' and because of her style no-one is ever in any doubt as to who is the MEP for the Highlands and Islands.

Friendly eyes in Brussels

In the way these matters are arranged, the Highlands and Islands have probably done reasonably well out of the British entry into Europe. Shetland, for example, certainly saw benefits from the Common Fisheries Policy. The Outer Isles were chosen as the United Kingdom location for one of three 'Integrated Development Programmes' in the Common Market. As it turned out, compared with continental competition, the Scottish Islands experiment in this regard was much the most successful. And much of that relative success was due to the special relationship that the HIDB had developed over the years with the Department of Agriculture and Fisheries (Scotland) which was responsible for administering the programme, largely funded from Brussels.

Sceptics, or perhaps just realists, have their reservations about the financial merits of British membership of the EEC. Whether in this grey area of 'additionality' much in the way of new European money is made available through the European Regional Development Fund, or whether it is used simply as a substitute for home-based Exchequer expenditure, is hard to discern. But it is probably true to say that the Highlands and Islands have attracted more capital in grants and loans through the ERDF and the European Investment Bank than would have been forthcoming otherwise.

In the early days of oil, for example, the Investment Bank provided finance of £4m to help launch the Lewis Offshore fabrication yard in the Western Isles, ill-fated though that was; and £16m towards the development of the Sullom Voe oil terminal on Shetland, and another £10m towards expansion of Shetland's Sumburgh airport, for a time the main helicopter operations base for the oilfields of the North Sea.

In 1988 the ERDF committed £73m to what is known as a 'National Programme of Community Interest' for the Highlands and Islands. Thisprogramme, planned to run for three years, is based on aims very similar to those of the Highlands and Islands Development Board—to increase output and employment, to maintain existing population, to help provide basic services, and to develop the potential of the high quality and diverse environment.

Before that 'National Programme' commitment, the Regional Fund had made significant contributions towards individual projects in the Highlands and Islands: more than £3m towards construction of the Kessock Bridge, which links Inverness with the Black Isle and the North; in 1979 alone £5m for road improvements to non-trunk roads from Skye to Caithness. In 1982 grants amounting to more than £40m were shared among a series of water schemes, sewage systems and the construction of the Kylesku Bridge—that last project relieving one of the classic gaps in Highland travel.

Some of the less obvious enterprises to benefit from the ERDF include the new and expanded Fair Isle Bird Observatory, the Balfour China company in Newtonmore, and the remote community of Glen Etive in Argyll—where, as a roadside sign confirms, a Hydro-Electric Board electrification scheme was grant-aided by the Fund. The advantages to the Highlands and Islands of all this activity, improving the infrastructure of the region, are obvious even to the casual visitor and much more so to those who live and work in the region.

Within the timespan of the HIDB, for example, communications into and within the Highlands have improved enormously. For better or worse, the journey by road between, say, Inverness and Edinburgh has been cut by half since the completion of the Forth Road Bridge and the upgrading of the A9. No less important, the road conditions north of Inverness, and to the west, have been greatly improved. Naturally, no native Highlander or Islander would ever be prepared to settle for what has been done, or for the budgets for future action, but the difference for those who can stretch their memories back 25 years or more is no less than amazing.

No houses for the young?

The same cannot be said for one of the most sensitive areas of domestic politics, where elected representative comes face to face with usually disgruntled con-stituent—housing. Apart from those areas on the Moray Firth and Cromarty Firth affected by the oil-related industry boom in the 1970s, and the obvious urban and tourist centres such as Inverness, Aviemore and Oban, most of the Highlands and Islands have gone through a rather stagnant period in public sector house-building. With reduced budgets and constant pressure for economy in local authority spending, council housing in many areas has remained virtually unchanged. Aggravating this is the fact that an unusually high proportion of private housing (almost 8%) consists of holiday or second homes; and this in turn makes it difficult, particularly for young couples, to find the kind of house they would like. There is still bitterness, too, in some areas, at the prices relatively humble properties can command because of the demand for second homes. This is seen as another factor militating against young local people who want to live and work where they have been brought up.

At the same time this is a rather double-edged argument. With the de-regulation of crofts and the availability of building plots on croft land, many a crofter has proved to be a canny negotiator in selling to the highest bidder. It would seem that there is no simple answer to offset the momentum of market forces in this process. In attractive parts of the Highlands and Islands there is likely to be an ever-increasing demand for housing from incomers, more of whom apparently want to come and stay rather than just have a holiday home. Recent building projects at Boat of Garten on Speyside, to the south and east of Inverness, and at Ullapool in the west, to take only random examples, confirm that even if there is an imbalance between need and provision of accommodation, inevitably affecting the less well-off, there is under way a positive expansion in Highland housing.

Schools and hospitals

As to education and health, the Highlands and Islands are traditionally well-served by the professionals involved. Any shortcomings are due primarily to the geography of the area, and, of course, the effect that has on costs.

There are, for instance, more than 300 primary schools and 60 secondary schools in the area, catering for about 50,000 pupils. But the differences in location and population of communities means that a primary school might have a roll of 500 or might have only three or four pupils in one room. New schools have opened, but the closure of some rural schools has been inevitable as the number of pupils has fallen away. Following the work of the Munn and Dunning inquiries of the late 1970s, reforms have taken place in secondary education during the 1980s: a restructuring of the curriculum for secondary schools and a restructuring also of the examination system. These have been accompanied by changes in provision of courses for the 16 to 19 year olds.

Further education is covered by colleges in Inverness, Thurso and Stornoway; and appropriately, though only after much controversy, there is the Gaelic College—Sabhal Mor Ostaig—in Skye, which offers a two-year Higher National Diploma course in business studies and Gaelic, designed for people who wish to live and work in a rural Highland or Hebridean community.

The Highland Health Board faces the same natural hazards as the education committee, though these are compounded when dealing not with the young and able, but with the elderly, ill and infirm. Although the Board administers more than 20 hospitals throughout the region, the main centre for surgery and specialist facilities is the recently rebuilt Raigmore Hospital in Inverness.

Central casualty services are also provided at Broadford on Skye, Dingwall, Wick, Golspie and Fort William. But patients suffering from serious heart conditions, orthopaedic problems or cancer generally have to go to Raigmore for treatment, with all the inconvenience that involves for themselves, their families and the hospital transport services. Out of necessity and adversity, of course, are born ingenuity and invention; and one consequence of a widely dispersed Health Board area is that doctors in general practice tend to develop extra skills and insights which might not be called on in a city. They are usually as good at interpreting the rules and red tape of the NHS in their patients' best interests as they are at prescribing a pill or stitching up a hand caught in a straw-baler. Which certainly contributes to the overall health of the community.

Westminster Representation

At the 25th anniversary of the Highland and Islands Development Board, the area might be reasonably satisfied with the performance of its political practitioners as represented in Parliament: Jim Wallace, Orkney and Shetland; Robert Maclennan, Caithness and Sutherland; Charles Kennedy, Ross, Cromarty and Skye; Sir Russell Johnston, Inverness, Nairn and Lochaber; and Mrs Ray Michie, Argyll and Bute— all Liberal Democrats; Calum MacDonald, Western Isles, Labour; and Mrs Margaret Ewing, Moray, SNP. Westminster, like the Palais de l'Europe, is never left unaware for long of the concerns of these constituencies.

Looking back over this quarter of a century much, if not most, of what the politicians of the Highlands and Islands were demanding has been achieved. We have had a Highlands and Islands Development Board for 25 years, though now it is to be called something else; bridges have been built, roads laid, ferries improved, jobs created, though also lost, and a most recent trend of more people coming to live in the area. It is probably time for a new political agenda with another generation, which could easily be as exciting as the last.

JOHN KERR Fleet Air Arm 1943–46. *Alloa Journal*, reporter 1946–50. National Trust for Scotland, Deputy Secretary, 1950–60; freelance with *Glasgow Herald* 1960–69; Scottish correspondent, *The Guardian*, 1969–78; News and Current Affairs, BBC Scotland, 1978–87

Chapter 13

Sport, Culture and Communication

13a   Shinty, Ski-ing and Other Sports

Alex Main

Among dedicated followers of shinty there are zealots who would have us believe there was a day when the national game was played by every hot-blooded male in the land. Legend has it that camanachd—the sport of the curved stick—dates back at least 1500 years as a popular pastime of the heroes in Celtic history. Some would go further and suggest that the archaeologists actually got it wrong in their interpretation of stone-age drawings, thus creating a misleading impression for present-day cartoonists that early man was bent on bashing the female sex with a wooden club.

What the cave-wall chroniclers were really trying to depict, it is said, were irate shinty players brandishing their camans in pursuit of the cavewife who had run off with the ball, threatening to keep it until she either had help with clearing away the dinner bones or until something was done about the overgrown gorse at the cavern door.

The more recent explosion in all forms of recreation leaves open the question of which is the largest participant sport practised north of the Antonine Wall. But who would dispute that sport and leisure have emerged in the later twentieth century as important contributors to the quality of Highland life?

On a given winter's day, for instance, upwards of 10,000 can be observed ski-ing the slopes from Cairngorm to Glencoe, Drumochter to Aonach Mor. From the valleys below it might appear at times as if the pistes had been invaded by great armies of ants, where not all that many years ago they lay covered in virgin snow. The natural combination of mountain and weather has been used to develop a sporting industry which is now reckoned to be worth in excess of £13 million a year to the Spey Valley alone, where it supports 700 full-time and 2000 part-time jobs. The conservation and environmental argument can be debated elsewhere, but the massive investment sparked off by the popularity of ski-ing has also helped in the development of an all-year-round programme of virtually every sporting and leisure pursuit imaginable.

Developments of this kind have served to focus an international tourist spotlight

177

39   A game of Shinty, Skye v Beauly. Photograph by Sam Maynard/Eolas.

on the entire Highland area, enabling it to project itself, as never before, not just as a wilderness of unrivalled scenic beauty, but also as a vast winter and summer playground.

In any assessment of the Highland sport of the past 25 years, it is worth looking back just a little further to consider how a multi-million pound industry was pioneered by a handful of enthusiastic locals and a group of Second World War veterans. The latter were in search of the thrills and excitement they first experienced when being trained on skis in the Canadian Rockies in preparation for combat in the northern wastes of Europe.

Pre-war ski-ing in Scotland had been the sport of a fortunate few, usually those who lived close to the slopes or who could afford the time and money to travel to them. The Scottish Ski Club was, of course, active in the south, but far from embarrassed by strength of membership. Highland Ski Club was formed a few years after the war ended. Its founder president, Ron MacPhee, who had his first taste of ski-ing during RAF aircrew training in Canada, recalls the start: 'There were other lads who had been serving with the Lovat Scouts for whom ski instruction had actually been part of their combat drill. When we returned home after the war, still excited by what we had experienced on the mountains of Canada, it seemed only natural to try it out back home. After all, there were plenty of mountains and snow here too.'

The club's inaugural meeting only attracted an attendance of six, but as the word spread so too did the membership, with the club adopting as its motto *Is Leam sa na Beanntan*—the Mountains are Mine. At weekends a hired bus took the early enthusiasts from Inverness, stopping at pick-up points along the way to Aviemore, where all then piled aboard an open Model T Ford truck—the only vehicle of size capable of negotiating the narrow, bumpy track leading to Glenmore. From there it was a three-mile upward hike through the forest and over Windy Ridge to Coire Cas, now the site of the huge ski car park.

Ron MacPhee remembers this. 'At first we only had a few pairs of skis between us. They were fold-up German mountain skis which we acquired by mail order from the Army and Navy Stores in London. Eventually we had our first mechanised tow—a rope supported on steel poles which stretched several hundred yards up the hill and was driven round a cylinder by an ageing agricultural tractor.'

In time, with the development of proper road access and the opening of ski-schools and equipment hire shops, Highland Ski Club became superfluous to such a commercialised scene. But if the ski boom tended to overshadow all else by its spectacular level of capital investment and crowd-drawing power, another sporting revolution was taking place throughout the Highlands and Islands.

In many sparsely populated communities in the mid 1950s or later, swimming pools, golf courses, bowling greens, running tracks and their like could be enjoyed only by rare visits to distant towns. Such limited facilities for sport as there were locally often disappeared through school closures and the decline of village halls. If the population drift was to be halted, it was obvious that the people would require not only jobs but a quality of leisure and recreation. Island, regional and district local authorities tackled the task with vigour, despite limited budgets and often with the welcome cash help available from the HIDB and other government-funded agencies. Each local authority now has its own Sports Council, through which grants are channelled to clubs and individuals.

It would be unfair to single out particular projects, groups of sports or individual local authorities when reviewing the transformation of the Highland sporting scene. Who could decide, for instance, which had more impact or social importance—a modern athletics stadium at Inverness or a new bowling mat for a village hall in north Sutherland?

A simple illustration might be the dramatic increase in publicly and privately owned swimming pools. Where once these might have been counted without using up the fingers on one hand, there are now modernised or brand new ones at Thurso, Wick, Brora, Golspie, Tain, Poolewe, Dingwall, Alness, Inverness, Culloden, Nairn, Grantown on Spey, Nethybridge, Aviemore, Fort William and Portree. Each of the main islands of the Shetland now has—or is about to have—its own swimming pool, in most instances as part of mini-sports centres connected to the local junior secondary school. Primary schools which do not have easy access to these 12 metre pools have been equipped with swim-training tanks. The cost of each mini-centre has been in the region of £11 million (construction costs are high in Shetland) but the public use of the facilities has been remarkable, with annual attendances in the region of 50,000 expected at even most northerly Unst and Yell, where the local population is only around the 1000 level.

Highland Region was the first regional authority in Scotland to appoint a Sports Development Officer. Alistair Kidd has held the post since 1980 and enthuses over how, through co-operation and co-ordination of initiatives in the districts, a whole new range of coaching in sport has been made available. 'Coaching has developed to such a degree that it is now possible to hold classes where we can even elevate students to actual coach status' he boasts modestly.

It may be a minor point in the overall scale of sporting development, but Alistair Kidd also likes to remind his counterparts in the populous Central Belt that there isn't a single blais pitch for soccer or rugby in the North of Scotland—all are on grass. He looks to the further development of village halls as mini-sports centres and for an expansion of the facilities available at the five main schools in Inverness. Each area of the Highland capital could have a sports centre of its own, rather than building a single major one somewhere on the town perimeter.

The upsurge in community sporting activity is confirmed by the existence of the Highland Sports Association for Disabled People. Funded mainly through the district councils, with administrative and often venue assistance provided by Highland Region, the Association enjoys considerable voluntary assistance and is responsible for an all-year-round programme culminating in an open sports day at Inverness each year for as many as 500. Young and old are transported from far and wide for an all-in cost, including food, of just £1 a head. Many have already made their mark in national and international competition.

A financial top-up from the HIDB, to match what clubs or communities have been able to raise through their own and local authority resources, has often meant the difference between new premises, better equipment, or other needs becoming available sooner rather than much later. On average the HIDB is disbursing £250,000 every year to sports and recreation in one form or another. Grants range from £100 to a maximum of £15,000, but the Board is willing to seek special Treasury permission to give higher grants as they did, for instance, with the Aonach Mor development and the Islay swimming pool.

Dr John Watt, senior social development officer at the HIDB, explains 'If the Board's efforts to sustain and even increase the population are to succeed then sport and recreation has an important part to play. New buildings or equipment cost the same whether you are in the city or out in the country. The difference is that in the city sports clubs normally have much greater fund-raising potential, if only by virtue of the size of population around them. We do what we can to help sparsely populated communities and less affluent clubs to get over their financial hurdles.'

Long distances and high travel costs, however, still inhibit the amount of competition available to sports clubs in the Highlands and Islands. 'If we had an extra one million pounds to spend tomorrow we could use it all on the provision of mini-buses' Dr Watts reflects. 'For instance there is an archery club at Lochbroom, but to achieve the desired level of competition they may have to make a round trip of two to three hundred miles. It becomes a very costly exercise when there are just a few of you.'

Without HIDB grants towards travel it is unlikely that up to 100 soccer teams from the Northern and Western Isles, as well as the Highland mainland, would now be competing for the Highland Amateur Cup. When the competition began in 1978 with a £75 HIDB grant to purchase the trophy there were only 24 teams taking part. The Board's present level of support to the competition is £6000.

Exotic sports such as hot-air ballooning, mountain-bike racing, sand yachting and deep-sea angling have been finding the Highlands and Islands an ideal venue for national and international competitions. Who, a few years ago, could have envisaged competitors in their hundreds, often entire families among them, plotting and mapping their way through the forests and foothills in such an imaginatively named sport as orienteering? Curling and ice skating now take place

40   Sailing, Aviemore. Photograph by Oscar Marzaroli.

almost solely on indoor rinks. (Whole generations of curlers and skaters, however, may have missed something in never having had the special thrill of performing in the great outdoors.)

Traditional sports such as bowling, sailing, golf and football are being played by greater numbers than ever before. There was a time when many such activities were either not available or were beyond the pocket of most. Waiting times on first tees are a rarity, except at some weekend peak times, and green fees may well be the cheapest in the golfing world. With almost 50 courses to choose from, including the renowned links of Dornoch and Nairn, golf is another sport that has not only become more widely available but is now also a very valuable marketing commodity for the tourist industry.

The semi-professional soccer scene may no longer have the spectator-drawing power of the 1950s and 1960s, but the reason for the drop in numbers is more likely to lie in the greater opportunities for participating, in preference to watching, rather than because of any drop in standard on the field of play. The Highlands are still without representation in the Scottish League, however. The continuing absence of an invitation to membership appears to be as much a stumbling block as are the administrative and partisan problems which inhibit the initiative being taken from this end.

And what of the national game itself? Jack Richmond, publicity convenor of the Camanachd Association, has no doubt that the present healthy state of shinty has much to do with the improved prosperity and employment potential of the area in the past 25 years. Had it not been for the fish-farm development, how else would places like Kinlochshiel be able to continue to find young men to make up a team?

As it is, to attend the final of the Camanachd Cup is an experience never to be forgotten, either by the knowledgeable enthusiast or the casually curious. You don't require to be a committed supporter of Newtonmore, Kyles or Oban to feel involved in the sizzling passion generated by the competitiveness, skill and—dare I say it—sometimes primitive ferocity of the occasion. Primitive? The caveman may have had something to do with it after all.

ALEX MAIN A native of Inverness and a reporter of the news scene in the Highlands and Islands since 1948, initially with the *Inverness Courier*—where he is now Editor—and successively between 1955 and 1989 with the *Press and Journal*, *Scottish Daily Mail*, *Scottish Daily Express* and *The Scotsman*.

13b   Museums and Theatre

John Kerr

One of the fascinating side-effects of all the effort that has been concentrated on economic development in the Highlands and Islands in recent years has been the upsurge of enthusiasm for local tradition and heritage.

A quarter of a century ago, the National Trust for Scotland, the Saltire Society and a handful of individuals stood almost alone in actively promoting the preservation of Scottish tradition in the form of buildings grand and humble, folk ways, landscape and the history of the nation at large. Now this cause has been adopted by government departments, local authorities and community organisations very much as a fact of life. The heritage trail is fast becoming something of a super-highway: and nowhere more so than in the Highlands and Islands, rich as they are in tradition and with an ever-controversial history.

The model for much of what has been developed over the past 20 years or so must be the Highland Folk Museum at Kingussie. Created by a dedicated scholar and social historian, Dr Isabel Grant, *Am Fasgadh* as it is known—from the Gaelic for 'The Shelter'—houses a magnificent collection of Highland dress, relics of ancient crafts, furniture and farm implements as well as having alongside reconstructed examples of primitive thatched cottages similar to the Black Houses of the Outer Isles. For most of her lifetime Dr Grant supervised and built up her folk collection single-handed. It was not until relatively recently that the Scottish universities and local government took a hand in the administration and upkeep of *Am Fasgadh*, although it had for long been recognised in Scandinavia and America as an outstanding record of the Highland way of life. The West Highland Museum in Fort William and its collection of rare Jacobite relics is another pioneering enterprise, still flourishing, which owes its quality and survival to the care and attention of a few individuals during the years before the concept of the heritage centre became fashionable.

Even now, in a more receptive cultural climate and with more public funds available, it is interesting that most of the local projects of this kind have been conceived and driven through to completion by small bands of local enthusiasts.

The quite remarkable 'Timespan' presentation at Helmsdale in Sutherland, midway between Inverness and John o' Groats, takes the visitor on a historical journey from the days of the Picts and Vikings, by way of the Highland Clearances and the Kildonan Gold Rush, through the rise and decline of crofting and fishing to the modern industrial revolution based on off-shore oil. It took a local committee seven years to research the events depicted here dramatically in sound and vision; an endeavour well justified by the results. There is a really chilling impact across the centuries from the tableau of the Sutherland factor, Patrick Sellar, evicting a crofting family with their meagre possessions and setting fire to their pathetically spartan cottage. On a more cheerful note, the impression of Highland prospectors panning for gold in Kildonan in 1869 could hardly be more lifelike, and there is a jolly goldfield ballad on the soundtrack to go with it.

On the other side of the country the Gairloch Heritage Centre in Wester Ross, another recent addition to the presentation of Highland lore, also offers good value to the enquiring visitor. One striking reflection of the way of life in this part of the country around the end of the century is a series of photographs in sepia of the Open Air pulpit which served as a focus of worship for the Free Presbyterians of Shieldaig for more than 20 years until they finally got a church built in 1920. A huge congregation, including a substantial contingent of small children, is disposed in serried ranks on a hillside which on most Sundays must have chilled to the marrow any faint hearts among the faithful. Nowadays all the creature comforts are readily to hand for the pilgrim who seeks shelter from the elements or a change of pace from Highland history—the Gairloch centre offers an admirable catering service to refresh and restore the flagging spirit: fresh lobster from local pots feature on the menus in season.

The local influence is strong, too, at Tangwick Haa museum on the North Mainland of Shetland. Originally the Laird's house at the end of last century, the Haa was rebuilt and restored with the help of grants from the Shetland Amenity Trust—one of the benefits of the oil age. And all the exhibits were donated by the people of Northmaven, a vigorous community who have outlasted their laird. The main emphasis at Tangwick Haa, obviously, is the sea, with records ranging from the operations of Catalina flying boats from Coastal Command which flew from Sullom Voe during the Second World War, to a list of all shipwrecks on that stretch of the Shetland coastline since 1851—out of 42 wrecks, six were the victims of German U-boats.

In Orkney, local involvement is represented by the Islands Council who own Tankerness House Museum in Kirkwall. In contrast to the reconstruction of a cottage kitchen, which is such a popular feature of the folk history movement, Tankerness offers the grander impression of a well-off merchant's drawing room dating from about 1820: propriety then seemed to take precedence over comfort. In addition to antiquities from Orkney's distant past of more than 5000 years ago, the Tankerness collection includes two handsome paintings by the distinguished Orcadian artist Sir Stanley Cursiter, once the Queen's Painter and Limner in Scotland.

One of the most recent heritage centres in process of development is the locally organised museum at Grantown-on-Spey. Here, even the pay desk at the entrance is an interesting relic from the age of steam—a handsomely curved oak counter salvaged from the ticket office of the town's now disused railway station. It was designed for sliding coins back and forth between passenger and cashier in the days when shillings and pence had some monetary value. From before the age of steam there is a tableau tribute to 'the good' Sir James Grant (1738–1811), one of the 'improving lairds' of the Highlands, who planned the new town of Grantown some 200 years ago. The Square at the north end of the High Street in particular suggests a more enlightened civic outlook than might have been expected from the gentry of the time. Cynics, of course, have been heard to say that the real reasons for the new town was a desire by Sir James to clear the old village off the doorstep of Castle Grant and keep the clansmen at arm's length.

But that kind of conflict of view, like the old sores of the Clearances in Sutherland, which are still slow to heal in some hearts and minds, is very much part of the essential fascination of growing public enthusiasm for looking back to our roots and the roots of our neighbours. Grantown-on-Spey, where the heritage centre reflects a long sporting association with salmon angling and ski-ing, is as different as can be from Gairloch, where the fishermen are shown mending their nets and using three-pronged flounder spears. The Orkney drawing room in Tankerness House is as different as can be from the croft living-room at Helmsdale's Timespan. And yet in each case the heart is essentially Highland or Island: and it can only be good for the Highlands and Islands, not to mention the rest of the country, that the roots and traditions of highlanders and islanders should be cherished and made known through such a thriving new wave of heritage development.

Music and the arts are no longer confined to Britain's highly-populated southern cities. All over the Highlands they are celebrated both at amateur and highly professional level. One of the world's major, though small scale, international musical events is held each year in Kirkwall, Orkney. The week-long St Magnus Festival, begun in 1977 and coinciding with the summer solstice in June, attracts music lovers from 'a the airts'— as well as a large, appreciative and increasingly knowledgeable local audience. One of its co-directors, Sir Peter Maxwell-Davies, who came to live on the remote island of Hoy in the early 1970s, wrote his opera *The Martyrdom of St Magnus* for that first festival, performed in the glorious twelfth century St Magnus Cathedral: an opera which has since been performed all over the world. The festival, in which the Scottish Chamber Orchestra takes part, includes concerts, recitals given by visiting artists such as Vladimir Ashkenazy and Julian Bream, and poetry readings. An additional dimension is given by the participation of local schoolchildren, who perform highly sophisticated and demanding works with unselfconscious professionalism.

The theatre, too, has been making a lively contribution to the life of the Highlands and Islands in the 1970s and 1980s. The founding and development on many cultural fronts of Eden Court Theatre in Inverness has given music, drama and art not only a secure base in the north but also a strategic jumping-off place from which the good news in all artistic forms can be launched on tour to parts seldom before reached by such activities.

41   Eden Court Theatre, Inverness. [HIDB]

It was the changing times, during the past 25 years or so, which produced one of the most uproariously funny—and at the same time politically aware—plays in modern Scottish theatre: John McGrath's *The Cheviot, the Stag and the Black, Black Oil*. A satire on several estates, it might be called, covering what Mr McGrath would regard as the misuse of land from the time of the Clearances to the coming of North Sea Oil. With the touring company '7.84', the author took his anti-establishment message all over the country and it was never better received than when in Highland or Island territory. The Minister of State at the Scottish Office at the time, Lord Polwarth—a Border laird who was really only a temporary Tory politician—had been challenged on some issue of land use in oil development and, while hedging a direct reply, was injudicious enough to suggest that all was well because '*I have a plan.*' This provided John McGrath with the theme of a hit song for his play, and the introductory line, '*My name is Lord Polwarth and I have a plan ...*' became the subject of great political hilarity and certainly shook the foundations of the Scottish Office at St Andrew's House. (The title of the theatre company—7.84—was intended to remind observers that 84% of the country's wealth was owned by 7% of its people. It is alleged, though the story may be apocryphal, that this message, prominently displayed on the back window of John

McGrath's Volvo estate car, caused a petrol pump attendant north of Inverness to remark to McGrath 'There's no need to boast about it, though'.)

The Mull Little Theatre, based on the energies and talents of the Hesketh family, has also done stalwart work in taking entertainment to remoter communities. The company is less committed in the political sense than 7.84, but no less dedicated to the theatrical tradition of getting the show on the road, and on the stage, regardless of the snares and pitfalls that always surround such enterprise.

More recently, with the encouragement of social grants from the Highlands and Islands Development Board and assistance from the Scottish Arts Council, an increasing flow of companies from central Scotland and even south of the Border have been touring in the north. The Cleveland Theatre Company from Stockton-on-Tees, Theatre Seanchaidh (Greenock), Cahoots Theatre Group (Glasgow), the Black Box Puppet Theatre (Edinburgh) and the Trestle Theatre Company (Barnet) are a few of the bands of good companions who have been helping to bring a widely varied range of theatrical experience into country and village communities.

Operating from the Highland capital of Inverness, Eden Court is mainly concerned with the presentation of incoming touring companies from Edinburgh, Glasgow and London, as well, of course, as visiting orchestras. But in recent years the theatre has developed a policy of mustering a touring company of its own and sending it around the farther-flung outposts of the north—so much so that a map recording their travels was a source of amazement and admiration for Mrs Thatcher's Arts Minister Richard Luce during an official visit to the theatre.

Since Eden Court was officially opened by the late Andrew Cruickshank in 1976, its artistic activities have expanded out of all recognition and beyond most expectations. Situated within yards of the swift-flowing River Ness, the building itself is of distinguished design. It provides for a large catchment area—Dornoch to the north and Speyside to the south are within comfortable travelling distance for an evening out—a remarkably varied programme of entertainment: drama, ranging from the classics to West End comedy, symphony concerts and chamber music, jazz in the foyer, art exhibitions in the corridors, films in a now well-equipped cinema, lunchtime poetry readings, pantomine for Christmas and New Year: the variety is apparently endless. And in addition the theatre is occupied by conferences for 30 days a year—the Scottish National Party, the Liberals as was, the Women's Rural Institute and Scotland's fish farmers have all at some time chosen to debate their policies and their future in the auditorium at Eden Court, which among other advantages offers the bonus of comfortable seats and a good acoustic.

Like many such an enterprise, Eden Court has had its administrative and financial ups and downs, even to the point of serious doubt being cast over its future. Its very inception was accompanied by much local criticism. There was a considerable public outcry (not least from the then editor of the *Inverness Courier*) against the expense to taxpayers and ratepayers alike in building, equipping and running it. At one time it was referred to as The White Elephant and a low bronze sculpture placed outside the main entrance (now removed to the side of the building) was known as The Droppings. But having survived teething troubles and other more mature difficulties, it would seem that the major theatre of the Highlands and Islands is set to continue in that role and to provide both a focal point and a launching pad for the performing arts. It has become an impressive creative centre of which the people of the Highlands and Islands can be properly proud.

The most recent attendance figures available show the great variety of interest and area covered by the Highlands and Islands 'Top Forty' Museums and Art Galleries:

1   Inverness Museum and Art Gallery
2   Highland Folk Museum, Kingussie
3   West Highland Museum, Fort William
4   Shetland Museum
5   Tomintoul Museum (and Information centre)
6   Gairloch Heritage Museum
7   Glen Coe and North Lorne Folk Museum
8   Auchindrain Museum, Inveraray
9   Falconer Museum, Forres
10 Pier Arts Centre, Stromness, Orkney
11 Dufftown Museum
12 An Lanntair Gallery, Stornoway
13 Tankerness House Museum, Orkney
14 Stromness Museum, Orkney
15 Museum of the Cumbraes
16 Isle of Arran Heritage Museum
17 Easdale Island Folk Museum
18 Combined Operations Museum, Inveraray
19 Mull and Iona Museum
20 Laidhay Croft Museum
21 Robertson Museum and Aquarium, Millport
22 Strathpeffer Doll Museum
23 Dingwall Museum
24 Shetland Croft House Museum
25 Tain and District Museum and Clan Ross Centre
26 Appin Wild Life Museum
27 Strathnaver Museum
28 Lyth Arts Centre
29 Wick Heritage Centre
30 McAlister Clan Centre, Tarbert
31 Groam House Museum, Rosemarkie
32 St Fergus Gallery, Wick
33 Nairn Fishertown Museum
34 Thurso Museum
35 Clan Gunn Heritage Centre, Wick
36 An Orkney Wireless Museum
37 Nairn Literary Institute Museum
38 Ivor Wood Museum, Orkney
39 Lochcroistean Historical Centre
40 Burghead Museum, Forres

These and many of the smaller museums are eminently worth attention, for visitors and residents, and not least for the younger generation.

13c   The Press in the North

James Gunn Henderson

Like newspapers the world over, the weeklies in the Highlands and Islands have radically changed in the past quarter-century, notably from 1980 onwards, and mainly for the better. They are more brightly presented, easier to read and handle, but not necessarily as good in content or balance. Spelling mistakes abound, sentence structure is as erratic as in the Sheriff Courts, and syntax for many journalists is just as well understood as if it were a community charge on corruption.

Sadly, comment and opinionated reporting is beginning to show outwith the leader columns, a trend to be regretted unless it is clearly presented as the views of a named author. Local newspapers have often been considered to be almost drably verbatim and my own was once known as 'the County Council minutes, with pictures'. We try harder nowadays to make council meetings interesting reading, not always an easy job. But I do recall a Caithness councillor once congratulating my old mentor David Oag, then editor of the *John O'Groat Journal* and a superb shorthand writer, with 'You make me read much better than I sound to masel'.

With the arrival of free weeklies (mainly in the populous areas, because door-to-door delivery cannot be profitable out in the country) standards are dropping further, with every hand-out and press release, from whatever source, being seized on to fill in the grey rectangles between the billowing and often bellowing adverts.

The weekly editor today, of free-sheets or paid-fors, is more hard-pressed by his company accountants than the scribe of old, and he has to permit advertising 'features'—a clever ad-man ruse to persuade the customer that this is an editorial page as distinct from a blatant advertisement—to bolster extra pages and enhance the profit margins. Sometimes these 'features' are well produced and informative, depending on the in-house standards, but many are lazily written and slack in pace to the point of boredom. Many principal advertisers must feel cheated and sold short with inferior editorial content, because the journalist has shown his lack of interest in the subject from the start—although I agree that not many people can wax lyrical on double-glazing or overhead cam-shafts.

The 25 years gone have seen the demise of some respected titles, like *The Northern Chronicle*, *The Football Times* (the Saturday evening edition of *The Highland News*), and the pace-setting *Highland Herald*, all Inverness-based. The only new paid-for weekly newspaper to be successfully launched is *The West Highland Free Press*, which deserves the special section devoted to it in this book because it is clearly politically committed, brash, anti-establishment, landlord-bashing and masterly in subjective reporting. Its style and panache have been secretly admired by many of us who would not admit to it as patently as I am doing now. Then who would buy a pro-Government, landlord-loving, estate marketing weekly paper made from pulped Sitka spruce from the Flow Country? (Answers, please, on a postcard, in not more than fifteen words, to 'Wogan, c/o *The Northern Times*, Golspie, Sutherland). The *WHFP* has taken on bigger brother *Stornoway Gazette* in the Western Isles, claiming greater readership in the Catholic southern isles—but that is to be expected, given the schism that extraordinary piece of local government reorganisation in 1975 widened rather than closed.

Groupings of newspapers have become more marked with better communication and the opportunities of group advertising and combined printing. The only remaining single-title 'independents' are *The Shetland Times*, *The Orcadian*, *The Northern Times* in Sutherland, *The Inverness Courier* and *The Nairnshire Telegraph*. *The Stornoway Gazette* was bought by *Galloway Gazette* group owner Ian Brown of Newton Stewart in 1979.

Security printers Peter Press Ltd of Berkshire, after being 'seen off' by Moray and Nairn Newspapers in an unsuccessful £600,000 bid for their titles in 1981, turned their attention to the Highland News Group in Inverness and Caithness. The late Provost Sandy Macrae of Dingwall had been responsible for that pairing—the *Highland News* with *The John O'Groat Journal* in 1961, having already acquired *The Caithness Courier* some time before that.

Peter Press chairman Peter Fowler, a former advertising executive and keen sportsman in the Highlands, with his second home in the notorious Highland Clearances strath of Glencalvie, had already acquired the county paper *The Ross-shire Journal*, which he had described as 'obscenely profitable'. From that firm base in Dingwall he had launched his bid for the Inverness group, having failed to take over the Elgin-printed *Northern Scot*, *Forres Gazette* and *The Strathspey and Badenoch Herald* of Grantown. The old *Courant & Courier* from Elgin had 'died a death' in the 1960s. Thus consolidated, with *The Lochaber News* slip edition of *The Highland News* and a similar slip *The North Star* for Dingwall, Peter Fowler's northern newspaper empire extends from Fort William to Thurso. But he is second string in circulation terms in all but Dingwall, where he personally owns the dominant *Ross-shire Journal*, and in Caithness. His main rivals on his southern boundary remain top dogs—*The Oban Times*—as do *The Inverness Courier* in his heartland and *The Northern Times* throughout Sutherland.

Down in the southernmost extremity of the Board's area, Rothesay-based *The Buteman* remains in the control of a local company, E & R Inglis, like the locally-owned *Argyllshire Advertiser* of Lochgilphead and *Dunoon Observer*.

One of the most revolutionary media developments to hit the Highlands was stillborn. This was the concept of Beaverbrook Newspapers executive John Vass in 1979, to facsimile-print Fleet Street dailies in a bespoke factory, aided by the HIDB, at the Longman in Inverness. From there he hoped to distribute the *Daily Express*, *Star*, and some of the 'heavies', to cut the costs of transportation and give these papers a 'head start' even on the Aberdeen-produced *Press & Journal*. Even though he had started his *Express* career in Inverness, Vass had been away in London too long to gauge the depth of prejudice against his employers still nursed by the print union SOGAT over the shut-down of the Albion Street plant in Glasgow in 1974, with the loss of almost 2000 jobs. The HIDB were criticised by the union for offering £150,000 in grant and loan to the £500,000 project without first consulting their members, opposed to fax-printing then because it meant only a small staff of technicians and press minders in Inverness. Vass tried to soldier on during the negotiations with the first of the Highland free-sheets, but in the end his fax plans were 'blacked' and he was obliged to fold his tent and leave for Edinburgh. The union even 'blacked' his gift to my newspaper of a Christmas carol insert, as an old pals' act. Now look at the fax printing from London's Wapping to Kinning Park in Glasgow of *The Times* and its most unlikely bedfellow, *The Sun*!

In the last ten years, local newspapers in the Highlands and Islands have become more conscious of the pervasiveness of the so-called 'electronic media'—radio and television—although modern type-setting and printing is almost entirely controlled by electronics and computers. BBC Radio Highland started up an English and Gaelic news and features service from studios in a converted mansion at 7 Culduthel Road, Inverness in 1976, followed by a commercial enterprise, Moray Firth Radio, broadcasting from a 'greenfield' site at Scorguie, Inverness, for the first time on 23 February 1982.

Grampian Television established a Highland base—after strong criticism that the area was being 'neglected' on the small screen—at the riverside in Inverness in June 1984, followed more than three years later by a BBC television team, working out from their Culduthel Road studios. It can now be almost guaranteed that a newsworthy item from somewhere in the Highlands and Islands will appear on the nightly BBC TV 'Reporting Scotland' and on Grampian TV's 'North Tonight'. It is also worth noting that many of those highlighted items, like so many 'exclusives' nationally, first appeared as headlined stories in the local weeklies, a rich source of ideas for news editors the world over.

On the other hand the impact of radio and television on the local weeklies, and indeed on the one provincial daily, the Aberdeen-based *Press & Journal*, has been considerable. While it has meant a sharpening up of news presentation with some analysis in greater depth, to offset the immediacy of voice and vision, it is in the advertising departments that the chill has been felt, with both commercial radio and television 'creaming off' some good accounts because of their right-now appeal. The tele-ad girls in the newspaper offices have a hard job convincing their prospective customers that a permanent record of their product or forthcoming event in ink or even with 'spot' colour is preferable to a jazzed-up jingle or a ten-second film clip, no matter how visually appealing.

A free-sheet 'war' broke out in Inverness in 1989, when *The Highland News* group stole a march on Thomson Regional Newspapers by launching *The Inverness Herald* ahead of the *Press & Journal's* own free-sheet. That has since been followed up by *The Nairn Herald* and *The Ross-shire Herald*, both slip editions produced from Highland Printers' Longman plant. It was said that the weekly group even 'stole' key personnel ahead of the TRN launch. In reply, the bigger provincial group recruited several members of the *News* editorial staff when they set up their competitive *Inverness Herald and Post*, followed soon after by the *East Ross Herald and Post* with a main street office in Dingwall. How long these two can battle it out is a bank manager's nightmare. The ironic twist here is that TRN have engaged in a £70 million national campaign of free-sheets with the generic title of *Herald and Post*—when the masthead's first name was very much identified with *The Highland News* acquisition of the old *Highland Herald*, a toothy tabloid of the 1950s, long ahead of its time.

Moray Firth Radio announced profits of about £38,000 in the year to 30 September, 1988, an increase of 12% on the previous year, not at all bad for a small station. Managing director Thomas Prag, who formed the station on leaving BBC Radio Highland, reported: 'We had hoped for slightly better results but the boom in national advertising seen by much of the radio industry last year has been less dramatic for the smaller stations. Once again we have had to rely on our own efforts to sustain steady growth.'

There are many newspaper managers who would be pleased with that size of interim result. One who may well be is Stuart Lindsay, formerly *The Glasgow Herald*'s reporter in Inverness, who scored the coup of the decade in 1988 by persuading Miss Eveline Barron CBE, proprietor of the oldest-established newspaper in the Highlands, *The Inverness Courier*, that he was the right man to sell to. She had resisted the blandishments of several newspaper tycoons, it is said, who door-stepped her with bouquets of flowers over a period of at least five years. The sub-title on the *Courier*'s masthead 'and General Advertiser' was never more apt, for local people bought it in the Barrons' day (she succeeded her uncle Dr Evan Barron, giving more than fifty years of family editorship) for its advertisements and eccentric leaders, rather than its news content of perhaps three pages over the two weekly issues, Tuesdays and Fridays.

How the scene has changed! Still front-page advertising, leaders not quite so eccentric or memorable, but from twelve pages it has swollen to thirty-two of a Friday, of which close to 70% is advertising. Filling the spaces in between is perhaps some of the most indulgent journalism seen in many a long day. Writers from all over ('Letter from London', 'Letter from Orkney', perhaps even 'Letter from Surabaya', but none, thankfully, so far, from France) are being given column inches and fat fees unheard of in the North before. It was disclosed in a recent industrial tribunal that the deputy editor is being paid substantially more now on a weekly paper than he was as chief reporter for the provincial daily. On, on goes the success of the *Courier*. It is selling 38,000 copies a week now, to the 25,000 of just a few years back, showing how the Highland Capital is burgeoning at the expense of the outback.

The influence of the Highlands and Islands Development Board on the continuance of so many local newspaper titles is considerable, with generous grants and loans to purchase or lease modern presses and computer terminals, new custom-built buildings or conversions and adaptations. The Board has perceived this assistance as necessary to maintain the chain of newspapers throughout its region to reflect the individual identities of the disparate communities. These papers employ many skilled workers, widely scattered throughout the HIDB area. The Board has also assisted in the development of community news-sheets, some of them now becoming commercially viable and forming what could be the nucleus of a cottage communications industry. There are papers like *The Ullapool News*, *The Assynt News* of Lochinver, *Ileach* of Islay, *De Tha Dol?* of Acharacle, which look established and set to run for years. In time, these could all be hooked up to computer terminals for the easy distribution of common 'intelligence', to use the stagecoach word for news.

So is there a *quid pro quo?* Are editors so influenced by the Board's generosity that they temper any criticism for fear that the next grant might not be forthcoming? Does management weigh on editors to 'tread carefully' when reporting some of the Board's wilder speculations, like the Breasclete fish processing plant or the Barra spectacle factory? In some 15 years of direct experience in dealing with the HIDB, I have not come across a single instance of any Board member or official attempting to suggest any such arrangement, nor even a hint from any of my colleagues that they have ever been so influenced either by the Board or by their own bosses.

Instead, let me finish with a success story of co-operation at its best, between a Government-backed development agency and a small firm of printers and publishers. In 1967 a Scottish-run, Reading-based business, Method Publishing Co Ltd, applied to the HIDB for a grant to enable it to relocate in the Highlands. Their forte was the publication of Ministry of Defence periodicals distributed to Service bases world-wide. At the same time, the Golspie management of *The Northern Times* applied for financial help to move from a corrugated iron, gas-lit building in Station Road to a new factory in Main Street, with modern printing equipment. Someone in the HIDB spotted the opportunity of a 'marriage' between the two, a printer looking for more work, a publisher looking for a printer ...

Now, twenty-two years later and in yet another bigger building, leased from the HIDB after a £210,000 conversion, Sutherland Press House contains three allied companies—the Northern Times Ltd, Method Publishing Co Ltd, and Seaforth Photo-Litho Ltd, giving employment to some 140 people, in Sutherland, England, Germany and Hong Kong!—and injecting well over £1 million annually into the local economy.

> JAMES GUNN HENDERSON has been editor of *The Northern Times* at Golspie since 1975. A native of Wick, he was a cub reporter on *The John O'Groat Journal* in 1948. After National Service in the Royal Army Education Corps, he joined *The Scottish Daily Express* in 1953. He was deputy chief of the Edinburgh bureau (21 reporters, 6 photographers) from 1960–65, deputy news editor in Glasgow from 1965–69. and news features editor 1969–75. He lives in a house overlooking the estuary of the River Fleet—perhaps the last legitimate Fleet Street editor.

42 (*overleaf*)   Press montage. A selection from the many newspapers serving the Highlands and Islands.

West Highland Free Press

AN TIR, ... CANAN, 'SNA DAOINE

30p

No. 928

Tories b
dealer I

Minister admi

The Government have been
forced to drop their controversial
plans for a ...

North STAR

ROSS-SHIRE'S BRIGHTEST WEEKLY!

Week ending Saturday, February 10, 1990   Price 26p

The Shetland Times

Founded in 1872   Friday, 27th October, 1989   Price 35 pence

Ross-shire Journal
and General Advertiser for the Northern Counties

...y on
...oil

...een "extremely
... the council's
...p the mess. Mr
... further along
...ar complaints
... carpets were
...he council's
...r with the construction.

Getting
ready fo
just one
jetty

by Peter Bevingt...

THE COUNCIL ar...
for extra busi...
ir Sullom Voe h...
hroughput of oi...
ninal slows dow...
next decade.
e number of com...
e pilot boats is al...
ed. The SIC's r...
urs department...
ing two empl...

Established 1875

Peacefully in
ital, Invergor...
bruary, 1990,
rdross Place,
loved wife of
ch loved step-
at 16 Ardross
lon, on Thurs-
ry, at 11 a.m.

MILLER. — Mrs Christina Miller, Anne, Tom and family
wish to thank most sincerely
all relatives, friends, management and staff of Forbes Shop,
Bakehouse and Cafe, neighbours, old and new, for their
kind expressions of sympathy,
flowers and help received in...

ROSS. — In lovin...
a dear friend,
died on 7th Febru...
— Sadly missed
Dundonnell.

SHEARER. — I...
ory of my dear ...
loving granny, P...
on 8th February, ...

The Orcadian

The Northern Scot
AND
MORAY & NAIRN EXPRESS

A POPULAR JOURNAL FOR SCOTSMEN AT HOME

First Published 1880

REGISTERED
AT THE

POSTAGE:
Inland 34p   Overseas 57p

ELGIN, FRIDAY, NOV...

THS
T — Willie and Mari are
... to announce the birth of
ighter IF...

GOLDEN WEDDING

...TICES

...NG
...LL

W
OU

AM MUILEACH
Community paper for Mull and Iona

MAY 1989
ISSUE NO 91.

ourn...

...ORTHERN COUN...

...90

Forres Elgin & Nairn Gazet...

NORTHERN REVIEW AND ADVERTISER.

John O'Groat Journal
AND WEEKLY ADVERTISER
FOR THE COUNTIES OF CAITHNESS, SUTHERLAND, ROSS, CROMARTY, ORKNEY AND SHETLAND

154th year — 7984   WICK, FRIDAY, JANUARY 12, 1990   PRICE

Queen Mother to receive Freedom of Caith

THE Queen Mother is to become the first individual to be honoured with the Freedom of Caithness District.

The district council will present Her Ma... stigious disti... mark her lo... the county an... her 90th bir...

The estee... Queen Moth... Caithness ov... illustrated b... only is Her ... individual to ... honour, in A... the first wom...

Freedom of the Royal Burgh of Wick.

The convener of Caithness District Council, Councillor John Young, suggested that the

Young stated: "The only freedom conferred by Caithness District was on the Queen's Own Highlanders in 1986 (no individual having received this hon-

her to mark her long association with the district and to honour the Queen Mother on her 90th birthday".

In pre... ticket, t... Miss Be... freedom reconde...

FRIDAY 26 JANUA...

rgyllsh Adve

Her Majesty — ceremony planned for August

ORTH'S ER ONE!
Tel: 62821
ck. Tel: 2966;
2821 .. 4990...

The Northern Times
AND WEEKLY JOURNAL FOR SUTHERLAND AND THE NORTH
FRIDAY, 17th NOVEMBER, 1989   30p

ery "Rose" uvet Cover e Set at
SS'S
o. Tel. 63815

Caithness Courier
MIDWEEK COMPANION TO THE JOHN O'GROAT JOURNAL
WICK, WEDNESDAY, JANUARY 10, 1990

124th year — 1112

ghlar NEW

Wick air link hop...

HOPES have been dashed of an early resumption of ... duled ai... Wick an...

BAIN MORRISON & CO
XMAS HOLIDAYS
We will be closed from Friday, 22 Dec at 3 pm until Monday, 8 January, 1990, 8 am.
We would like to take this opportunity to wish our r Xmas

Stornoway Gazette
AND WEST COAST ADVERTISER
GUTH NAN INNSE-GALL
Week Ending December 23, 1989

Subscription Rates: Local/Mainland £29.12; Surface Airmail from £43.68.

STRATHSPEY and BADENOCH HERALD
INCORPORATING THE STRATHSPEY HERALD AND THE BADENOCH ...
THURSDAY, JA...

ARG... WEE
5863 - Established 1877

THE Gover... million Gaelic Television ... whi... ll enable the amount of Gae...

The Inverness Courier
And General Advertiser
FOR THE COUNTIES OF INVI
TUESDAY, ...
ESTABLISHED DECEMBER 4, 1817

NAIRN, MORAY, SUTHERLAND & CAITHNESS

CHRISTMAS & NEW YEAR 1988

Campbeltown Courier

The Oban Times
&
West Highland Times
airle Thiriodh Ne...

13d   The West Highland Free Press

Brian Wilson

The early 1970s were still a time in which young people leaving schools or universities could afford to indulge themselves by doing what they fancied doing, without too much regard for the impact upon longer-term career prospects. How else could it be explained that four honours graduates of Dundee University decided to establish a local weekly newspaper based on the Isle of Skye?

I had grown up in a West Highland atmosphere; my father from Appin and my mother from Islay. The *Oban Times* came into the house every week, and my father contributed the notes from Dunoon. That was probably my first sniff of journalism. Later, when a developing political awareness told me that the maxim 'ownership means control' applies to newspapers as much as to anything else, the idea of a paper based in the West Highlands and Islands began to evolve. The catalyst was undoubtedly my peripheral involvement in the short-lived *Islander* which, in the summer of 1969, circulated in Arran, Kintyre and Islay.

A politically radical paper in an area which was supposed to be socially con-servative but which, my background told me, was a lot more interesting than that description suggested—the idea began to take shape. For a year we went our separate ways. I spent that time on a postgraduate journalism course in Cardiff, with the aim of learning some of journalism's skills without the need to be employed by a newspaper. I was already well aware that newspaper offices are strewn with people who wish they had started a paper but started taking a salary instead and then couldn't look back. 'What you've never had you never miss' was an essential ingredient of the *West Highland Free Press's* survival.

Having settled upon Kyleakin in Skye as a base, by dint of wholly unscientific examination of the possibilities, the paper made its first uncertain appearance on 4 April 1972. I suppose that if there was anything so grand as a strategy at that time it was to play the part of wholly conventional local newspaper until established, and then begin to work in some of the politics. But events rapidly overtook any such plan. Big issues began to present themselves and to demand a journalistic repsonse.

Blandness was not an option if the adventure was to be worth the extraordinary investment of energy and commitment.

The most effective political contribution we could make to many of the communities which the paper circulated in was simply to tell people what was going on. The established, establishment papers—the *Oban Times* and *Stornoway Gazette*—had convinced themselves that between them they had the west coast sewn up. But they steered clear of all but the most petty controversies and did not perform the basic function of telling their readers, within the peripheral circulation area which the *Free Press* had defined for itself, much of what was being done in their name. Local government, centred in Inverness and Dingwall, was run in virtual secret as far as the west coast was concerned. In the early days the *Free Press* probably won much of its credibility simply by transforming that state of affairs. And how the landed grandees of Highland local government resented it!

Many of the issues which started to come at us thick and fast were tied up in the ownership and misuse of land. When I wrote from the gut and attacked the landlords as they had not been attacked in print for long decades past, the wonderful discovery was that the great majority of readers loved every word of it. Far from this new paper being an alien imposition upon a contented population, as our enemies claimed and even I might have feared, it was giving expression to sentiments which were already there; had always been there; but for many years had lacked a vehicle for expression. I will always maintain that the *Free Press*'s greatest contribution to Highlands and Islands life has been to put landlordism on the defensive by treating it as the pariah which it was and is, thereby articulating the fundamental political instinct of the Gael—however paradoxically that may rest alongside other social attitudes.

It was a novelty too for a newspaper in the Highlands and Islands to look critically upon development proposals, whether from civil or military sources. The Scottish press had long since developed a pavlovian attitude towards any press release which promised 'jobs'. In the work-starved West Highlands and Islands there were particular difficulties in exercising critical faculties in the face of proposals which held out the prospect of employment. Within the first year of the paper's existence two such proposals emerged—the first for the creation of a naval base at Kyle of Lochalsh, in association with torpedo testing in the Inner Sound of Raasay: the second for the construction of concrete oil platforms at Drumbuie, also in the Lochalsh area.

The *Free Press* became the focal point for discussion on the merits and demerits of both proposals, which clearly could have a major impact upon small West Highland communities. There was never any serious doubt that the Ministry of Defence would prevail, and the Kyle base is there to the present day. But the Drumbuie debate culminated in a marathon public inquiry and refusal of the proposals, with a more suitable site at Kishorn being given the go-ahead instead. The Drumbuie inquiry widened in scope to become, in effect, an inquiry into the whole speculative oil platform industry, which involved every construction company in the land driving around the Scottish coast-line, looking for a site to which they might then win an order. The *Free Press* argued that the state should identify the most appropriate sites, which could then look forward to continuity of orders. The rightness of that argument has, I think, been borne out by subsequent events.

Our coverage of Drumbuie and the MOD plans for Kyle, alongside our ongoing exposees of landlordism in action and a generally inquisitive journalistic style, all helped to put the *West Highland Free Press* on the journalistic map. When the idea of supporting the venture was first put to them, the Highlands and Islands Development Board had clearly regarded it as a bad bet and so we started without help from anywhere—not a bad example, I often think, to my political foes who mouth platitudes about 'enterprise' but have never actually displayed any. However, within a couple of years the HIDB was anxious to be helpful.

During that time the paper was printed in Inverness and brought back to Skye for folding, collation and distribution—a formidable task which could not be sustained indefinitely. In mid 1974 we made the painful transition to printing on our own equipment in leased premises at Breakish on Skye. A tiny business, employing only those who had been involved from the outset, became a more substantial one with wages to be paid and equipment to be kept busy. It took most of the next decade to get the business on a near-even keel and often only an intense and irrational determination not to admit defeat kept it afloat.

Throughout good times and bad, however, the *Free Press* has remained true, I think, to its founding principles. Under Iain MacCormick's editorship it is still an articulate voice on behalf of the communities it serves, a respecter of the forces which have created them, and the intractable opponent of those who exercise unaccountable authority and influence over them. The political comment remains trenchant, but the primary obligation has always been to act as a good local newspaper, which the great majority of its readers buy as a local newspaper—and then find, I hope, that they get a little bit extra and different on top. As it matured the paper became better at saying what it is for as well as what it is against, and has played a significant role in the creation of community co-operatives, the formation of a strong Crofters' Union, various pro-Gaelic initiatives and so on.

Looking at the current issue of the *Free Press* I see many of the ingredients which have made it what it is—an excellent expose of the treatment of employees by a brewery-owned estate in Wester Ross; good campaigning journalism against the imposition of tolls on a Skye bridge; loads of historical material; a lot of humour (we have in Hector MacDonald the wittiest columnist in British journalism); a strong letters page; my own column ranging in subject matter from a defence of Caledonian MacBrayne to an attack on Mrs Thatcher for her performance over South Africa at a Commonwealth Conference ... It has always been an exciting and hugely enjoyable mix to put together, but the real heroes have been the readers, who have had the largeness of mind to accept a local newspaper which has never quite conformed to stereotype—and which, I hope, never will.

BRIAN WILSON—Dunoon Grammar School; Dundee University; University College, Cardiff. Founder editor of *West Highland Free Press*. MP for Cunninghame North since 1987.

13e   Television and Radio

Alastair Hetherington

As late as 1975, colour television in the Highlands reached only the immediate area of Inverness, a corner of north-west Caithness, and the east side of Arran. For all the rest, from Campbeltown in the south to Shetland in the north, only the old 405-line black-and-white pictures were available—and with no cover whatever in large parts of Lorne, Inverness-shire and further north. As to Vhf radio, there was none whatever anywhere in the HIDB's territory. But a combined operation of BBC and ITA engineering brought colour television to all except the remotest inland areas between 1975 and 1983; and Vhf, too, came to most of the Highlands and Islands in that period.

The costs of transmission were, of course, out of all proportion to the money coming from television licence fees and ITV running costs; but it was the agreed policy of governments and broadcasters that the services should be extended to all but the most extreme of remote communities. (Sir Kenneth Alexander, at a meeting with the broadcasting authorities when transmitter progress was slow, reminded them of their commitment to 'the Post Office principle' of universality; and in Lewis the BBC's engineers at the huge new Eitshal transmitter, working overtime on a Sunday to speed its opening, were forced to leave the island after being denounced from the pulpit in Stornoway—no landlady would take them, thus bringing work to a stop.)

As the transmitters extended their cover, a few enterprising people set about establishing their own 'self-help' relays. These were, at first, illegal. The earliest were off-shore oil rigs, where signals from the mainland were picked up and relayed. The broadcasting department of the Home Office chose to turn a blind eye to these—and indeed to similar small relays set up in Shetland, Sutherland, and further south. But credit for persuading the Home Office to change its policy lies with a butcher at Acharacle, in Ardnamurchan, who was determined to have a legal relay. In 1979, having written to the Home Office and having had no reply, he went to London and persisted in demanding an interview. He made such an impression on the broadcasting department that a month or two later Acharacle received the first licence for a community-owned television relay. It was soon followed by another licence for part of Strathglass; and in the next few years more than 120 relays were licensed. To the community or group of houses installing a relay, the cost can be anywhere between £1000 and £8000, depending on the distance and height between the receiving mast and the dwellings. The HIDB has given grants to help a number of applicants. The relays have brought a high-quality picture and good sound to people who had no television service.

In radio there has also been valuable development since 1976. BBC Radio Highland, based in Inverness, came on air in that year—averaging about three hours of programmes daily, half in English and half Gaelic. It also became a lively contributor to BBC Radio Scotland and to UK network programmes. It was followed in 1977 by Radio Orkney and Radio Shetland—each staffed at first by only two broadcasters and a secretary, and broadcasting for about 90 minutes a day with island news, discussion and local entertainment. When the proposal was first put to the BBC in London they dismissed it as 'impossible', but eventually the managing director of BBC Radio, Ian Trethowan, agreed (although quietly believing that the experiment would fail). In fact the two stations were a huge success from the day they opened, for the simple reason that Orkney and Shetland each had strong individuality and a great thirst for island news, information and debate. For some years the two stations achieved, in percentage terms, the highest radio audience ratings in the UK.

Again, credit goes to local initiative. A campaign was launched by Jo Grimond, then MP for Orkney and Shetland, backed by a young Orkney farmer who had worked part-time on a two-man radio station in Canada while on a one-year exchange there. They believed in their case and they won. BBC Radio nan Eilean, based in Stornoway, followed two years later—and the pattern was soon followed in the Scottish borders, Wales and Northern Ireland (with BBC Radio Foyle as perhaps the most important of all, because of its ability to bridge the gulf between Catholics and Protestants in Derry). Again the HIDB had been of help in contributing to the costs of small studios for Highland, Shetland, Orkney and nan Eilean. More recently, Radio nan Eilean has been expanded into Radio nan Gaidheal with additional staff and more share in Gaelic broadcasting. From Inverness and Stornoway, Gaelic is up to five hours a day.

Another newcomer to the air, in 1981, was IRN's Moray Firth Radio, serving a strip of the north-east coast from Wick in the north to beyond Elgin in the east. It, too, had support from the HIDB in its early days. It has good audience figures and makes a modest profit in spite of stiff competition for advertising revenue.

On the television side, in recent years Grampian Television has strengthened its Highland activities with two camera crews based in Inverness and feeding back to Aberdeen. The BBC similarly has one camera crew and reporter based in Inverness, which has led to a valuable increase in northern items—with excellent pictures—in the early evening 'Reporting Scotland'. From Fort William southwards, the ITV service comes from Scottish Television in Glasgow, and it too has been more active in the Highland areas.

But is it good for us to have so much television and radio readily at hand? Do we devote too much time to ephemeral viewing? That is for individual decision. At least it can no longer be said that Northern Scotland is deprived of what is available to the rest of Britain. Scottish programmes are twice as frequent compared with the 1960s, and the Highland element much stronger. Gaelic, too, has a firmer base. The public demand exists, and the broadcasters have tried to meet it.

13f   Crafts in the Highlands, 1965–1990

J ENNY C ARTER

John o'Groats is not what it used to be—an attraction merely by accident of situation, a real outpost of civilisation. Nowadays series of workshops smartly laid out by the HIDB draw the legions of visitors who arrive daily by coach and car. Pottery, candles, knitwear—all the old favourite Scottish crafts can be seen and purchased here.

'We sell a lot of our pottery to passing tourists,' says David Body, whose Scarfskerry Pottery operates from one of the units, 'and we sell our pots in several other small craft shops around the Highlands too.' But, he admits, 'most of our work goes south of the border to England.'

It's a situation which is not unusual among the many craftspeople in the Highlands who today are designing and making quality goods. From Orkney to Arran you will be able to buy some locally-made work in neighbourhood shops and a drive along any Highland road will still provide a good crop of 'Crafts Sold Here' signs. But no longer do top craftspeople spend valuable hours passing the time of day with summer tourists—these days they are off looking for wider markets, in England, in America, in Japan.

Twenty-five years in the Highlands have brought dramatic change to the scale and range of crafts businesses. Craft goods, which began to come into their own in the 1960s as a valued alternative to the mass-produced item, have always been to some extent luxuries. In times of economic pressure, craftspeople have always had to fight more than most for a share in the market. In the 1960s few had any idea of how to set about that struggle. Twenty-five years later survivors have to be expert in self promotion.

The early years

Prior to the setting up of the Highlands and Islands Development Board, support for small craft businesses was given nationwide through the Scottish Country

202

Industries Development Trust (SCIDT). It came largely through advice and set-up grants. After 1965 visits to craftsmen, grant-giving in the Highland areas and advice on technical and marketing matters were taken on by the Board's Crafts Liaison Officer, Mike Wilton, and to a certain extent through the Board's Industrial Promotion Division.

One of the first major tasks of the Crafts Liaison Officer was a census of craftworkers in the region, undertaken with the object of compiling a register. A simultaneous survey was conducted in the rest of Scotland—the first attempt to build up an overall picture of the industry, to assess its business needs and its potential for development. The fieldwork was done by two former Regional Development Officers of SCIDT (which was reconstituted in 1969 into the Small Industries Council for Rural Areas of Scotland—SICRAS).

The result of their work, the Crafts Survey Report submitted to the Board in 1969, makes fascinating reading. Think of 'crafts' businesses in the Highlands today. Names like Lynda Usher, the Isle of Mull Silver Company or Ola Gorie spring to mind—firms whose drive and professionalism have taken them to an international market and widespread recognition. In 1969 the picture which emerged was of a straggling, struggling community where boatbuilding was the dominant craft and where lapidary work and mink jewellery ranked alongside shellcraft and pebblework. The work was sold almost entirely locally—tourism and the crafts in the 1960s were inextricably linked. While the use of export agencies would undoubtedly have increased the potential market, few firms made use of such agencies—and indeed few were geared to quantity production. Nor was the level of professionalism high: a concern about the general lack of reliability in keeping delivery deadlines made itself felt time and again in the pages of this report.

The picture built up here was a broad one, but was to some extent distorted. The compilers of the 1969 report decided on 'a "cut-off" level of a maximum of five whole-time skilled persons employed in craft firms or enterprises', while acknowledging that this excluded certain flourishing and established crafts (Shetland knitwear and Caithness Glass, for example). The crafts scene was, perhaps, neither as depressed nor as small as the report appeared to indicate (although inclusion of firms with more than five employees would have added a mere 6% to the total number of firms covered).

Figures given showed that in 1969 364 crafts businesses were operating, with an estimated total turnover of almost £500,000. 'While these figures are encouraging and perhaps even surprising,' reads the summary 'it takes little imagination to see the possibilities of development of the industry to a stage where it exceeds the £1 million mark, providing craftworkers and proprietors are prepared to develop and expand their businesses in a thoroughly costed and carefully planned manner.'

This conclusion appears to have been extremely optimistic, bearing in mind some damning indictments made in the pages of the report itself, notably: 'The quality and design of goods produced by some craftworkers in many cases falls short of desirable standards and many visitors to Scotland must be surprised and disappointed with some craft goods offered for sale.' Tourists in the 1960s, it seemed, would buy almost anything as a memento of their visit and some craft-workers 'appear perfectly satisfied providing that they can sell what they make, regardless of the possible damaging effect on the reputation of Scottish craft goods.'

Perhaps it was not surprising that craftworkers seemed so little interested in upholding high standards, as it was clear that few made a good living from their craft: 'Doubtless many crafts will continue to be practiced despite proof that such work cannot be strictly economical. The person employing his or her spare time in a way which gives pleasure or satisfaction does not trouble with detailed costings.'

The need for raising standards was, perhaps, the most pressing point made in the report. It recommended attending exhibitions, submitting work to the Scottish Craft Centre (in Edinburgh) and seeking sales in competitive markets. It pointed out, above all, the need for training. In many cases such training was difficult to acquire, although 'on the job' training was provided by the Scottish Country Industries Development Trust's itinerant technical staff in wrought iron, wood-work, welding, weaving and engineering. Training in business management and in design took place under the auspices of the SCIDT, but only outwith the Highland area. Training, it was recognised, was a real need: 'The more awareness that can be created in the craftsman in all aspects affecting his business, the more likely are craft enterprises to become soundly based and run. There is much that could be done in this direction. On the marketing side, for instance, the craftworker not infrequently lacks appreciation of product packaging and presentation, dis-tribution methods etc. There is a real need for courses on these and allied aspects of a craftsman's business.'

The push for professionalism was about to begin.

Taking up the challenge

1970 saw the first Highland Trade Fair—a positive step forward for the promotion of small businesses, particularly crafts businesses in the Highland area. The Fair illustrated further the potential for crafts activities; not only was it seen to be possible to conduct craft businesses in geographically remote areas, but their presence did not have a detrimental effect on the way of life of these fragile communities—indeed, they were thought to enhance it. In areas where it was impossible to attract any other kind of manufacturing industry, craftwork had enormous potential.

Growth in the early years of the Fair, however, was not easy. The shortcomings of crafts products in terms of design and marketing awareness were all too obvious. The training requirements highlighted by the 1969 report became increasingly apparent. If the crafts were to expand and improve, training was paramount—an investment in the future. By 1973, ideas for a dedicated Centre in the Highlands were beginning to crystallise.

The turnover potential of £1 million estimated in 1969 had, by the mid 1970s, rocketed to £3.5 million, excluding Shetland knitwear and Harris Tweed. The value of this capacity for growth was very highly regarded by the Board, while the particular difficulties faced by craftworkers were acknowledged. A comprehensive report on their needs and the feasibility of setting up a training centre in the Highlands was commissioned from consultant David Pirnie.

'It was a very thorough exercise which took over a year,' comments Pirnie. 'The investigations involved visits to Wales, to rural parts of England and to Ireland, where conditions similar to those operating in Scotland existed. It included consultations with the other major development organisations in the country, SICRAS in Scotland (later subsumed by the Scottish Development Agency), the Crafts Advisory Committee in London (later to become the Crafts Council), education authorities and the Scottish Education Department, the colleges of art and design.'

The findings of the study were overwhelming: the need for training was recognised without exception. But at the same time it was clear that what was really wanted was far more positive marketing advice, information, technical

43   Orkney chairmaker. [HIDB]

guidance, help with design and product development. Most craftsmen practising in the Highlands felt the effects of their remoteness, but were deterred from seeking assistance by the level of bureaucracy which had to be overcome.

At the time of the study the educational institutions, with the exception of the Scottish College of Textiles in Galashiels, had little interest in working craftsmen. The need for a specialist service was perceived by the HIDB.

'The operation envisaged was to be "one-door-access",' said Pirnie. 'The focal points were to be training, development, marketing and information.' But as he explained, the scale of the proposals for the establishment of 'Highland Craftpoint' grew and grew. 'Our intention to provide an information service necessitated a library. Training required workshop areas, teaching demanded a seminar room, while exhibitions required a substantial display area. Highland Craftpoint was designed to have workshops equipped and staffed to deal with ceramics and metalwork, to cope with everything from the needs of the hand-worker to crafts businesses working on a more or less industrial level. While textiles ranked with jewellery and ceramics as one of the largest areas of production, the excellent relations with the College of Textiles obviated the need for a large textile workshop in the Centre.'

44   Tweed mill, Shawbost, Lewis. Photograph by Oscar Marzaroli.

The location was to be within 15 miles of major public transport, in an attractive area and within easy reach of leisure and service facilities, including accommodation. In addition to its year-round function as a consultancy and training base, the Centre was to include a Visitor Centre for the summer months. A site in the attractive little town of Beauly, on the old A9, was chosen.

Highland Craftpoint—the early years

On 29 July 1979, following approval from George Younger, Secretary of State for Scotland, Highland Craftpoint was incorporated as a company limited by guarantee, not having a share capital. David Pirnie, who had been consultant on the project, was appointed Director. The first chairman was Rear Admiral David Dunbar-Nasmith—then Deputy Chairman of the HIDB—who had been a driving force behind the venture. Two years later the premises at Beauly were opened. Funding came largely from the HIDB, with one-third of the total costs being contributed by the Scottish Development Agency. (In the first year of its operation, the SDA's contribution to running costs was £61,345 and the HIDB's £123,230.) SDA funding enabled craftspeople from outwith the Highland area to attend courses and instruction at Highland Craftpoint, and gave them the benefit of the advisory services offered by the Centre.

Highland Craftpoint was designed to present a 'total package'. The range of services was integrated, and any removal from the range was perceived as being detrimental to its total effectiveness. Yet the concept remained continually under threat. David Pirnie wrote in May 1984, 'The concept of integration which forms the basis of the company's services and structure has proved appropriate and generally successful ...sustaining it, in practice, has not been easy, nor has it been continuously successful. It is a demanding concept, and periodically pressures of work and individual staff priorities have provided powerful arguments for abandoning principle in favour of expediency.' It was a concept, indeed, which was not to survive.

Reacting to change

While in the early years the policy of offering an integrated service remained unchanged, new elements were introduced—the marketing element expanding, for example, when Highland Craftpoint took over the administration of the Highland Trade Fair, and with the introduction of *A Buyer's Guide to Retail Products* for the Region. It was necessary and right that the company should respond to change, although not all the proposed changes met with approval.

In 1984 the company announced that it would focus its attention more on development, while training—originally the prime reason for its existence—was to be undertaken more on an individual than a group basis. This plan was not well received and under pressure from the SDA, supported by the HIDB and by the industry, Highland Craftpoint was forced to restore the former level of short group courses.

By 1985 it was becoming increasingly clear that duplication of some of the services offered by Highland Craftpoint on the one hand and by the SDA on the other (such as the presentation of two separate trade fairs and of two Buyer's Guides) was causing confusion. Less than a year later the HIDB instituted a far-reaching review of the company, prompted in part by notification from the SDA that it was unlikely that its current level of funding would be sustained. (In the year 1985–6, the HIDB's grant-in-aid was £553,187, the SDA's £147,600).

'Craftpoint' emerges

The result of this stringent review, which took place alongside wide-reaching discussions about the organisation of the crafts administration in the SDA, was a restructuring of 'Highland Craftpoint' and the final disappearance of its original 'total package' concept.

On 1 April 1987 the company became 'Craftpoint'. It was given the remit to operate on an all-Scotland basis, concentrating solely on marketing aid. Its training function was transferred to the HIDB and conducted through the Board's Business Unit, still based at Craftpoint's premises in Beauly. Exhibitions, which had originally formed part of Highland Craftpoint's overall strategy but had latterly lost ground to a specialised Trade Promotion Centre within the premises at Beauly, were now dropped altogether in favour of marketing in the field. This included trade promotions such as the organisation of the annual Trade Fair at Aviemore (which in 1986 had opened its doors to craftpeople from south of the Highland Line for the first time) and the promotion of Scottish work at overseas fairs. It also included the production of a *Buyer's Guide* on a national basis, the publication of a regular bulletin giving industry and market monitors, and the highlighting of fruitful fields for market development.

Looking back—and forward

Crafts in Scotland in 1990 present a picture very different to that early fragmented, haphazard and somewhat sloppy scene. Businesses have grown in number—Craftpoint's 1989 estimate of crafts businesses in Scotland was 3031, with an estimated turnover of £50 million, with the balance of business north and south of the Highland Line at 40 north, 60 south.

There is no doubt that the overall level of professonalism, both in design standards and marketing awareness, has risen dramatically. Firms such as Ortak (which started business 20 years ago with only one employee and now, with a staff of 70, is the second largest employer in Orkney) owe a great deal to the support of the HIDB and Craftpoint. 'Our factory is on a lease from the HIDB,' explained Malcolm Gray, Managing Director, 'while we have had considerable

24 Easdale Island off Seil Island, by Oban: the island's Folk Museum (top centre) provides a pictorial history of the slate industry and domestic life of the villagers. Scottish Museums Council.

25 Highland Folk Museum, Kingussie. Scottish Museums Council.

26 Some of the many shades of Shetland yarn.
T M Hunter, Brora, Sutherland.

28 Ross-shire Crafts, Clashnamuiach.

27 Iceberg Glassblowing, Drumnadrochit, Inverness-shire.

29 Carra Print, Tobermory, Isle of Mull.

help from Craftpoint in terms of specialised courses on casting, precious metals and stone setting. We now produce 900 pieces of jewellery a day and still can't meet demand. We attend 17 trade shows a year, including five in the States.' Marketing help from Highland Craftpoint gave the Isle of Sanday knitters a start as a co-operative venture, while sponsorship for trade fairs has helped promotion considerably. 'We're much more aware of market trends,' says Managing Director Elspeth Sinclair. 'We know now to watch fashion trends, although we refuse to be slaves to fashion.'

David Grant, Managing Director of Highland Stoneware at Lochinver, says categorically, 'We wouldn't be where we are today without the help of the HIDB. They helped us financially, with marketing and with our premises. We have help with setting up our business systems and we work closely with two management units who have helped us to improve our efficiency and have tailor-made software for us. We started from nothing and now we employ 30 staff.'

45   Kingussie Pottery. Photograph by Oscar Marzaroli.

There have, of course, been failures. Knitwear, which went through a boom period in the 1970s, has slumped considerably; many of the smaller, less professional businesses went to the wall. Other businesses have also suffered from changing trends in fashion and the vagaries of the national economy. Ceramics, which enjoyed a boom at the beginning of our period and then fell into disfavour, seem to be enjoying a revival. Little can change the fact that the Highlands suffer from their remote geographical position, while the fact that 54% of Scottish crafts are still sold locally underlines the continuing importance of the seasonal tourist trade.

Perhaps it has been an inevitable corollary of the HIDB's involvement that craftwork in the Highlands has always been viewed more as a manufacturing industry than as a branch of the arts. However fine their design work, crafts firms in the Highlands are overwhelmingly production based. Perhaps this is no more than a logical extension of the age-old role of the village craftsman—the potter providing vessels for the community, the weaver using local wool to provide warm cloth. Unfortunately, many 'craftspeople' still see poorly made, badly designed knick-knacks as a way to making a good living. There are still too many hairy haggises and tartan dollies around for us to be at all complacent about our souvenir industry. There *are* high quality goods being made in the Highlands, if you know where to find the makers. It is perhaps ironic that you will purchase the best more easily in London's smart craft galleries or up-market New York stores than in Inverness or Thurso.

Has the shining hope for the future which prompted the ambitious Highland Craftpoint project been fulfilled? The administrative structure of craftwork in Scotland has undergone—and is still undergoing—considerable change, and Craftpoint must necessarily be a part of any reorganisation. The radical restructuring it has already undergone to some extent reflects a change in the climate of the crafts world since its inception. Its future role, and the status of Highland crafts, will remain in jeopardy until plans for the overall future of crafts in Scotland are resolved.

JENNY CARTER began her career in book publishing with William Collins in Glasgow and worked as Senior Commissioning Editor in charge of Scottish books for Johnston & Bacon in Edinburgh. She moved sideways into writing books and magazines and was appointed editor of *Craftwork* magazine (which she edited for five years) by the Scottish Development Agency. She now has her own editorial agency in Edinburgh, specialising in writing, editing and production of journals for industrial, financial and commercial organisations. She writes on a freelance basis for newspapers and magazines on crafts in Scotland.

Chapter 14

The 'Top Country' Story

Alastair Hetherington

This final chapter looks forward to the future, as well as assessing the past. And it fills one or two gaps.

Looking forward: in 1989 the HIDB launched its biggest investment, to be completed by 1992. Jointly with British Telecom, it is creating a new all-digital communications network, giving small and large interests instant links with London, Zurich or Tokyo—or, for that matter, with Lochmaddy, Baltasound or Ardersier. It means installing a completely new Telecom system, replacing some 43 telephone exchanges. The network will offer from home or office voice communication, video and graphics, data and text, and other services. You will be able to buy and sell from home, hold conferences (but remember that jokes can be misunderstood on a multi-link meeting) and conduct almost any other business or personal exchange.

The network, when complete, will be of immediate value to the many small enterprises that have established themselves in the Highlands and Islands. There have, inevitably, been failures among these but there have been a much greater number of successes. Among the latter, though it may be invidious to pick names from so many, there are:

Arran Provisions at Lamlash
R K Carbon Fibres at Muir of Ord
The Dufftown quarry operated by an Aberdeen company
Mountain Technology in Glen Coe
Judith Glue's knitwear in Orkney, with a big mail order trade
K W Wooster International's plastic injection moulding at Campbeltown (having moved from Northamptonshire)
Zonal's recording tapes at Invergordon (having moved from Surrey)
The numerous fish farming activities on the West Coast and in the islands
—and towards a thousand others

All these are developments of the 1965–1990 period, and all have had help from the HIDB. It is a remarkable achievement. And all these, potentially, will be able to benefit from the new Telecom network.

211

A golf course and its makers

Travelling in the Highlands or among the Islands almost always brings a surprise or two. In the autumn of 1989 the Hetheringtons, having not been in the far North-West for five years, had cause to visit Durness. Looking for the regional councillor—a veteran from the founding of Highland Regional Council in 1975—they were told that he was on the golf course. *What golf course?* There had been none five years before. The new one was the answer—on ground looking across Balnakeil Bay towards Faraid Head. *Would he be playing golf? No, he would be green-keeping.* So they went to the course, found him on his grass-cutting motor, and heard the story.

In 1971, not long after returning home to Durness after 12 years in the RAF, Francis Keith planned a course. The land belonged to the DAFS (the Department of Agriculture), and they were willing to see a golf club there; but the Sheepdog Club (43 croft holders who used the land) voted against it by a margin of one. Then in the autumn of 1986 Councillor Keith—who also runs an 11 acre caravan and camping site, together with a pub and restaurant—decided to make a little course on the caravan site for use in the winter only. That whetted the appetite of some of his neighbours, including some of the crofters; but it had to be closed next spring when the campers came.

That spring the Sheepdog Club invited Keith to design a nine-hole course on the original land, which he did very quickly. But then the Nature Conservancy Council appeared on the scene and said 'no'—to which Keith replied that he had had planning consent for a golf course in 1971 and had been practising on the site himself ever since, thus keeping the consent alive. The NCC still objected, saying among other things that the revised course was not all on the same land as in 1971; so Keith redesigned it no fewer than five times to satisfy them. There was further complaint, but in the end Keith created his course in 1988, with nine holes and its magnificent view over the Bay. The work was almost all done by unpaid volunteers, even when having to move some tons of boulders. The club, which has had a small grant from the HIDB for its tiny club house, has 70 members, paying £40 a year each, and in addition one thousand 'visitor rounds' were counted in the summer of 1989.

This is a case of successful community enterprise if ever there was one. Without injury to the environment—as far as the layman can see—it has created a valuable asset for residents and visitors alike. And, incidentally, it is almost certainly the most northern golf course on the British mainland, being a fraction further north than the courses at Reay (near Dounreay) and Thurso.

Environmental issues

In its modest way, the Durness golf club illustrates some aspects of the conflict between preservation and development. As Dr Morton Boyd has recounted in Chapter 9, for nearly 40 years the Nature Conservancy Council has had a statutory duty to protect the environment, to establish nature reserves and SSSIs (Sites of Special Scientific Interest) and to conduct scientific research. It has done a vast amount of excellent work, but, though Dr Boyd may disagree, it has also brought upon itself more public hostility than it need have done. In its earliest days— before his time at the NCC—it provoked criticism and derision by drafting by-laws for the Cairngorms, with summary fines for anyone found camping without consent anywhere among the mountains. While its research and preservation work have been of the highest standards, its public relations have not.

At Durness the case against allowing golf was that the grassy little hills rising to some 170 feet above the sea were of special value for their *Primula Scotica* and Mountain Aven. The counter view, put by Francis Keith and others, was that *Primula Scotica* was to be found all along the north coast of Sutherland and in Orkney and that the Mountain Aven was to be found in many other limestone areas. Again, for those who are not botanists, ecologist or ornithologists, it is far from easy to form a judgement on environmental issues.

In his chapter, Dr Boyd has rightly touched on some of the great achievements of the NCC in Scotland. Among them have been:

— the protection and revival of the Old Caledonian pine forests;
— the protection of predatory birds and the revival of, among others, the magnificent sea eagles;
— the saving—with the National Trust for Scotland and others—of the Drumbuie lands near Kyle of Lochalsh from becoming an oil construction yard;
— the good relations and agreements with the oil companies in Shetland and Orkney;
— the research on red deer, with the Red Deer Commission, and their analysis of excessive numbers (still damaging to land);
— and the 'world class' nature reserve occupying the whole island of Rum.

It has to be remembered, too, that in its early days the NCC was under-funded and lacked the resources needed for identifying and surveying likely SSSIs. The resources came only from the 1981 Act, and even then the distribution lay with the headquarters in England.

For those who are not scientifically trained, it is indeed hard to make sound judgements. One may start from the dictum of Prince Charles. 'In the wilder areas' he said in the summer of 1989, 'conservation must come before recreation'. Durness can hardly be classed as a 'wild' area, nor does there seem to be any great risk to rare plants, birds or animals. The extension of ski-ing areas in the Lurcher's Gully area of the Cairngorms is another matter. Part of the case for extending ski uplift facilities is that, even with this extension, the ski-ing areas will take no more than two per cent of the Cairngorm mountain territory. Part of the counter argument is that the extension will move into an area of much higher scenic and natural value than the existing ski-lifts in Coire na Ciste and Coire Cas. Already Coire an t-Sneachda (the next to the west) has been partly invaded. It is not surprising, therefore, that in the autumn of 1989 the Countryside Commission for Scotland, after an extensive assessment, concluded that the Lurchers Gully development ought not to be approved. That was their advice to the Secretary of State for Scotland; if accepted, it will protect an area of exceptional beauty.

Another case of conflict, the so-called 'flow countries' of Caithness and Sutherland, has been what Professor George Houston in Chapter 4 called 'a Quango War'. That, happily, appears to have been settled in 1989 by a working party of all the primary interests; as a result there is hope of continued planting and employment. The working party's report mapped and categorised the land into four groups—unsuitable, undesirable, possible and preferable—providing an agreed basis for further forestry.

Agriculture: a farmer's view

Though farming barely exists in much of the Highlands and Islands, it is a major element in Orkney and in the rich regions round the Moray and Cromarty Firths. The soil is fertile, the climate dry, and there is much sunshine. Farming is still a substantial employer, though these days there is much more hiring of manned equipment.

Farming has changed during the HIDB's period. The first change was brought about by political intervention, when security of tenure was granted to tenant farmers. This has safeguarded the future for many farmers' families, but it has also had an adverse effect, in that there are now virtually no farms being re-let—no new tenancies are available for young people, who are now denied the opportunity of a start on their own.

A related change has taken place since crofters have been able to buy their crofts. Many did not choose to avail themselves of this option, but a number of those who did so have now re-sold them. With the relaxation in planning laws, permission for development has become easier and big gains have been made, causing some observers to comment that these crofters were not in love with the land, but only with its development value (a criticism levelled equally at some landowners).

Over the years the HIDB has been helpful, as farmers gratefully acknowledge, particularly with marketing. The Board also does a lot of 'pump-priming' on an individual scale.

Overall, financially, farmers are not as prosperous as they were. No farmer, it is said, can now live without an overdraft, and in many cases borrowing is at an astronomic level, causing grave anxiety. Nonetheless, the standard of living is reputed to be higher in spite of (or because of) the overdrafts and most of the farming community would probably agree that it is a better life today.

As to agricultural workers, they have always been at the bottom of the pile. Now they are better paid, but not in comparison with others. Traditionally those living in 'tied' houses have not had to pay rates, so the community charge has affected the way in which they are paid. Employers have had to increase their pay and 'gross it up' so that they receive enough to pay their community charge. (On the subject of the community charge, opinions vary between outright opposition—James Shaw Grant has spoken of its adverse effect, particularly on the more remote areas, in Chapter 3—and tacit approval: some observers have commented that the charge already appears to be proving its worth, with councillors being more prudent in budgeting and saying 'We must not and will not overspend'.)

Twenty-five years ago there were 21 dairy units between Beauly and Ardersier. Now there are four. Costs have risen due to a number of factors—shorter working hours, government regulations, pasteurisation requirements—and during the past ten years there has been Treasury encouragement to go out of dairying. Farmers have turned instead to beef cattle, which, besides being a viable business, have the advantage of being easier to manage. Sheep farming is less certain at present, though the problem may be temporary. Egg production, in spite of 1988's setbacks, is still profitable: there are regular checks against disease and those producers who survived the scare now get more for their products.

The optional 'set aside' policies (whereby farmers are paid to leave fields lying idle) look disastrous in the North. The government introduced the policy due to surpluses accumulated because of EEC regulations: but these surpluses are really more those of people such as Lincolnshire wheat farmers. Crops in the Highlands are not in surplus. With the resurgence of the whisky industry every ounce of malting barley is snapped up eagerly.

As one experienced farmer has said,

> In farming, above all, you have to go with the rules and adapt them. You must produce what the market wants. Until recently the rule has been to provide a plentiful supply of food. We are told that the former mountains of foodstocks have been reduced or eliminated; but perhaps it should be remembered that the seven good years were followed by seven lean years: an over-full larder may not be such a bad thing.
>
> It should not be forgotten that the countryside today is the way the people themselves have made it. Farmers are criticised by environmentalists and we do not get enough credit for what we have done. You get the odd farmer who takes hedges down and creates a prairie, but they are the exceptions. We cannot live in a timelock; you cannot hold back progress. We have a balanced countryside today and the people in it are looking after it well.

It is good if farmers believe, overall, that their lives are better; and it is good that much thought is being given to future generations, even when that may lead to conflict. As George Houston, Morton Boyd, John Foster and others have indicated, the long-term preservation and improvement of the land remain crucial—and priorities are not simple to decide.

Policing the Highlands and Islands

The number of small police forces (33) in Scotland was reduced in 1968 after some amalgamations, but the major change took place in May 1975, with the formation of eight large Forces. Today the Northern Constabulary, with its headquarters in Inverness and responsibility for policing one sixth of the land mass of the British Isles, is 631 strong, with up-to-date equipment and a computerisation programme which no small force could ever justify. Even at that, the Northern force is small compared with those further south—but the crime rate is well below the national average. Argyll, of course, remains within the Strathclyde force—the biggest of the Scottish eight.

Shetland provides an example of the change. Until 1940 it had two tiny forces—those of Zetland County and (separate) the Lerwick town police. From 1940 to 1969 Shetland had a single force, latterly with ten policemen. (The Chief Constable, giving evidence to the Royal Commission on the Police in 1960, was asked what he would do if on a Saturday night there was a fight in Lerwick between Shetland fishermen and Norwegians. 'I'd take the sergeant and we'd go and deal with it', he said. At that time there were only six in Lerwick—the chief, the sergeant and four men—and one each in Scalloway and Yell. I remember it, having been a member of that Royal Commission.)

In 1969 the Northern Constabulary was formed, at that time taking in only Caithness, Orkney and Shetland. Soon after that, and with the coming of oil, Shetland's force went up to 21. And with reorganisation in 1975 the Northern Constabulary was extended to Inverness, together with Ross and Cromarty, Sutherland and the Western Isles. Today Shetland has a Chief Inspector, an Inspector and a Detective Inspector, six sergeants and 27 constables.

Not all of the work of the Northern Constabulary is connected with crime or accident. One community initiative on their part is 'Outreach' at Foyers—a centre located beside Loch Ness, recently refurbished with help from the HIDB and the Manpower Services Commission—to which youth groups from all over the region are invited to go for a week at a time, receiving tuition and safety training in outdoor activities such as climbing, hillwalking and water sports from members of the force.

Children in trouble

Since the introduction in 1971 of Children's Hearings in the Highlands and Islands—as in the rest of Scotland—young offenders have been dealt with in an atmosphere of greater understanding than previously. Under this system children who are not serious offenders are no longer required to appear in the intimidating atmosphere of a courtroom. They will attend—with their parents—a hearing with a Children's Reporter, representatives from the Social Work Department, and three lay people, who form the Children's Panel. The informal surroundings under which their case is discussed have produced a more sympathetic attitude.

Whereas in the early 1970s, due to lack of facilities, very few children with difficulties could be placed in residential schools within the area, now many more can be placed within the Highlands. Today very few have to go outwith the region, to Aberdeen, Perth or elsewhere. In any case, the numbers involved are small: only 40 or 50 will be put into residential care in any one year and of these only two or three are sent south.

Troublesome teenagers are less of a problem nowadays than the sad difficulties of younger children. The authorities are now dealing with a far greater proportion of severely neglected or abused children, whose cases occupy most of the time and attention of the Children's Panels—not that there are greater numbers of them than in other areas, but here there has been success in discovering them. In many ways the Highlands and Islands have led the whole country in dealing with such cases. By no means all vulnerable children have been fostered or sent to care in a residential home: there has been positive emphasis on helping parents with difficulties, and on improving parenting skills. This policy has been rewarding in terms of maintaining united homes and encouraging happier family lives for both generations.

Highland health

Two great changes have been the building of health centres and the opening of the new Raigmore Hospital in Inverness, splendidly equipped and now used by much of the Highlands for all but minor or routine treatments.

Until the 1960s most medical practices in the rural Highlands were single-handed and were 'home visit' rather than surgery-based. Because of distances involved and the lack of public and private transport, doctors at that time tended to make more home visits. It was disappointing to arrive home from a 25-mile journey only to find a message requesting a call from the same vicinity, so there used to be an elaborate system to contact the doctor on his rounds. He or she would phone in from a callbox, or a message would be left with someone on that day's visiting list who had a telephone. Sometimes a helpful telephone owner was prepared to flag down the doctor, or even to tie a red rag to a tree, to alert the passing doctor that a message awaited him: many travelling miles were saved in this way. To some extent these arrangements still exist, as bleepers cannot work in hilly areas.

Surgeries now have greater numbers of patients, most of whom come by car: generally only the very ill, frail or aged expect to be visited at home. As a result, unless enquiries are made during a surgery visit, the present-day doctor is likely to be less familiar with the patient's home circumstances. In areas of larger population, practices have tended to be amalgamated, or single-handed practitioners have taken on partners, with the result that it is sometimes difficult for a patient to see the doctor of his choice. The amalgamated practices form groups, working from purpose-built, grant-aided surgeries staffed by receptionists and secretaries. Nursing services are integrated to some extent. District nurses employed by the Health Board attend to patients in their homes; practice nurses, employed and paid by the general practitioners, work within the surgery, dealing with matters requiring nursing skills.

Doctors are now able to live where they choose instead of in what were, in many cases, effectively 'tied houses'. This has relieved the present-day doctor's wife of many duties and responsibilities. In the past she was required to man the telephone, deal with callers at the surgery, and provide tea and comfort for those in distress. Invaluable, uncomplaining, unpaid and devoted, she was an unsung heroine of the earlier era.

At one time local cottage hospitals catered for most of the run-of-the-mill needs of rural communities. Casualties were dealt with, out-patient speciality clinics were held regularly; surgical operations, maternity services, radiology and physiotherapy were available. The closeness of the hospital to the community meant that friends and relations could easily drop in for a visit. Now most patients go to Raigmore, and, because of distance and expense, visitors are naturally less frequent: a lengthy stay in hospital can be a lonely experience these days.

Doctors, quite rightly, make use of the excellent radiological, pathological and clinical services available at Raigmore. No longer is it necessary to do the limited pathological tests which used to be done in the surgery. General practitioners of earlier days had, because of transport problems, to deal with a wider range of medical treatment than perhaps do their present day colleagues. Today medicine tends to be more compartmented and specialised.

TV is constantly showing medical and health programmes and discussing new treatments. These have both good and less desirable effects. People learn that they are not the only sufferers, and carers realise that they can exchange problems with others. On the other hand such programmes may lead to unreal expectations of treatments and cures. Patients have become much more demanding as a result: a new treatment featured on television or in a magazine can result in an immediate rise in surgery attendance. Such programmes also tend to awaken fears in the apprehensive viewer, who, though perfectly healthy, may imagine that he is suffering from one or all of the diseases discussed.

Nowadays there is a different approach on the part of the community. In the past, as he went amongst them, the local doctor was seen as a figure to be greatly respected, often regarded as a highly valued friend and counsellor. Perhaps because of those changes which have taken place, making the doctor less closely identified with local communities, people are more apt to voice open criticism. The dramatic advances which have brought more effective treatments and medicines have also created changes for doctor and patient alike. Much has been gained: something has inevitably been lost.

The inner and smaller islands

Much of this chapter has been about mainland matters. The island communities of the Northern and Western Isles have been discussed in earlier chapters. But—not to be forgotten—off Scotland's fragmented west coast lie a myriad of exquisite islands, some large, some small, some simply uninhabited rocky splinters. Each has its own character.

Arran has mountains, beaches and seven golf courses, which bring it many visitors. Whereas in winter it has a population of 4000, in summer it goes up to 12,000 or more; nearly half the houses on the island are holiday homes. It also has a number of small farms, with cattle which are mostly shipped to the mainland for their final fattening. Its biggest employer is Arran Provisions, set up in 1974 by a Birmingham fraud squad officer who wanted to come home to the land of his father and grandfather; it makes unusual mustards, a variety of jams and other special foods, and most of its produce goes to the mainland to be sold. In its development it has had useful help from the Highland Board. Proximity to Glasgow gives Arran some advantages, and whereas the visitors and holidaymakers used to come mainly between June and August, the season now runs from mid-March to the end of October.

Bute is the nearest neighbour—once the most popular holiday place on the Clyde, with attractions both for the wealthy and for families of modest means, but less popular since ro-ro ferries opened access to more distant places and because of the growth of cheap package holidays in Spain or Greece in the 1960s and 1970s. Bute nevertheless continues to attract holiday people, and it still has a number of prosperous farms.

Islay, one of the more prosperous of the islands, with its five whisky distilleries producing the distinctive, peaty malts much enjoyed by the connoisseur, has also produced a significant anti-environmental backlash. During the barnacle goose war of 1986 the celebrated environmentalist David Bellamy visited the island in order to protect the winter habitat of this migratory bird against the depredations of the distillery company which planned to plough up the peatland. To his dismay, Bellamy found the island's population united in favour of the distillery company's proposals. Barnacle geese, it seemed, were viewed as 'black and white eating machines', whereas the golden malt represented the islanders' livelihood.

Islay's neighbour *Jura* is one of the most glamorous of islands. Viewed from Kintyre, Mull or elsewhere, its dramatic hills—'the paps'—present an image of the lonely Inner Hebrides, long since deserted by most of its crofting inhabitants. There are few houses, one road, one hotel and some lovely beaches. It was here that Orwell retreated to write, towards the end of his life. The Paps make excellent climbing, but with some hard going over loose rock in parts near the tops.

Mull, because of its 'white settler' population, is somewhat unjustly referred to as the Officers' Mess. It has its own beauty, includes a miniature railway personally built by a group of railway enthusiasts (with HIDB support) and has a colony of resident artists. It, and even more its tiny outlier Iona, attract a vast number of visitors each summer. *Iona* is the jewel of the Hebrides, with its extraordinary atmosphere, its exquisite colours and long sea views to the chain of small islands of which it is a part. And, of course, it is St Columba's island.

Skye, possibly the most visited of all the islands apart from Arran, retains part of the Gaelic culture now abandoned in the islands further south. It is here that the wealthy entrepreneur Ian Noble founded the Gaelic College. *Colonsay, Coll, Tiree* (nowadays an international centre for sail-boarding); the *Small Isles* of *Rum* (not to be mis-spelt Rhum—a point on which Dr Morton Boyd is firm), *Eigg* and *Canna*; the *Summer Isles* ... each has a quality and a character of its own. On these islands descendants of the old Highland community now live alongside people who have arrived from other parts of Britain and from the rest of the world who, by a process of osmosis, are now Highlanders themselves. (On Lewis a year or two ago we met a small Gaelic-speaking Vietnamese boy.)

Grants and loans from the HIDB, particularly for tourism, crafts and fish-farming, have helped to sustain previously dwindling island populations.

Ferries for the Islands

For this variation on a well-known saying, we are indebted to the Managing Director of Caledonian MacBrayne:

> *The earth unto the Lord belongs and all that it contains Except alone the Western Isles—*
> *He left them to MacBraynes.*

He left them, Colin Paterson says, probably because He realised the complexity of the operation. To cope with 23 islands, using 51 terminals, Cal Mac has 31 ships. Of the vessels, 12 are major ferries with a capacity of up to 120 cars, 15 are minor ferries which can carry six to 28 cars, two are for passengers only and two are launches. Annually they carry more than five million passengers, one million cars and over 100,000 commercial vehicles and coaches. It is a measure of development that from carrying some four million passengers in 1982, CalMac by 1988 was carrying 5,354,522 people, and still more in the splendid summer of 1989.

No less significant, P & O had raised its traffic to Orkney and Shetland, particularly with the introduction of a third major vessel, the St Sunniva, in 1986. The P & O figures for the years 1979 to 1989 show an increase of passengers of no less than 59% to Orkney and 24% to Shetland. Cars carried were up by 70% for Orkney and 34% for Shetland. In freight, while there was a drop in the P & O services to Shetland, the Orkney ferries carried 15% more.

The great change, as noted by John Foster in Chapter 8, came from the roll-on, roll-off (ro-ro) ferries. They opened great new areas to tourists and to longer-term visitors. Although it might be argued that Noah invented the first ro-ro, with the animals going in two by two and out again afterwards, the first of the major ro-ros on the Clyde was the *Glen Sannox* in 1957. (The smaller *Arran* had come three years earlier.) The *Sannox* was built both for stern loading of vehicles and for side loading, and for many years she was the fastest passenger vessel on the west coast of Scotland. The *Caledonia*, bought from Norway in 1970, was the first in the fleet to have bow and stern doors. This was followed by conversion of the *Clansman* two years later.

CalMac itself came into being only in 1973, with the merger of the Clyde-based Caledonian Steam Packet and the inner and outer isles services of David MacBrayne. Both had been taken over by the Scottish Transport Group in 1969. The merger enabled the new company to have a common policy on fares, charges, schedules and design. It was an important advance for their sea-going empire, with 23 islands, many peninsulas and an extraordinary range of traffic.

With such a scattered and thinly populated area, the shipping service has to have government support. But it is a matter of pride to Colin Paterson and his staff that in real terms the subsidy has been reduced since 1983—thanks to the increased traffic and better management. By the time this book is published it will be less than one quarter of CalMac's revenue.

In the late 1970s there had been talk—in Europe as in the UK—of introducing a Road Equivalent Tariff. The argument was that islanders were having to pay five times the cost per mile to travel to and from the mainland compared with travelling the same distance on the mainland. 'RET' was even included in the Conservative election manifesto of 1979. But in the end it was shelved in the urge to cut public spending. Since 1985, however, the EEC has provided generous 'regional grants' for new vessels—the first to any company in Europe having been for the mv *Hebridean Isles* at 40%. Recent grants have been at 50%.

Colin Paterson reckons that to introduce 'RET' would cost £10m a year at 1990 levels, and he says that already CalMac's policy is to support island dwellers by providing cheaper fares through books of tickets for multiple journeys. At the same time, of course, tourists can obtain a reduced rate by buying 'island hopping' tickets for extended journeys. That has been part of a successful marketing drive.

Another popular innovation was—and is—the computer booking system. It is now possible, by telephone or visit to nearly all the CalMac terminals, to book your car on to the majority of ferry crossings. The company grossly underestimated the response, but has been delighted by the result. Having found that it works, a majority of travellers now use the booking system, which has encouraged tourists to visit more of the islands.

One troublesome—and, for CalMac, expensive—problem has been the Transport Department's blanket legislation after the Zeebrugge disaster in 1987. It took little account of the different style and structure of Scottish west coast vessels as compared with those on the English Channel. CalMac's ships have a single vehicle deck compared with the two or three decks on the Channel runs and the number of heavy commercial carries is never as great. Travellers on the Dover or Folkestone crossing must indeed be conscious of the apparent top-heavy style of the ferries there.

CalMac has a good record in safety matters. It has also shown a remarkable ability on occasions to cope with the foulest weather—as on Good Friday of 1989, when the ferocity of the sea seemed likely to stop all crossings in the Clyde. Nevertheless, by bringing the old *Glen Sannox* back into service along with the *Isle of Arran*, all those wishing to cross to or from Brodick had been delivered by midnight.

Nostalgia may cause some travellers to regret the loss of such beautiful cruising vessels as the old *Duchess of Montrose*, *Duchess of Hamilton* and *St Columba*. Their kind became a casualty to the coming of ro-ro and there is nothing comparable to them now—except the old privately-owned *Waverley*, with its paddles still churning in spite of great age. (The old *Queen Mary* can still be seen in the Thames near Waterloo Bridge, but with the wrong colours and not much of its former charm.) Much as we may miss the old cruising beauties, since so many of us want to take our cars or lorries from or to the islands, we must be thankful for the CalMac and P & O services.

Conclusion

So what has changed over these 25 years?

In his poem *For the Old Highlands*, Douglas Young laments the passing of 'that old, lonely, lovely way of living in Highland places; the harmony of folk and land is shattered—the yearly rhythm of things, the social graces, peat-fire and music, candle-light and kindness; now they are gone it seems they never mattered much, to the world.' Too romantic, perhaps, but some would share his regret for that passing.

Yet a country that does not change from year to year—perhaps even from day to day—is dead. The Highlands and Islands of Scotland, lying far out on the northern tip of Europe, have been changing constantly since Neolithic man and woman came to settle here, building their communal homes, beginning to husband their animals, farming their land and creating their awesome stone circles—perhaps as much as 4500 years ago.

And change will continue. The landscape itself, though it appears to be immutable, alters with the tides and with the winds: settlements and villages in Orkney and along the Moray Firth have been lost for many centuries under drifting sands. Here and there the sea has invaded the land. Forests have grown, matured, died and given way to peat bogs. Animal species which once inhabited the countryside have long since disappeared. Weather patterns have altered.

Now we are talking about a short space of time: 25 years. Too short a measure, it might be thought, to make a perceptible impact on the life of a community. Yet this quarter-century has probably seen faster and more dramatic alteration in the life of the Highland community than any previous quarter-century in its history, apart perhaps from the post-1745 period. Certainly 1965–1990 has seen a remarkable acceleration in the process of change.

Many of the changes have been common to those taking place in the rest of Britain—in the rest of Europe—but because of the vastness of the area and the thinly spread population the effects have been more pronounced and dramatic than elsewhere. Others have been particular to the region itself, though the pace of change may have been forced from outside.

Looking at the contributions in the foregoing chapters from our team of writers, chosen for their knowledge and experience of their subjects, it is evident that there are anxieties. Mistakes have been made and the consequences have been damaging and will continue. There have been difficulties arising from well-intentioned attempts to 'plant' industry, in the way that one might plant a forest, expecting it to grow and prosper without first studying the condition of the soil and the effect of the weather on the young saplings—or, perhaps, failure to apply sufficient fertiliser in good time. The result in some cases has been disappointment, financial loss, increased rather than decreased unemployment, bitterness, and an exploited environment—though remedial action has been taken, as with the industrial estates at Alness and Invergordon.

The two main indigenous industries, farming and fishing, are experiencing serious difficulties. George Houston makes particular reference to the recent problems of farming in Chapter 4. In the case of fishing, 'overkill' is due partly to shortsightedness and the lack of adequate protection during the negotiations over our entry into Europe. James Nicolson and all the writers with seafaring constituents have spoken with alarm about the future of fishing and its consequences on communities whose livelihood has come from the sea since man took to the waters in coracles. It is hard to foresee how these problems are to be resolved.

There is a long-running anxiety over the sale of large tracts of territory to buyers from overseas, who have no interest in the land other than that of capital appreciation. There are worries, too, about the effect of the demands which large-scale and ever-growing tourism is making on community life. In many ways this industry is replacing the old industries of harvesting the earth and sea, which developed the particular characteristics of the Highlander or Islander over successive generations. Derek Cooper is particularly despondent in that respect and is right to remind us that the 'benefits' which come with the influx of visitors eager to experience the wild and to behold the beauty may, in the end, damage irreparably that which they come to seek.

The effect of the influx of permanent residents from outside the region is a constant thread throughout the chapters. People have come to settle in ever-growing numbers, drawn by the isolation and magnificence, the quiet pace of life, the attractions of easy travel and wonderful amenities. How often, driving along an empty single-track road overlooked by mountain, moor, and rushing river, do we hear on the car radio of another five-mile tailback on the M25 and give thanks for our own good fortune. Certainly there must be sympathy for refugees from an increasingly uncomfortable and unattractive south; and the Highlander is by tradition a hospitable and welcoming host. But there is a wariness too, and a sense that if not carefully watched the invasion may get out of hand. It is said that already two dozen people commute daily from Dalcross Airport at Inverness to Heath Row (flying time one hour and 20 minutes), arriving there at 8.20 a.m., in time to do a day's work and return to Inverness for a late meal in the evening. An entire new town is being constructed on the hill to the south of Inverness, with expensive houses, a golf course and all the sophisticated amenities that accompany such development. All this the indigenous Highlander looks at with some concern: on the one hand there can be no holding back from inevitable change—but is it wise to rush headlong into an unknown future?

As James Shaw Grant has said in Chapter 3, 'the past 25 years has presented a bewildering series of variations on the theme of decay and regeneration'. But looking back over the various chapters which make up this book one must be struck even by the very headings of the chapters: *A New Confidence, A Better Life, A Cloud of Gloom Dispersed*, and Anne Lorne Gillies's *Absurd Sense of Optimism*. Throughout almost every page there comes a clear sense of increased pride: the

Highland way of life, the language and the environment are no longer despised, but envied.

Increased comfort and prosperity: there are new roads and bridges, frequent (but not cheap) air services. Most families have a car and a telephone, houses are warm against the winter weather. Health services, if less personal, are better equipped and more efficient. Education—always a Highland 'plus'—is changing and many would say for the better: no longer do so many Highland children have to go to one of the big central secondary schools, living throughout the term in a hostel. For many, new schools have opened locally, within a reasonable daily bus-ride.

Unemployment—though blackspots remain—is lessening, and training for new jobs is there for the asking. The Highlands are no longer viewed as a place which the young must leave in order to succeed. At one time—in the 1960s—there was a call for a university in the Highlands, to be sited at Inverness. That call was not met, nor will it be, but the Technical College at Inverness provides a wide range of courses, both for the region's school-leavers and for the more mature seeking re-training. Tourism and fish-farming, despite attendant worries, are bringing prosperity and even wealth to families whose forebears scratched a poor living from a rain-and-wind-swept soil.

The production of oil in the region has, of course, had a dramatic impact. It has given increased prosperity to the Moray and Cromarty Firths—and, for a time, to Kishorn and Lewis in the west. It has brought undreamt-of wealth and a new self-esteem, not only to the mainland but perhaps most of all to the once deprived communities of Shetland. To Orkney too, though it was always richer, there has been great benefit—and without injury to the historic and scenic wonders of the Orkney islands. To the Western Isles, though they have so far enjoyed a lesser gain—but a gain nevertheless—it is off their shores that further development may come.

And now sophisticated new communications systems will bring the Highlands and Islands into the mainstream. Whichever way you look at it, distance is no longer a safeguard, a refuge or a restriction.

Of the HIDB itself, whose Silver Jubilee we commemorate in these pages—together with its possible demise—let us say this: over the years there have been wise and far-sighted decisions and much goodwill, which, with the tremendous financial input through the Board, have led to great improvements. There have also been mistakes and criticisms. But it cannot be doubted that overall the Board has justified the worthy intentions of its founders. It remains to be seen how the Government's new Enterprise concept will work in its stead: we wish it well.

On the whole, this book and its contributors have given a positive and encouraging verdict. The Highlands and Islands of Scotland are adapting well and, given certain safeguards, prospects for the twenty-first century are good.

30   New Bridge and Old Ferry, Ballachulish, Argyll. Photograph by John Foster.

31   *Suilven* at Ullapool. (HIDB)

32   Kessock Bridge, Inverness. Photograph by Peter Davenport.

33   Kylesku Bridge, Sutherland. (HIDB)

Appendix

TABLE I   BOARD ASSISTANCE BY SECTOR 1971 (AT 1988 PRICES)

	Grant (£'000)	Loans & Equity (£'000)	Employment Created	Employment Protected
LAND DEVELOPMENT	92	799	34	14
of which: Farm Development	50	727	24	12
Horticulture	0	0	0	0
FISHERIES	181	848	55	5
of which: Fishing Boats	78	751	55	5
Fishing Farming	0	0	0	0
TOURISM	1,789	350	241	20
of which: Hotels	1,396	215	162	20
Other Tourist Accommodation	110	0	16	0
Catering	180	100	52	0
Recreation & Tourist Amenities	70	16	3	0
MANUFACTURING, SERVICES & PROCESSING	2,247	1,865	629	32
of which: Fish Processing	174	129	82	0
Boat Yards & Marine Engineering	43	32	8	2
Crafts	57	46	45	14
Construction	0	12	12	0
Service Industries	461	394	62	2
TOTAL	4,310	3,862	959	71

Notes

The figures above relate to assistance approved by the Board—not payments. Cases withdrawn after approval are thus included.

Part-time or seasonal jobs are valued at half a job, and part-time seasonal jobs at a quarter.

Service industries excludes tourism and services directly related to land development and fisheries.

TABLE II   BOARD ASSISTANCE BY SECTOR 1976 (AT 1988 PRICES)

	Grant (£'000)	Loans & Equity (£'000)	Employment Created	Employment Protected
LAND DEVELOPMENT	538	1,612	78	36
of which: Farm Develoment	86	903	15	28
Horticulture	122	210	21	4
FISHERIES	839	2,740	138	36
of which: Fishing Boats	191	2,424	96	34
Fishing Farming	626	281	38	2
TOURISM	3,231	2,058	350	106
of which: Hotels	1,221	793	152	94
Other Tourist Accommodation	1,166	579	72	3
Catering	295	176	56	0
Recreation & Tourist Amenities	255	191	38	0
MANUFACTURING, SERVICES & PROCESSING	1,613	4,163	843	270
of which: Fish Processing	117	613	133	58
Boat Yards & Marine Engineering	189	343	78	16
Crafts	96	95	74	16
Construction	117	106	42	15
Service Industries	280	1,006	176	18
TOTAL	6,237	10,575	1,409	448

Notes
The figures above relate to assistance approved by the Board—not payments. Cases withdrawn after approval are thus included.
Part-time or seasonal jobs are valued at half a job, and part-time seasonal jobs at a quarter.
Service industries excludes tourism and services directly related to land development and fisheries.
Above totals include some expenditure not allowed on a sectoral basis.

TABLE III   BOARD ASSISTANCE BY SECTOR 1981 (AT 1988 PRICES)

	Grant (£'000)	Loans & Equity (£'000)	Employment Created	Employment Protected
LAND DEVELOPMENT	1,629	2,555	118	47
of which: Farm Development	789	2,143	33	35
Horticulture	116	70	12	1
FISHERIES	1,788	3,400	219	61
of which: Fishing Boats	196	2,431	130	31
Fishing Farming	1,391	337	69	2
TOURISM	3,287	1,140	265	48
of which: Hotels	1,540	513	124	42
Other Tourist Accommodation	944	372	58	2
Catering	129	69	38	0
Recreation & Tourist Amenities	210	74	26	2
MANUFACTURING, SERVICES & PROCESSING	4,555	3,633	1,014	237
of which: Fish Processing	210	460	102	14
Boat Yards & Marine Engineering	176	182	16	12
Crafts	96	77	76	1
Construction	660	343	106	2
Service Industries	1,016	850	221	68
TOTAL	11,262	10,733	1,616	395

Notes
The figures above relate to assistance approved by the Board—not payments. Cases withdrawn after approval are thus included.
Part-time or seasonal jobs are valued at half a job, and part-time seasonal jobs at a quarter.
Service industries excludes tourism and services directly related to land development and fisheries.
Above totals include some expenditure not allowed on a sectoral basis.

TABLE IV   BOARD ASSISTANCE BY SECTOR 1986 (AT 1988 PRICES)

	Grant (£'000)	Loans & Equity (£'000)	Employment Created	Employment Protected
LAND DEVELOPMENT	1,523	747	232	50
of which: Farm Development	536	563	80	16
Horticulture	53	35	23	4
FISHERIES	2,063	2,848	280	37
of which: Fishing Boats	185	2,494	101	18
Fishing Farming	1,830	252	164	15
TOURISM	4,397	1,254	604	25
of which: Hotels	1,923	495	266	1
Other Tourist Accommodation	1,305	371	117	10
Catering	320	143	102	6
Recreation & Tourist Amenities	754	195	99	2
MANUFACTURING, SERVICES & PROCESSING	5,797	1,477	1,131	374
of which: Fish Processing	1,326	194	240	162
Boat Yards & Marine Engineering	114	48	24	0
Crafts	47	31	20	5
Construction	46	7	16	0
Service Industries	1,532	407	409	17
TOTAL	13,780	6,326	2,247	486

Notes
The figures above relate to assistance approved by the Board—not payments. Cases withdrawn after approval are thus included.
Part-time or seasonal jobs are valued at half a job, and part-time seasonal jobs at a quarter.
Service industries excludes tourism and services directly related to land development and fisheries.

TABLE V   BOARD ASSISTANCE BY SECTOR 1965–1970 (AT 1988 PRICES)

	No of Cases	Assistance Approved (£'000)	Jobs Created
Manufacturing	320	15,385	2,340
Tourism	380	13,992	1,300
Fisheries★	255	10,251	740
Agriculture	60	2,586	40
Miscellaneous	205	5,441	700
Non-economic	205	1,046	10
TOTAL	1,425	48,701	5,130

Notes

The figures above relate to assistance approved by the Board—not payments. Cases withdrawn after approval are thus included.

Assistance to fish processing units and boatyards is included under manufacturing.

Board Assistance corresponds to the seven crofting counties of Argyll, Caithness, Inverness, Orkney, Ross-shire, Sutherland and Shetland.

TABLE VI   MANUFACTURING & SERVICES DIVISION ASSISTANCE TOTALS 1971–1988 (AT 1988 PRICES)

	No of Cases	Grant (£'000)	Loans & Equity (£'000)	Employment Created (FTE)	Protected (FTE)
Mining & Quarrying	64	2,216	2,382	297	127
Fish Processing	232	10,199	6,886	2,430	999
Boatyard & Marine Engineering	100	2,519	2,985	564	256
Crafts	551	2,810	3,018	1,765	314
Printing & Publishing	126	1,682	3,483	468	202
Other Manufacturing	884	26,770	24,390	6,850	2,271
Building Industry	247	4,749	6,288	1,613	594
Service Industry	1,344	12,769	7,730	3,364	645
Transport	134	2,837	2,728	408	98
Training NES	10	187	246	76	12
Marketing NES	6	52	195	20	27
Other NES	69	3,891	1,654	569	88
TOTAL	3,767	70,682	61,986	18,423	5,633

Notes

The figures above relate to assistance approved by the Board—not payments. Cases withdrawn after approval are thus included.

Part-time or seasonal jobs are valued at half a job, and part-time seasonal jobs at a quarter.

Service industries excludes tourism and services directly related to land development and fisheries.

Nairn, Bute and Arran were not eligible for Board assistance until 1975, Cumbraes until 1980 and Forres and Upper Moray until November 1986.

NES—Not elsewhere specified.

TABLE VII   TOURISM DIVISION ASSISTANCE TOTALS 1971–1988 (AT 1988 PRICES)

	No of Cases	Grant (£'000)	Loans & Equity (£'000)	Employment Created (FTE)	Protected (FTE)
Other NES	26	449	99	28	0
Hotels New	61	5,587	1,924	661	8
Hotels Improvements/Extensions	1,307	28,225	10,461	2,807	857
Self-Catering	870	13,816	4,805	707	60
Bed & Breakfast	362	1,898	703	254	24
Other Accommodation	432	5,080	1,815	508	94
Staff Quarters	22	369	33	18	10
Catering	407	4,410	2,218	1,280	52
Marine Recreation	370	5,062	2,841	517	76
Other Recreation/Tourist Amenities	601	9,286	2,283	1,042	177
TOTAL	4,458	74,182	27,183	7,822	1,357

Notes
The figures above relate to assistance approved by the Board—not payments. Cases withdrawn after approval are thus included.
Part-time or seasonal jobs are valued at half a job, and part-time seasonal jobs at a quarter.
Nairn, Bute and Arran were not eligible for Board assistance until 1975, Cumbraes until 1980 and Forres and Upper Moray until November 1986.
NES—Not elsewhere specified.

TABLE VIII   FISHERIES DIVISION ASSISTANCE TOTALS 1971–1988 (AT 1988 PRICES)

	No of Cases	Grant (£'000)	Loans & Equity (£'000)	Employment Created (FTE)	Protected (FTE)
Equipment & Ancillaries	273	433	1,018	82	175
Fishing Boats: New	268	4,593	17,314	512	142
Second hand	848	2,102	36,257	1,441	513
Services	42	1,253	1,284	97	33
Fish Farming	515	21,140	6,998	1,168	163
Freshwater Fisheries	17	71	21	8	0
Other NES	13	88	182	14	9
TOTAL	1,976	29,680	63,073	3,322	1,036

Notes

The figures above relate to assistance approved by the Board—not payments. Cases withdrawn after approval are thus included.

Part-time or seasonal jobs are valued at half a job, and part-time seasonal jobs at a quarter.

Nairn, Bute and Arran were not eligible for Board assistance until 1975, Cumbraes until 1980 and Forres and Upper Moray until November 1986.

NES—Not elsewhere specified.

There were no equipment and ancillaries cases prior to 1983 and none in fish farming before 1973.

TABLE IX   LAND DIVISION ASSISTANCE TOTALS 1971–1988 (AT 1988 PRICES)

	No of Cases	Grant (£'000)	Loans & Equity (£'000)	Employment Created (FTE)	Protected (FTE)
Farm Development:					
General	1,208	5,933	11,519	566	316
Sheep	283	616	1,219	121	53
Beef	391	711	4,118	112	81
Dairy	166	1,024	3,165	90	103
Crops	29	170	387	24	34
Horticultural Development	248	1,364	1,699	368	64
Machinery Syndicates	772	1,878	578	44	104
Contracting Services	444	2,372	1,338	445	63
Services: Agriculture, Horticulture and Forestry	372	2,834	2,019	363	172
Slaughtering/Processing	58	1,184	444	113	28
Other NES	114	938	1,176	161	35
TOTAL	4,085	19,025	27,664	2,407	1,053

Notes

The figures above relate to assistance approved by the Board—not payments. Cases withdrawn after approval are thus included.

Part-time or seasonal jobs are valued at half a job, and part-time seasonal jobs at a quarter.

Nairn, Bute and Arran were not eligible for Board assistance until 1975, Cumbraes until 1980 and Forres and Upper Moray until November 1986.

NES—Not elsewhere specified.

Index